Mohab Abou-Elkawam

Nomads of a Global Industry

D1613374

Mohab Abou-Elkawam

Nomads of a Global Industry

Seafarers and the Marine Environment : The Quest

LAP LAMBERT Academic Publishing

Impressum / Imprint
Bibliografische Information der Deutschen Nationalbibliothek: Die Deutsche Nationalbibliothek verzeichnet diese Publikation in der Deutschen Nationalbibliografie; detaillierte bibliografische Daten sind im Internet über http://dnb.d-nb.de abrufbar.
Alle in diesem Buch genannten Marken und Produktnamen unterliegen warenzeichen-, marken- oder patentrechtlichem Schutz bzw. sind Warenzeichen oder eingetragene Warenzeichen der jeweiligen Inhaber. Die Wiedergabe von Marken, Produktnamen, Gebrauchsnamen, Handelsnamen, Warenbezeichnungen u.s.w. in diesem Werk berechtigt auch ohne besondere Kennzeichnung nicht zu der Annahme, dass solche Namen im Sinne der Warenzeichen- und Markenschutzgesetzgebung als frei zu betrachten wären und daher von jedermann benutzt werden dürften.

Bibliographic information published by the Deutsche Nationalbibliothek: The Deutsche Nationalbibliothek lists this publication in the Deutsche Nationalbibliografie; detailed bibliographic data are available in the Internet at http://dnb.d-nb.de.
Any brand names and product names mentioned in this book are subject to trademark, brand or patent protection and are trademarks or registered trademarks of their respective holders. The use of brand names, product names, common names, trade names, product descriptions etc. even without a particular marking in this work is in no way to be construed to mean that such names may be regarded as unrestricted in respect of trademark and brand protection legislation and could thus be used by anyone.

Coverbild / Cover image: www.ingimage.com

Verlag / Publisher:
LAP LAMBERT Academic Publishing
ist ein Imprint der / is a trademark of
OmniScriptum GmbH & Co. KG
Heinrich-Böcking-Str. 6-8, 66121 Saarbrücken, Deutschland / Germany
Email: info@lap-publishing.com

Herstellung: siehe letzte Seite /
Printed at: see last page
ISBN: 978-3-659-78530-6

Zugl. / Approved by: PhD Thesis Cardiff University 2015

Nomads of a Global Industry: Seafarers and the Marine Environment

Mohab Abou-Elkawam

ABSTRACT

This research study offers a contribution to the field of framing environmental policies in several ways. First, it makes explicit the ways in which a nomadic professional group such as seafarers frame and interact with the growing demand to protect the environment in general and the marine environment in particular. Due to the nature of their profession, this group is able to roam the world and compare the effectiveness of environmental regulations in various countries. The shipping industry is composed of different types of shipping companies, some of which can be described as more environmentally aware than others, an issue which would affect the frames of seafarers regarding compliance to environmental regulations as discussed in this study. Moreover, this research opens up a social qualitative inquiry in areas scarcely attended to by previous scholars especially when focusing on the relationships and tensions between seafarers and their personal and professional commitments to their global work place; the marine environment. This study argues that such differences not only impact on the social construction of seafarers regarding environmental protection but also affects their framing of daily compliance practices as well. This allows us to review the institutional and instrumental policies carried out by different ship owners in different parts of the world and verify how this impacts on the compliance practices of this professional group in the context of a demanding and challenging regulatory environment.

CONTENTS

CHAPTER ONE – Introduction

1.1 Background to the research

The sea was presented throughout history as a space "outside" society; for those who lived by the sea as a friction free surface, non-territorial and existing solely as a space of distance between places. These images obscured the material reality experienced by those who derive their living from the sea and play a crucial role in the social construction of the sea as a void space (Steinberg 2001). In the last thirty years this image has changed. The sea is seen by some as an asocial space of movement, by others as a wealthy social space liable for development and yet by many as a common space that provides crucial resources for the social system. Each of these views leads, not surprisingly, to conflicting regulations and governing policies (Van Dyke et al. 1993).

These policies not only reflect on the regulations dealing with ocean governance regimes but also have significant implications on the main industry using the ocean; the shipping industry. This industry is, unlike other commercial sectors, intensely mobile: the ships are transferable with relative ease to a very large number of world locations constrained only by tonnage and size. Globalisation and global economic evolution is continually strengthening and extending the significance of maritime transport within this process of globalising trade (Selkou and Roe 2004).

Within this evolution of global trade conducted primarily by sea, the issue of regulating the marine environment emerged among many attempts to prevent more environmental degradation both inland and at sea. Throughout the 1970s and the 1980s, significant growth was observed in the number and scope of international institutions regulating international waters alongside the development of complex international alliances of environmental movements and organisations leading to multi-layered regulatory levels for the world's oceans (Held et al. 1999). These multi-layered regulations relating to the marine environment were not free from long-standing problems in compliance, monitoring and enforcement (Mitchell 1994a).

1.2   Key assumptions

This research started with the assumption that there are only three ways to influence peoples'
behaviours towards the marine environment: technical constraints, legal instruments and moral
constraints. This assumption also recognised that technology can be used to limit the scope of
undesired behaviour and where that fails legal remedies may be sought and ultimate appeals
may be made to moral and ethical principles. This key assumption launched this research
project on a journey to unravel how various stake holders in the maritime industry socially
construct the issue of marine pollution and how this is reflected upon their different perceptions
and views about compliance to an established marine environmental convention such as
MARPOL 73/78. MARPOL is the most established environmental convention that deals with
ship-based pollution.

1.2.1 The Definition of Marine Pollution

In order to deal with, detect, and enforce legal instruments or prosecute polluters, the first step,
on the one hand, is to clarify and define the term "Marine Pollution" utilised by most
enforcement agencies and their staff. The term "marine pollution" as it is commonly
understood, refers to an action or a situation that changes the quality of sea water for the worse.
The Oxford English dictionary defines pollution generally as "the action of polluting or
condition of being polluted, defilement; un-cleanliness or impurity". Both definitions do not
clarify or explain the term "pollute" which is a pre-requisite for any operation of law (Meng
1987). The working definition of marine pollution by the joint group of experts on the scientific
aspects of marine pollution (GESAMP) is: "the introduction by man, directly or indirectly of
substances into the marine environment (including estuaries) resulting in such deleterious
effects as harm to living resources, hazard to human health, hindrance to marine activities
including fishing, impairment of quality for the use of seawater and reduction of amenities"
(GESAMP 2006).

On the other hand, socio-legal theorists are defining 'pollution' as "the ephemeral result of an
act or pattern of deviance posing problems of discovery and detection"(Hawkins 1984). From
this latter definition it is quite clear that, in contrast to some other forms of deviance, marine
pollution, if considered as an act of deviance, constitutes some inherent problems of

10

enforcement as it, in most cases, lacks solid evidence. The indicators which can be taken for granted by enforcement agencies as evidence usually decays especially in the case of intentional discharges of oil in the high seas given the right weather conditions (which contributes to the natural dispersing of oil). This nature of "detection difficulties" could be one of the contributing factors to the low levels of compliance to maritime conventions seeking to regulate the marine environment. In order to introduce the issue of compliance, a general overview of the gravity of the problem of ship- source pollution follows in the next sub-sections.

1.2.2 The Existing Regulatory Framework

Various forms of international regulations have attempted to control various aspects of the maritime industry. The most important and widely accepted of these regulations have emerged from the International Maritime Organisation (IMO) and the International Labour Organisation (ILO). However, the social standards that ILO conventions cover are not as widely ratified by nations as the more technical standards of the IMO (Alderton and Winchester 2002b). Along with the evolution of globalisation, national government parties to IMO and ILO have enacted a series of internationally agreed conventions related to matters of ship safety, pollution prevention and the welfare of seafarers. The most important of these are the IMO's safety of life at sea convention (SOLAS 82), the prevention of pollution from ships convention (MARPOL 73/78) and the standards of training, certification and watch keeping convention (STCW95) with its mandatory and recommendatory sections (OECD 2002). In February 2006, another major ILO convention was finally adopted namely the seafarers' bill of rights, known as the Maritime Labour Convention MLC 2006, which is a single international social instrument accepted as the 'fourth pillar' of the global maritime industry (ILO 2006).

Nevertheless, the global implementation and enforcement of the aforementioned conventions has never been a simple and straightforward task as it might appear. A series of shipping accidents in the 1980s and 1990s, including the "Scandinavian Star" in the Baltic Sea, "Exxon Valdez" in Alaska, "Sea Empress" in Milford Haven and "Erika and Prestige" in the Bay of Biscay, highlighted the imminent need for the improvement of maritime safety and environmental protection through stricter and more uniform application of existing regulations (Richards et al. 2000). Unfortunately, these accidents triggered a set of uni-lateral policies by

11

individual European states to protect their shores from the devastating effects of marine pollution. Naturally, such policies are seen by the IMO as a further compromise to the global implementation of international maritime conventions.

This brief discussion clearly indicates that the effectiveness of IMO safety and pollution instruments depends primarily on the consistent application and enforcement of their requirements by individual national governments usually referred to in the maritime sphere as "flag states" (Singhota 1995). Acknowledging this necessity, the IMO introduced an additional sub-committee namely the Flag State Implementation (FSI) subcommittee. Its primary objective is to identify the necessary measures to ensure effective and consistent implementation of IMO conventions, paying attention to the particular difficulties faced by countries in this respect (IMO 2006c). Since the introduction of this FSI sub-committee, it seems that events of an environmental nature and problems regarding security (after 9/11) are defining a qualitative shift in maritime policies at the present time both at international and regional levels. Although economic objectives have not been totally set aside, it could be said that concern for geo-strategic and environmental aspects are being especially emphasised (Suarez de Vivero and Rodriguez Mateos 2004). An example of this shift was the agreement signed between Spain, France and Portugal in November 2002 (in the aftermath of the sinking of Prestige), where all three countries agreed to ban the transit of single-hulled oil tankers over 15 years of age through their territorial waters and exclusive economic zone (EEZ) with immediate effect (IMO 2006a).

Focusing on the case of enforcement of IMO's main regulatory instrument for the prevention of pollution to the marine environment – MARPOL 73/78 – some scholars still argue that the compliance levels by state parties are not reaching the desired levels especially after having been in force for more than 25 years (Brookman 2002; Cormack and Fowler 1986; Van Leeuwen 2004; Wonham 1998). On the one hand, efforts to negotiate consensus to impose sanctions on non-compliant flag states or even detected individual polluters are usually not successful (Alderton and Winchester 2002a; Raftopoulos 2001). Seeking solutions, in 2003 the IMO introduced the "Voluntary IMO Member State Audit Scheme" - soon to become mandatory - which is intended to provide an audited member state with a comprehensive and objective assessment of how effectively it administers and implements the key IMO technical treaties that are covered by the Scheme.

On the other hand, deliberate discharges from oil tankers have traditionally been the biggest source of oil pollution from ships, greater than the much-publicized accidental spills. Previous research around this topic focused on empirical evaluation of the compliance process over time identifying policies to increase compliance by flag states and shipping companies (Mitchell 1994). Such approaches underline the importance of a qualitative study in trying to unravel the actual reasons of non-compliance with environmental maritime conventions by various players in the maritime industry (Khee and Tan 2005). In the same context and among the issues that is liable for a social inquiry is the cost-conscious nature of the shipping industry and its implications for the compliance process to the different marine environmental regulations. To fully introduce the tensions surrounding the marine pollution problem it is important to trace the origins of this longstanding debate.

1.3 The International Problem of Oil Pollution from Ships

1.3.1 Historical Background

Since the late 1960s, with the evolution of Tanker trade and dependency of oil as a primary source of energy, many studies have attempted to estimate the flow of petroleum hydrocarbons into the marine environment. One of the most authoritative estimates was produced by the US National Academy of Sciences (NAS) in 1973. This study concluded with a quite staggering final report estimating 6, 713, 000 metric tons of oil to have entered the world's oceans in 1973, with at least 1, 500, 000 tons attributed to operational discharges from all types of ships (M'Gonigle and Zacher 1979). It is worth noting that these figures were estimated before the implementation of the MARPOL convention in 1983.

More than a decade later another study was carried out by the GESAMP working group at the request of the IMO. This study focused primarily on improving the estimates of oil entering the marine environment from transportation sources, as a sort of testing of the efficacy of annex I of the MARPOL 73/78 convention (IMO 1990). The study estimated that 570,000 metric tons of oil entered the world's oceans from marine transportation (International Oil Spill Conference 1999). If we exclude accidental discharges, the remaining figure attributed to operational discharges only will still be very close to half a million tons in 1989 six years after the MARPOL 73/78 convention came into force. This is still far from being acceptable (see fig. 1.1).

More recently, a prominent reconnaissance study for oil spills was carried out in 1999 by the European Commission research units to monitor the extent of compliance with MARPOL73/78 convention. The study chose a special area (according to Reg.10 annex I of MARPOL) of the Mediterranean Sea since it is the maritime route to Europe for oil produced in the Middle East. It is estimated that 360 million tons and refined products are transported annually through the Mediterranean sea representing approximately 22% of the world trade (EEA 1999). The study was composed of a reconnaissance carried out over the entire Mediterranean region acquiring 1600 'ERS 1' and 'ERS 2' satellite images during 1999. Within this sample of 1600 images, 697 were found to contain at least one oil spill signature with a total of 1638 spills. The spills covered an estimated area of 17, 141 square kilometres with an estimated amount of 13,858 metric tons (Palvakis et al. 2001). It is worth noting here that discharging any oil effluents in a MARPOL special area is totally prohibited.

Figure 1.1 1989 Estimated annual input from marine transportation, total: 570,000 tons, Source: IMO 1990

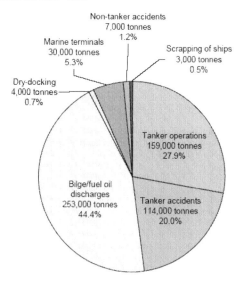

1.3.2 The MARPOL Convention

The first international agreement regulating intentional oil pollution was the OILPOL convention in 1954. This classic convention's primary rule system prohibited discharges above a specified limit within specified zones (i.e. 100 parts per million – 50 miles from shore). The monitoring of such 'discharge standards' was to be carried out solely by concerned coastal states (Pritchard 1985).

The OILPOL convention was subjected to numerous amendments during subsequent years with the evolution of the dependency on oil as an energy source. In 1969, in the aftermath of the grounding of the 'Torry Canyon', the focus turned to reducing the amount of oily effluents discharged into the marine environment from ships. The agreement reached kept the controlled discharge zones but added that all tankers need to keep discharges in terms of rate (60 litres per nautical mile) rather than oil content and that total discharges are to be limited to 1/15000 of a tanker's cargo capacity (Mitchell 1994a).

A conference in 1973 introduced the comprehensive form of the "International Convention for the Prevention of Pollution from Ships" (known today as MARPOL) which included refined products as well as crude oil. The 1973 version constituted five annexes (including annex I for oil) to address liquid chemicals, harmful packaged substances, and sewage and garbage discharges by ships (Brookman 2002). This version essentially maintained the same 'discharge standards' that had existed before the conference (M'Gonigle and Zacher 1979). The controlled zones remained at 50 miles, though special areas (i.e. total prohibition of oil or oily effluent discharges) were designated as the Mediterranean, Baltic, Black and Red Seas and in the Persian gulf. However, the new introduction of discharge monitoring technical equipment was the controversial aspect of the 1973 version of MARPOL. The convention required certain equipment to ensure compliance with what was later termed the 'discharge standards'. Such standards mandated oily water separators (OWSs) and monitoring devices to be installed on all tankers delivered after 1979 (Cormack and Fowler 1986; Pritchard 1985).

Due to the low compliance and enforcement difficulties of the MARPOL/73 convention, the then International Maritime Consultative Organisation IMCO (now known as the IMO) called for a conference that produced a protocol which became integral to the 1973 version; together known as MARPOL73/78. This version added some construction requirements to certain large tonnages of existing and new tankers such as the fitting of crude oil washing systems (COW) and segregated ballast tanks for the purpose of reducing the discharge of dirty ballast (i.e. seawater contaminated with cargo residues) in the sea. With growing opposition from the influential oil industry and some major tanker owners, the dynamic process of amending this convention continued with significant amendments in 1982, 1984, 1987, 1990 and finally 1992 when the convention required that all new tankers are to be built with double hulls or equivalent spill protection construction standards (IMO 2002; Mitchell 1994a; Mitchell 1998). Within this context, it is important to highlight that Annex I of MARPOL (oil) came into force in 1983 after being ratified by the required number of state parties representing the required tonnage which, arguably, should represent a norm for the current generation of seafarers. As of 31st of December 2005, 136 countries, representing 98% of the world's shipping tonnage, became parties to the convention.

From the above, it is clear that nation states did not find it difficult to make agreements, upgrade, amend or change them in continuous attempts to control the 'marine pollution' problem for more than half a century. Nevertheless, the compliance with MARPOL and other instruments aiming to control and reduce pollution in the marine environment are still far from any politically or socially acceptable standards (Cormack and Fowler 1986; Raftopoulos 2001). On the enforcement front, MARPOL's adoption of explicit requirements for states to detect and prosecute violations, as well as earlier efforts to increase fines imposed for dumping infringements failed. Some scholars in this area argue that this failure was mainly due to the lack of successful establishment of a harmonised mechanism for increasing the incentives of governments (i.e. flag states) to undertake these activities (Mitchell 1994b). In subsequent chapters of the thesis, I analyse whether any of the compliance system changes outlined here have achieved their intended results from the point of view of my respondents and their daily experience with compliance requirements of the MARPOL convention.

1.3.3 Seafarers and the Illicit Discharges of Oil

The most recent reports about MARPOL violations have consistently been linked to the behaviour of seafarers (Fingas and E. Brown 2007; Mattson 2006). The most prominent violations detected are the oily water separator (OWS) by-passing violations in vessels' engine rooms as evidence of deliberate oil discharges in the sea. News about such violations could be read on a nearly daily basis in maritime specialised newspapers and journals. These offences - if discovered - result in huge fines for shipping companies and occasionally in criminal prosecution for both the company and individual seafarers involved. For instance, a major Norwegian shipping company was fined US 6.5 Million dollars for OWS violations and the Chief Engineer of the vessel could be facing a sentence of up to five years imprisonment (LLOYD'SLIST 2006b). In another similar case in US waters, the company was fined US1.5 Million dollars after proving that four of the company's US flagged car carriers committed repeatedly OWS violations (LLOYD'SLIST 2006a).

1.4 Uniqueness of the Research Problem

The uniqueness of the problems of marine environment governance lies with attempting to regulate actions and spaces outside the sovereign authority of the states (Van Dyke et al. 1993). Arguably, some of the difficulties in implementation and enforcement may be attributed to the long standing historical notion of the "freedom of the seas" (Grotius 1916), which is still stipulated in the United Nations Convention on the Law of the Sea (UNCLOS). This global umbrella convention for ocean governance also enshrines the relatively new concept of "common heritage of mankind" which was an issue for debate throughout the 14 years consumed in negotiating this convention. UNCLOS was introduced as a way of thinking about the impact new technologies would have on the further exploitation of natural resources – resources that were beyond national jurisdictions (UNCLOS 1983). Since adopting the convention in 1982, the implementation of UNCLOS's many agreements has not been an easy task. For instance, the agreement on the scope and scale of environmental 'threats' to the sea was difficult to achieve. Consensus was also not reached on who is responsible for such 'threats' and how the costs should be allocated to ameliorate their consequences. Even when agreement was possible in aspects relating to state responsibilities about regulating their own flagged ships, international organisations have lacked the authority to ensure enforcement (Held 2000).

On an individual level, the nomadic seafarer faces a dilemma trying to cope with the requirements of three tiers of legislation namely international, regional, and local. Whilst shipping as a global industry is being regulated mainly on an international level, the seafarers will also need to comply with regional sets of marine environmental legislations (e.g. on the EU level). Not only this, but he will face the complexities of local regulations of each country his ship is trading with as soon as he approaches that country's territorial waters and ports. These different tiers of legislation led to seafarers on board ships, in many cases, striving to achieve contradictory roles which influence their framing of the marine pollution regulatory process. On the one hand, they are asked by their management to behave, simultaneously, like a cost-conscious, competitive, risk taking, virtuous, and standards' conscious professional (Haines and Sutton 2003). On the other, the different levels of commitment to comply with marine environmental legislations result in ambivalence, stress and confusion for seafarers. Therefore, this research will endeavour to identify the means by which such trans-boundary professionals frame and view their commitments towards the marine environment and how they react to such frames on the daily practical level on board ships.

1.5   Aims of the Research

This is a piece of qualitative research that involves talking to seafarers about their perceptions of marine pollution in an attempt to identify the effect of the key frames through which they make sense of their daily actions and environmental compliance practices. The study will also look at how seafarers link their frames and actions to their shipping companies and to the main regulatory bodies governing marine pollution issues. In short, I am trying to understand how seafarers as a nomadic professional group perceive requirements in relation to marine pollution regulatory instruments, how they discharge responsibilities in this respect, and how they socially construct and rationalise such responsibilities. It is clear from this study that seafarers are experiencing many difficulties – especially on the technical side - in their attempts to comply with mandatory legal instruments (e.g. MARPOL). In the light of the above discussion, I may declare the aims of this research as follows:

- To explore and analyse how seafarers socially construct the marine pollution problem, how they view possible solutions, and how they frame and react to compliance issues with relevant marine environmental regulations.
- To show and explain why technically- based regulatory instruments may not be the only solution for trans-boundary marine pollution problems.

For achieving such aims it is important to introduce, briefly, the framing concept employed throughout this thesis. This thesis draws on frame analysis developed by Goffman (Goffman 1974) which has been applied to environmental conflicts (Lewicki et al. 2003) and in the area of social movements (Benford and Snow 2000). Recent work on global social movements has extended these uses by developing a reflexive framing approach (Chesters and Welsh 2005a; Chesters and Welsh 2006a). Framing thus applies to both the interpretation of environmental disputes and assessing the sense making devices activists use to orientate themselves in relation to contentious issues. In this study aspects of these approaches are used to interpret the seafarers' relationships with wider environmental stakes, marine pollution and their working practices.

1.6   Contribution of the Research

This research offers a contribution to the field of framing environmental policies in several ways. First, it makes explicit the ways in which a nomadic professional group such as seafarers frame and interact with the growing demand to protect the environment in general and the marine environment in particular. Due to the nature of their profession, this group is able to roam the world and compare the effectiveness of environmental regulations in various countries. The shipping industry is composed of different types of shipping companies, some of which can be described as more environmentally aware than others, an issue which would affect the frames of seafarers regarding compliance to environmental regulations as discussed in this study. Moreover, this research opens up a social qualitative inquiry in areas scarcely attended to by previous scholars especially when focusing on the relationships and tensions between seafarers and their personal and professional commitments to their global work place; the marine environment. However, in the course of this study some important questions emerged:

- Are the marine pollution problems simply to do with regulations?
- Should we even be thinking about the link between environmental compliance and technology solutions?
- Is technology the problem or the people using it?
- How do the frames of seafarers shape their daily compliance practices?

To attend to the above questions, this research looks at the frames of seafarers working onboard three different strands of shipping companies and different geographic locations around the world and using different types of technology solutions as mandated by marine environmental conventions. This study argues that such differences not only impact on social constructions of seafarers towards environmental protection but also affects their framing of daily compliance practices as well. This allows us to review the institutional and instrumental policies carried out by different ship owners in different parts of the world and verify how this impacts on the frames of seafarers towards environmental compliance. Hence, this study includes the outcome dimension with a view that implementation can only take place adequately if there is a change of practice of those subject to the provisions of the regime.

1.7   Research questions and strategy

The research will be structured around the following Primary Research Question:

How do seafarers as a nomadic professional group perceive and react to growing environmental concerns and new stringent marine environmental regulations in the pursuit of best practice?

Subsidiary research questions that the research project needs to address are:

- Are there incentives, other than regulatory enforcement, which can promote environmentally proactive practices by seafarers to deliver advances in the quality of the marine environment?
- How do seafarers interact with new regulatory and monitoring regimes (e.g. port state control, flag state control, vetting inspections) in terms of their contribution to improving environmental compliance?
- What factors contribute to the assumption that technology solutions are not working effectively in terms of monitoring pollution levels? What are the implications of this for companies and seafarers?
- To what extent can maritime education and training institutions promote environmental awareness of current and potential seafarers?

To achieve my goals the institutional environment is also subjected to enquiry: my focus is on the significance of pressure from the main maritime governing body, or more specifically the 'International Maritime Organization' (IMO). The importance of international environmental legislation, and especially the MARPOL 73/78 convention as the main marine environmental protection international treaty in force, is also discussed in depth. I start by looking at the institutional factors at the main governing body (i.e. the IMO), moving on to review the administrative culture in different shipping companies and finish by focusing on the daily environmentally related frames and actions at the bottom level of the compliance chain (i.e. the seafarers). As for the interests and incentives to compliance, I study both those in the specific category of a shipping company and among the sea-going decision making staff. The former are believed to evaluate the policy in question according to its costs and benefits, while the latter are supposed to follow and encourage their crew members to comply with the detailed requirements of the environmental maritime conventions. By looking at these three tiers, I combine the policy makers' insights with elements from regime target groups' social constructions of the marine pollution problem in a holistic way. This is necessary to study the impacts of environmental frames on the daily practice of seafarers, and it may also be fruitful to propose some viable approaches to tackle the on-going compliance problem.

1.8 Thesis Structure

Chapter two reviews the key literature underpinning this research and provides my critical insight on the existing reflexive modernisation, risk and trust extensive fields. The key research literature spans several disciplines indicative of the inter-disciplinary nature of the research topic. Bearing in mind the huge span of reflexivity and risk literatures, I focus upon areas directly relevant to my research questions and themes evident from my pilot study. This allowed me to be selective and to link established theories about reflexivity, risk, and trust to the context of my study. The relatively new concept of 'reflexive framing' with its literature also provided a coherent theoretical background for many of my empirical findings as I discuss in chapter two. Chapter three displays the most prominent expert regulatory tool used by maritime legislators to mitigate marine pollution by shipping (i.e. the Marpol convention). This convention is widely ratified by the majority of maritime nations but the onus of daily compliance measures still rests with seafarers as this chapter explains.

Chapter four sets out the methodology employed in this study and explains the rationale behind the choice of method. This chapter also constitutes an initial analysis of the pilot study interviews conducted back in the early summer of 2006. In this chapter, I discuss the methods used to create this thesis describing the practical methods employed in the collection of the various sources of data. Next, I describe the process of analysis and discuss the use of theory in this text. The aim of this chapter is to give the reader insight into the empirical and analytical foundations of this text. Furthermore, I also want to show how my experiences from the time when I collected and analysed data also provide many insights into the research question(s).

The following four data chapters take in turn the different aspects of the 'global influences', 'faceless interactions', 'face work interactions', and 'conflict management and practice' inspired by how seafarers socially construct environmental protection and their accounts regarding what influences their frames and actions.

The final chapter (summary, conclusion and further work) brings the four aspects together and discusses the relationships between them, showing the importance of their interaction on the decisions and outcomes affecting the main problem of this research.

1.9   Concluding Remarks

This chapter introduced the reader to the wide and complex ideas governing, affecting and underpinning this research project. When the ocean is considered as such a complex system, the role of science becomes one of providing representative organizational models based on the interaction and integration between ecological and social elements and processes (Vallega 2001). At this point lies the real value of the social science prospect in this research study with its contribution to the understanding of "human kind by human kind", especially in terms of human behaviour towards the marine environment in both spatial and temporal dimensions (Smith 2002). The next chapter explores the key body of literature inspiring this research project.

CHAPTER TWO – Literature Review

2.1 Introduction

Seafarers, as a labour group, 'construct' their own frames of marine pollution risk through multiple resources. These resources are either on a personal level as citizens, reflexively coping with the persistent calls to protect the environment in contemporary society, or as professionals having to comply with an array of marine environmental legislations. In this chapter I will engage with three major areas of literature. The first two are focused on the issue of reflexivity and pollution risk(s) and are essentially a pre-requisite for the third area of literature discussing the current marine environmental regulations and the problems with environmental compliance practices in the shipping sector.

The chapter is divided into five sections; the first section, selectively reviews some of the relevant strands of the vast 'reflexive modernisation' literature and its embedded concept of 'risk' in late modern society. The second section links the reflexivity notions to the vital issue of 'trust' and trust relations between individuals and reviews the theorisation of different types of 'trust' relations in the literature. The third section moves on to critically compare different approaches to presenting and interpreting the concept of 'ecological modernisation' and the resultant legal, environmental, and social practices by nations, corporate players, and individuals. The aim is to highlight and define the relevance of such overarching literature on interpreting and analysing the environmental practices of seafarers as individuals and as professionals. The review sets the scene for the rationale behind the employment of the 'framing' paradigm as the chosen vehicle for interpreting and analysing this study's data. It further explains the reliance on the more recent concept of 'reflexive framing' as a rigorous analytical tool and why it is best suited to the aims and objectives of this particular study.

The fourth section presents the current status of marine environmental regulatory instruments. The focus of this section is to clarify the increasing environmental demands put on seafarers as a professional group in terms of complying with marine environmental regulatory instruments. In this section, I will briefly discuss the literature surrounding the 'audit culture' and the dominant reliance on technology as two of the main regulatory tools utilised by maritime policy makers in mitigating marine pollution. These two regulatory tools exemplify the most prominent portals of interaction between seafarers and the overarching environmental regulatory system governing marine pollution. Finally, the fifth section briefly presents the concept of the global environmental frame (GEF) and the reasons behind my choice of the 'framing' and the more recent 'reflexive framing' analytical concepts to interpret and make sense of this study's data.

2.2 Reflexive Modernisation: A Maritime Context

This section explores selected strands of literature around the theory of 'reflexive modernisation' which is primarily associated with the names of Anthony Giddens (Giddens 1990, 1991) and Ullrich Beck (Beck 1992; Beck et al. 1994) . Whilst the perspective seems to have generated vigorous debate in sociology, its impact on my interpretation of the data is prominent. Most importantly, it helps me to examine how the 'reflexive self' in a state of late modernity is defined and how it revokes traditional thinking about environmental issues. In this context, it is important to note that whilst theories of reflexive modernisation have stimulated such sociological debate, it has been subjected to very little empirical verification (McKechnie and Welsh 2002) hence the importance of this qualitative study.

Through exploring the relevant strands of existing literature, this section argues that theories of reflexive modernization are directly relevant to the concerns of this study around marine pollution. In particular, I aim to show that the notion of reflexive modernization and its subsidiary concepts (e.g., risk and trust) can provide a powerful theoretical frame within which to place and understand some of the recent transformations of marine environmental regulations and the current difficulties in compliance. I draw upon the reflexive modernization theory to describe and explain the broad changes, reform, and pressures that have emerged in the last two decades in the maritime sector resulting in different frames and actions by seafarers as discussed in the following sub-sections.

2.2.1 The 'Reflexive' Citizen / Seafarer

We cannot exclude seafarers from being citizens - as well as situated professionals - living in this late modern era. As Giddens, Beck, and Lash contend (Beck et al. 1994) in relatively

24

different ways, citizens are being increasingly 'reflexive' in today's world. On the one hand, Giddens refers to reflexivity as a condition and outcome of a post-traditional society contending that citizens take decisions on the basis of a more or less continuous reflection on the conditions of one's action (Giddens 1994a). On the other hand, Beck sees 'reflexivity' as a critical re-appraisal of one's risk position in today's 'risky' society. He asserts that this 'reflexivity' can go forward and be mobilised by individuals without the tools of 'scientific and expert knowledge' (Beck et al. 1994). In other words, Beck argues that individuals do not necessarily rely on institutional and scientific experts when deciding on the mobilising of their actions. For the purpose of this study, it should be clear that Giddens deals with reflexivity as a means of change whilst Beck sees reflexivity as 'more of the same' using 'critical reflection' as his means of change. In this respect, both approaches are proving to be useful to my interpretation of the seafarers' interview accounts. For example, in this study, we can see how seafarers are continuously monitoring compliance and non-compliance practices by their peers on board ships and by others of different nationalities or by those who are working for different shipping companies. Doing this, and specifically from their extremely mobile workplace positions, they are also assessing and evaluating risks to the environment, their health, and the well-being of their children and future generations as well. These are areas that, historically, seafarers lacked sufficient knowledge of, as they themselves admit except in recent years after becoming increasingly subjected to globally mediated calls to protect the environment.

In this respect, seafarers' orientation of the impacts of pollution on the marine environment are clearly influenced by what is circulated in the mass media about environmental issues. Within the context of the reflexive modernisation process, it is argued that individuals may become more informed by an array of communicative facilities around them. They reflexively reflect on these instantaneous audio/visual facilities creating their own interpretations of the world changes around them which forces them to critically reassess their own role in such debates (Adam et al. 2000; Beck et al. 1994). In this context, Boden (2000) suggests that the instantaneous flow of information that characterises contemporary society is one of the main resources of reflexivity. She argues that as computers, telephones, and televisions are merging into a singular communicative environment, the very idea of interaction is taking on a new meaning (Boden 2000).

However, for my own study's purposes, I am particularly interested in the claim of the reflexive modernisation theory that as a result of this information digestion process, people, progressively become more sceptical of state and expert advice (Beck 1992; Ekberg 2007). The argument is that people are also more likely to distrust external sources of information, preferring to rely instead on themselves and their ability - on the individual level - to interpret the growing 'risks' within the contemporary information society (Beck 1992; Bickerstaff et al. 2008b; Webster 2004). In this study, this argument is taken into consideration when attempting to verify the reasons and consequences of distrust on the environmental practices of seafarers.

This individualisation process – among a labour group such as seafarers – results mainly in implications on practice and, potentially, on environmental behaviours and attitudes of people (Lupton and Tulloch 2002; Matten 2004). These behaviours may or may not be in compliance with the growing body of legislative instruments targeting marine pollution problems (Brookman 2002; Mattson 2006; Mitchell 1994b; Mitchell 1994c). Here, I raise some important questions about how these pollution risks are understood and if framed as potential risks, how are they managed by seafarers.

2.2.2 The Reflexive Citizen

Theorists of reflexive modernisation focus on the issue of uncertainty, radical questioning and doubt by citizens living in the contemporary risk society (Beck 2000; Giddens 1990; Giddens 1999). This uncertainty is attributed to a whole set of what they term 'manufactured risks' that could be divided into economic, political, professional, environmental, and personal health risks (Beck-Gernsheim 2000; Rose 2000; Van Loon 2000; Welsh 2000b). As a result of such 'manufactured risks', Beck (1990, 1994, 2009) argues that in today's risk society we have developed a sort of prognostic catastrophic potential which fuels uncertainty and provokes profound political consequences. It could be argued that this prognostic feature of risk perception among maritime policy makers could be one of the reasons behind the recent accelerating pace of adopting a growing set of marine environmental regulatory instruments in the last decade (e.g. Marpol Annex VI, Ballast water management convention, Anti-Fouling convention... etc.). Arguably, in a global industry like shipping, it also led policy makers to rely heavily on techno-fixes to minimise intentional pollution risks especially in the area of

26

monitoring the discharge of pollutants from ships, a strategy that proved to be problematic for seafarers as discussed further ahead in this thesis.

Along similar lines and in response to his critics, Beck (2000) explains that the concept of 'risk' is a 'peculiar intermediate state between security and destruction'. This characterisation of risk is a long way from the classic scientifically calculated risk (i.e. risk = accident X probability). He argues that contemporary risk societies are characterised by the paradox of more and more environmental degradation – perceived and potential – coupled with an expansion of law and regulation. This is an argument that could be coherent in reviewing the plethora of marine environmental legal instruments adopted in the last decade. He also asserts that in the contemporary 'risk society', the perception of threatening risks determines thought and action (Beck 2000). In this thesis, I take these arguments a step forward towards better understanding of environmental practices resulting from such potential and perceived pollution risks among seafarers. In doing this, I provide an account focusing on the tensions between workplace roles and practices and the perceived wider citizenship and 'environmental' responsibilities by this labour group, an area ignored in the literature discussing the risk positions of contemporary citizens.

At this point, and for the purpose of further exploring the 'relevant' strands of literature, I need to raise several important questions around arguments put forward by Beck (2000) that are potentially important to the data analysis of this study. Firstly, how is the notion of 'self-transformation' of risk (i.e. linking technical risks to economic, health, and political risks) affecting the perceptions and actions of seafarers about mitigating marine pollution? Secondly, what are the potential means of re-gaining the lost trust in the producers and decision makers of risk (i.e. policy makers) and the risk takers (i.e. seafarers)? Thirdly, if the risk concept is changing the perceived relationship between past, present and future - as Beck (1990) argues - what could be the effect of such perception on the daily environmental practice of seafarers as a nomadic professional group?

2.2.3 Response to Risk Perception

Central to my argument in this thesis is how the 'risk' literature describes the movement of risk from the periphery to the fore-front of individual perception (Beck et al. 1994). I take this argument further to explore the implications of such centre-staged environmental perceived/actual risks on the framing of environmental pollution by seafarers. Throughout this study, many seafarers imply that influential social actors push forward the environmental agendas in maritime policy making by enhancing the 'perceived' risks of shipping to the marine and coastal environments. However, this could be another consequence of a dominant phenomenon of distrust in policy makers that potentially reflects on the seafarers' environmental practice as discussed in the next section. To strengthen my argument, I approach MARPOL as a working expert system intended to harness expert knowledge of the regulation of the marine working environment. This will be discussed in the next chapter.

These insights will aid in the interpretation of data regarding the assignment of blame by seafarers to policy makers, ship managers, and even their peers on board depending on the available resources of information and their own observations and experiences (see chapter five). In this context, this study needs to locate the specific resources that this particular labour group (i.e. seafarers) is experiencing in order to facilitate a better understanding of perceived/actual pollution risks in the shipping sector.

2.3   Trust

The establishment of the relationship between trust relations and environmental practice is crucial for this study. In this respect, it is important to highlight that whilst Giddens' work is developed primarily with the relationship between layman / person and expert in mind, the concepts he develops can also be applied in the case of interactions between experts and situated professionals. In this sense, I am approaching the maritime regulatory sphere as an abstract system whose integrity depends upon effective regulations, regulatory monitoring and auditing, and workplace practices (i.e. shipboard environmental practice). In this respect, trust relations are crucial in maintaining an effective maritime regulatory sphere in both the internal working environment and the wider public arena. Hence, for present purposes it is important to outline the key aspects of Giddens' work on trust and their relevance to this study.

In this study, seafarers are bound by legal and professional codes and regulations that expose them to various forms of interactions with people they consider as being experts (e.g. auditors and inspectors). An example of such interaction occurs when policy makers send their agents to fulfil the monitoring and auditing mandatory requirements of adopted regulations. Another form of interaction takes place when junior and senior ranks on-board ships interact regarding proper professional practice, where trust should be maintained. Here at these 'portals of access', using Giddens' (1990) terms, the chance of seafarers realising the expert's professional shortcomings could be enhanced. This may precipitate a situation of compromised trust relations as a result of the different nature of seafarers who are situated professionals possessing adequate knowledge about shipboard technicalities and who cannot be classified as lay public (see chapter six).

In this respect, Giddens (1990) asserts that the reflexivity of modern social life is reliant upon the constant examination of social practices in the 'light of incoming information about these very practices'. One of the key areas where this sort of examination occurs is at what he calls 'junction points' at which lay individuals interact with 'expert systems'(Giddens 1990, 1991). At such encounters 'trust' is built, maintained or compromised, depending on the expert's performance. This type of face-work interaction, in Gidden's view, also reflects the overall trust in the wider 'abstract' systems whether it is legal, social, or administrative. He argues that the realisation of the areas of ignorance which confront the experts themselves as individual practitioners and in terms of overall knowledge may undermine the faith on the part of the lay individuals (Giddens 1990).

In this context, and to clarify the reasons for the growing public distrust in 'expert systems' in general, Giddens (1990) contends that no one can become a highly credentialed expert in more than a few small sectors of the 'immensely complicated systems which now exist'. Furthermore, he argues that every expert could be considered as a lay person in the face of the multiplicity of 'other' abstract systems that influence their life (Giddens 1994a). Reflecting on this argument, the complexity of the ship's various areas of environmental audit where seafarers interact with agents of the 'abstract system' is investigated in this study in order to depict a clearer picture of trust relations in a professional setting.

2.4   Trustworthiness in Professional Settings

2.4.1 Face-work interactions: Personal Trust

Giddens classifies the process of regarding a person or a system as being 'trustworthy' into two categories: the first is that trust that could be established between individuals who are well known to one another and who, on the basis of long term acquaintance, have 'substantiated the credentials which render each other reliable in the eyes of the other' (Giddens 1990:83). This argument is exemplified in this study by the seafarers' trust in their peers and superiors on board a ship depending on the established ethos of the seafaring profession dictating the hierarchal structure and responsibilities on board. This usually emanates from an established assumption among seafarers that more senior and experienced persons should be trusted and their practices should count as exemplary.

Following this, it is important to highlight that the small society on board a ship is still bound by traditional ethos to a large extent. One of the main on-board workplace cultures is respecting the quasi-military hierarchal structure of ranks and roles. Based on Giddens' arguments, I contend that the high level of direct or face-work interactions in the confined work place on-board a ship and the mutual exchange or display of professional skills evokes either trust or mistrust (Giddens 1990, 1991). Seafarers in this process seek shared feelings of commitment to an important cause (e.g. saving the marine environment) within a feeling of group belonging in what could be a search for - using Giddens term - 'ontological security'. The trust between peers on board provides, maintains, or undermines the sense of 'ontological security' especially when the system in question is as abstract as 'the environment'. For Giddens the objective of the reflexive self lies in attaining a sense of ontological security in relation to both their personal biographical selves and their wider social relationships (Giddens 1990).

In this respect, personal trust is regarded as an expectation of individuals and their exercise. Giddens refers to the process of trusting individuals as a matter of 'face-work' commitments where other actors' honesty and probity are looked for (Giddens 1990). He defines the direct interactions occurring in face-work situations as vital to building or undermining trust, calling these 'access points'. However, Giddens' arguments around face-work interactions always assume that such interactions occur between lay individuals and experts possessing more scientific or professional knowledge – or at least perceived to be so. In this study, seafarers interact frequently with what they perceive as 'experts' at identified 'access points' in various occasions at sea and in port. For example, these interactions occur during multiple auditing and inspection procedures either by external audit groups or by internal company management representatives. Seafarers usually expect that such personnel should be at an expert level in exercising professional experience and practical knowledge. While some of these encounters cannot be classified as regular but rather occasional, Giddens still highlights that in such irregular face-work situations experts need to provide even more evidence of their own and their system's reliability (Giddens 1990:85).

Following this theme, Giddens argues that individuals, who had unfortunate experiences at a given access point, where the technical skills of the 'experts' in question are relatively low level, may decide to opt out of the expert-lay relationship. In a similar context, some seafarers in this study, after experiencing extremely conflicting views from different auditors and inspectors, chose to resort to their own professional judgement so as not to confuse themselves with what they perceived as non-professional demands (see chapters four and five). In this context, Giddens, in his extensive account regarding the relationship between lay persons and experts, emphasises that face-work trust relations ordinarily demand attitudes of integrity and unflappability in professional practice. Nevertheless, he concludes his discussion by assuming that everyone is aware that the real repository of trust is in the abstract system rather than the individuals who represent it (Giddens 1990, 1991). This is an issue for discussion in the next sub-section.

2.4.2 Faceless Trust

The second category is the trust in 'abstract systems' which does not primarily pre-suppose any direct encounters at all with the individuals or groups who are, in some way, responsible for these abstract systems. Giddens empathises that, in late modern society, the development of faith in symbolic tokens or expert systems which, taken together he terms 'abstract systems', is vitally important (Giddens 1990:80). He argues that the counter-factual, future oriented character of late-modernity is largely structured by trust vested in abstract systems, which by its very nature is filtered by the trustworthiness of established expertise. Here, it is important to note that for the purposes of this thesis I approach MARPOL as a working expert system intended to harness expert knowledge of the regulation of the marine working environment (see chapter three).

In this way, the faceless version of 'trust' can be defined as a state of favourable expectation regarding other experts' actions and intentions. However, on the road to reaching such favourable expectation Giddens notes that trust, especially in institutional abstract systems, rests on vague and partial understanding. He recognises that trust differs from weak inductive knowledge as it presumes a 'leap to commitment and an irreducible quality of faith' (Giddens 1990). In other words, and in contrast to face-work interactions, impersonal trust is more the expectation and predictability of expert laden institutions and the way embedded actors are using rules, routines, and authority. Hence, trust in abstract systems is a faceless commitment relying on what is expected from these professional, expert laden institutions. For example, in this study, seafarers expect an international institution responsible for global maritime governance and laden with experts such as the IMO to fulfil its role in providing at least some of what its slogan says: 'safer ships and cleaner oceans'. However, the quality of professional performance of the expert systems' agents (e.g. auditors and inspectors) plays a major role in either maintaining or compromising faceless trust as discussed in this thesis.

Based on this theoretical approach, I may argue that Giddens did not / failed to explore the potential consequences of maintained or compromised trust relations on the faceless level. In this study, measures devised by expert systems to reduce marine pollutions risks lead to further compromising trust as discussed in chapters five and six.

Generally, however, this clear emphasis in Giddens' work upon the importance of trust towards specific abstract systems brings some important analytical questions to the surface. First, what are the mechanisms of building trust, in this research, between professionals on one side and experts representing the abstract system on the other in lieu of the usual lay person-expert encounter? Second, if seafarers are situated professionals and competent in various aspects of technological aspects on board a ship, do they consider themselves at the same level of knowledge in environmental matters? What are the effects of environmental knowledge communicated via the mass media on the professional environmental practice of seafarers?

2.4.3 Trust and Reflexivity

Giddens contends that people in late modern societies, upon reaching the state of trust in abstract systems, may feel more secure. However, this trust cannot supply the mutuality which personal trust relations offer. Following this theme, he argues that the transformation of mutuality has notable implications on the individual; first, it leads to the construction of the self as a reflexive project, an elemental part of the reflexivity of modernity whereas an individual strives to find his/her identity amid multiple strategies and options dictated by abstract systems. Second, it generates a concern for self-fulfilment which could be seen as a positive appropriation of circumstances in which globalised influences impinge upon everyday life (Giddens 1990:123). Third, in professional settings, when and if reflexive individuals invest their trust in abstract systems, they trust the credentials and legitimacy conferred, as Giddens contends, through professional codes of practice, qualifications, accreditation, licensing, performance, and reputation (Giddens 1990:87). For Giddens, the objective of the reflexive self lies in attaining what he terms 'ontological security' in relation to both their personal biographical self and their wider social relationships. In this thesis, the interest is in the seafarers' sense of self security in their workplace under multiple professional and multi-layered legal compliance tensions.

This study will show that seafarers are trying to reach a state of 'ontological security' in relation to environmental protection influenced -in part- by the global mass media which inevitably impinge on their daily environmental practice on board ships. It will also become clear that seafarers in their pursuit of such self-fulfilment are more aware that their current environmental practice shapes future outcomes. Recognising this, they are engaged in a process of 'self-transformation' of risk (Beck et al. 1994). In other words, linking potential marine pollution risks to the economic welfare of their countries, the health of their children, and political reputation of their nations...etc. This reflexive process and its implications on the daily environmental practice of seafarers is one area of enquiry in this study.

If it is agreed that trust is an element of being a reflexive individual in late modern society, then the above discussion clarifies the dominant orientation of reflexive individuals towards promoting a better quality of life and reducing risks to health and the environment. In doing this, people - and seafarers in this study - try to assess and insure the safety, security, and survival of life on earth. These shifts are described by Beck and Giddens as recent shifts to ecological politics (Beck 1995; Giddens 1994a). However, there is still a need to verify the impact of such shifts on the practice of reflexive professionals such as seafarers.

2.4.4 Trust in Symbolic Tokens

Giddens maintains that it is our trust in symbolic tokens and expert systems that gives rise to faceless commitments (Giddens 1990:80). One of the most trusted symbolic tokens is 'money' which is, arguably, enjoying a higher level of trust than other components of abstract systems such as science and technology (Giddens 1990:1-34).

Giddens uses money as the example of the symbolic tokens process, whilst doing this he argues that for social institutions to function there must be trust and faith. In Giddens' view, Institutions are of course "abstract" social concepts that assist society to flow and function properly (Giddens 1990:1-34). In this study the concepts of 'symbolic tokens' and 'faceless trust' in 'expert systems' are adopted to explore how seafarers trust their own shipping companies and – at times – the policy making institutions involved in regulating marine pollution.

In this study, the sense of trust in 'money' or, in other words, economic revenue, is perceived by seafarers to be a prime factor influencing their shipping companies' environmental policies and decisions. As a consequence to such trust, a prominent type of 'faceless commitment' is detected among seafarers from different backgrounds and shipping companies. Put simply, seafarers, as reflexive individuals and professionals, are aligning their environmental practice to fulfil economic and profit demands of their respective shipping companies. However, in doing this, they are challenged with situations where they find themselves pursuing incompatible goals as discussed in chapters five and six.

As a result of the dominance of the idea that economic revenue is a key priority for ship owners, seafarers are found to be vulnerable to various practices to fulfil such demands. In this context, the literature suggests that abstract systems are accused of de-skilling late modern individuals and professionals, not only in the workplace but also in all sectors of social life that they engage in (Giddens 1991). By 'deskilling', Giddens refers to a process of marginalising

34

localised and – at times – professional knowledge, opening the door to the pervasive effects of dominant abstract systems to re-skill individuals with its own influential ideas. For example, in this study, many experienced seafarers in lieu of depending on the detailed provisions of the MARPOL convention to define their specific daily compliance tasks report that they are, instead, focusing on fulfilling the economic revenue demands of ship owners even if this clearly contradicts legal obligations and/or professional practice.

2.4.5 Environmental Risk and Trust

Beck has made it clear that scientific expertise plays an important role in the way the general public conceive modern risks, including environmental risks. Therefore, amidst the current rise of public concerns about these risks, it is assumed that the public awareness of such risks is highly mediated by expert knowledge and expert bodies monitoring and managing these risks (Beck 1992). In this context, and foregrounding marine and chemical pollution as examples of late modern risks, Beck argues that 'trust' is usually undermined when scientific experts fail to provide reliable policy recommendations because of the incompleteness of the available expert knowledge (Beck 1992).

Along similar lines, Giddens identifies one main characteristic of the new risk situation is experts disagreeing with each other. He argues that policy makers often get confused by ambiguous 'expert' research conclusions and disrupted interpretations (Giddens 1998). In this study, seafarers face a paradoxical situation in relation to environmental practice on both personal and professional fronts. On the one hand, they must rely on the expertise of scientific advisors to maritime policy makers and attempt to comply with the resultant marine environmental instruments on a relatively abstract level. On the other hand, they are confronted and confused by contradictory claims of other experts, on the face-work level, forcing them to resort - at times - to personal values to be compliant with professional obligations (see chapters five and six).

2.4.6 Transition of Risk and Trust

The study of seafarers' perceptions of pollution risks exemplifies the tension between material and socially constructed risks. In other words, this study observes the shift from actual to perceived risks in the form of a transformation from invisible to visible to virtual pollution risks along the temporal dimension (i.e. in the last few years- as seafarers argue). Seafarers talk about the journey across time from the normality of dumping various types of pollutants at sea just a few years ago. Following this, they mark the transition to a collective initiative of better environmental practices - or at least their hope to contribute to some - influenced by interactions with abstract systems and mass media campaigns in the last few years. Finally, many seafarers talk about future risks as potential harms to human health and are aware of the adverse effect on future generations as a result of the current status of pollution from shipping. Such perceptions and awareness lead them to speculate that the near future will carry more strict environmental measures that they will need to be prepared for to be better on the personal side whilst - in the same time - making sure they remain compliant professionals as well. However, the outcome of such expectations varies according to the category of shipping company and/or the geographic area of trade as we discuss later in this thesis.

In this respect, Beck (2000) suggests that technological risks of the risk society not only cross geo-spatial and geopolitical boundaries, but also cross temporal boundaries. This is also discussed by Giddens in the form of what he terms 'time space distantiation' (Giddens 1990). The above discussion about pollution risk perceptions in the past, present, and prospects for a 'stricter' future by seafarers exemplifies this line of thinking. What is more, this study examines the impact of such phenomenon on the classification - by seafarers - of certain parts of the world as 'dump free' while other areas are 'dangerous to dump' in a process that is directly linked to trust and distrust in abstract and expert systems.

Concerning the spatial aspect, Giddens and Beck maintain that one of the consequences of globalisation is that dependency on a specific place decreases and that individuals instead gain access to many different places (Beck 1992; Beck et al. 1994). This argument not only refers to physical access to different places but to access to a network of places as a result of globalised forms of communication as well. They argue that as a result of this process individuals develop a sense of commitment connecting many different networks of places. One of the main outcomes of such reduced place dependency is considered to be that rule-based behaviour is replaced by reflexivity. Hence, individuals no longer submit to traditional norms and values but instead develop a critical and reflexive attitude both towards the overarching social structure and towards their own conceptions, which they have previously taken for granted (Giddens, 1984).

In this context, I argue that seafarers in this study are not only subjected to physical access to many geographic places around the world but also to the globalised networks of environmental information affecting their framing of environmental issues. Doing this, they frequently talk about the transition from the normality of polluting activities by them and their peers a few years ago to recent, more responsible environmental attitudes. In this context, and bearing in mind Giddens' arguments, this study calls into question the link between reflexivity and de-traditionalisation at an empirical level. This will help gain a better understanding of the factors behind this transition and locate the difficulties that may be hindering better environmental practice by seafarers. Arguably, reflexive risk perceptions is one of the prime factors influencing citizen's perceptions in today's global 'risk society' (Beck 1992, 2009; Beck et al. 1994).

It is clear from the above discussion that there is a strong link between theories of risk and theories of trust. When risk and trust combine they relate inversely, thus in an environment of high risk (e.g. on board a ship) trust is assumed to be low and in an environment of low risk trust is high (Lash 2000). In this context, this study identifies implications of the variance between shipboard 'risky' environments in different categories of shipping companies (see the following chapter) not only on trust relations between seafarers and abstract systems but also on resultant environmental practice. However, the seafarer, inevitably, due to the mobile nature of his workplace is subjected to various different interpretations of the overarching concepts - linked mainly to risk and trust concepts - that influence maritime policy makers, such as the 'anticipate and legislate' precautionary approach. For example, it is clear that legal drafting of an environmental instrument such as MARPOL clearly coins the concept of ecological modernisation with its embedded precautionary and technology approaches (see section 2.4). Moreover, the seafarers themselves as a global workforce are 'assembled' from different parts of the world, different nationalities, and various cultural and training backgrounds. Naturally, this has an impact on how they frame marine pollution and regulatory instruments designed to mitigate or reduce the risk(s) of marine pollution. For this reason, the next section reviews and critically discusses the implications of applying this concept in the maritime regulatory domain.

2.4.7 Beck Vs Giddens on Reflexivity

Having mentioned that both theorists' approaches are beneficial to my work, it is important to compare Beck's and Giddens' approaches to reflexivity in order to establish the reasons behind considering both theoretical arguments in this study and to acknowledge the marked differences in their interpretations to the issue of reflexivity.

For Beck (1992), on the one hand, the notion of reflexivity is "more of the same" resulting in more perceived risks and more attempts to control / mitigate such risks by utilising the same classic means. In this context, McKechnie and Welsh (2002) argue that it is not clear with Beck's approach to reflexivity how action would be initiated or mobilised. In other words, how the heightened notions of risk can be transformed into critical reflection (i.e. action). In this context beck extends his argument to suggest that global institutions are increasingly becoming hollow in terms of legitimacy triggering a bottom up approach (e.g. people's science courts – beck 1992). In this study, some seafarers realising their increasing commitments towards protection of the marine environment, are showing strong self-reflection / self-critique signs but still rather ambivalent about the means to change.

On the other hand Giddens (1990, 1991) advocates the notion of "reflexive Subjects" who are engaged in a continuous process of self-monitoring and attempting to refine their customs and practices upon acquiring new information. Giddens' argue that such processes may result from the complex lay/expert relationships and the trust and distrust in modernity expert / abstract systems (i.e. global institutions – money). With Giddens reflexivity / reflection becomes more personal than institutional and we can sense more implicit rather than explicit attempts of change. In this study, some seafarers, while developing a sense of distrust in expert and abstract systems are attempting to explore means of change by refining and improving their long acquired customs towards marine pollution.

Seafarers in the pilot study are waving signs of a heightened sense of risk regarding marine pollution and the need for change in practices regarding environmental compliance, both are elements that will be explored and debated throughout the data chapters of this thesis as seafarers attempt to arrive to a state of professional wellbeing (ontological security). It is worth mentioning here that some scholars criticise the sort of certainty advocated by Giddens (1990) in his explanation of ontological security as a 'carapace' - a hard exogenous shell - preferring to approach ontology as a process of 'becoming' rather than a process of 'being' (McKechnie and Welsh 2002). Moreover, for this study, it is important to acknowledge that both approaches have marked limitations regarding the scarce direct engagement with capital and economic relations which, arguably, could be influential factors in framing environmental disputes.

2.5 Ecological Modernisation

One of the most influential approaches to engaging with environmental risks lies in the extended body of work on ecological modernisation (Andersen and Massa 2000; Mol 1995; Young 2000). Ecological modernisation (EM) arises as a set of theorisation around studies of chemical industries on land, operating with a relatively homogenous workforce drawn from a common culture. It is broadly understood as the 'implementation of preventative innovation in production systems (processes and products) that simultaneously produces environmental and economic benefits' (Hajer 1997; Mol 1995, 1997, 2001). In the maritime context any regulatory approach attempting to apply this will encounter mixed shipping crews, multiple monitoring and auditing authorities, different jurisdictions, and a disparity of training backgrounds among ships' crew and staff (Bloor et al. 2006; ILO 2004; Lane 2000). Nevertheless, it is clear from the design of the MARPOL convention and other recently adopted marine environmental instruments (e.g. Ballast water Management convention BWM, MARPOL Annex VI) that there is a high tendency towards applying core ideas of the EM approach such as the 'precautionary principle' and the 'BATNEEC' principle (best available techniques not including excessive costs). In this sense, ecological modernisation theorists argue that EM harnessed technological innovation driven by growing environmental demands and market competition may herald a positive sum solution to what has been a zero-sum problem (i.e. imposing emission restrictions on industry while there is functional dependency on business) (Hajer 1997; Mol 1997).

Focusing on the area of pollution abatement, management, and prevention, Gouldson and Murphy (1997) use the term 'Ecological Modernisation' to describe the recent shift towards a more holistic and preventative approach to pollution prevention and waste minimisation which, potentially, brings associated benefits to both the environment and the economy. In general terms, those who promote change in this way claim it leads to innovation and technological developments with micro-and macro-economic benefits, such as improved competitiveness and employment gains, beyond the efficiency and environmental gains initially hoped for (Andersen and Massa 2000; Gouldson and Murphy 1997). In this section I will briefly discuss and review two main themes of the ecological modernisation literature relevant to the adoption and implementation of marine environmental conventions. These are the precautionary approaches to regulating pollution abatement from shipping and the reliance on technology solutions to reach this goal. Such approaches are seen to be growing steadily within the area of marine environmental regulations in the last two decades with implications on the seafarers' framing of environmental issues. This is conducted to clarify the seafarers' difficulties with the non-uniform attempts to implement this approach by different governing bodies, countries, and shipping companies.

2.5.1 The Precautionary Approach

The precautionary notion represents one of the main pillars that the EM concept is based upon. This approach is mainly a policy principle rather than a natural scientific concept. It was introduced to highlight the idea of anticipatory policy and to introduce an approach to replace the highly criticised 'react and cure' formula of the early 90s (Hajer 1997; Mol 1995). In that context, the precautionary principle may prompt environmental policy makers to decide on action even if there is no clear scientific evidence of a causal link in what could be termed a 'no regrets scenario' or a 'win win strategy' (Vanderzwaag 2002). However, in the case of cross-boundary marine pollution many functional frustrations of operating this approach were due to the heterogeneity of cultures, legal systems, economic capacity, and the political will of various nations to actively implement the resultant legal instruments (Mitchell 1994a).

Secondly, the precautionary principle concept usually places stress on showing the new role of science and technology in policy making. However, it is clear that recently, science and technology as an example of an abstract system are not maintaining the high level of 'trust' they once enjoyed by citizens (Frame and Brown 2008; Webster 2004). Nevertheless, science and technology remains entangled in the centre of the maritime policy making processes to date. A conclusion which can be reached relatively easily when looking at, for example, the numerous new technologies suggested treating trans-boundary invasive species in a ship's ballast water tanks. Based on scientific studies, these species are proven to cause bio-diversity imbalances, health and economic problems when transported in ships' ballast tanks throughout the world (MacPhee 2007). At this point, it is important to note that the reliance on scientific reports by the GESAMP (see introduction chapter) group of experts commissioned by the IMO contributes to the high dependency on tech-solutions by maritime policy makers (Wells et al. 2002; Wells et al. 1999). Whilst these are purely scientific reports, they often flag up concepts like 'multiple stresses' and 'critical loads' on the marine environment from shipping-based pollution, strongly suggesting scientific and technical remedies that may still be causing implementation problems (Mitchell 1998) .

In this respect, the anticipatory component of the 'precautionary principle' elicits an accelerated pace of risk-based technology solutions despite the seafarers' practical difficulties in dealing with them. Naturally, this could lead to compromising the seafarers' trust in technological solutions as they often find themselves either unable to operate the newly introduced sophisticated devices or struggling with existing technology solutions as discussed further ahead in this study. Clearly, this link between the precautionary approach and risk-based ideas provides a clearer image of the conceptual and practical tensions that seafarers experience daily on the shipboard level. This is an issue for more detailed discussion in chapters five and seven.

2.5.2 Different Countries: Different Approaches

Inevitably, seafarers roam the world as an inherent nature of their profession, facing different cultural understandings and applications to the notion of precaution in relation to pollution issues. In western developed countries, eco-modernist thinking, on the public level, conceptualises the environment as a public good or a resource, instead of the idea that it is basically free good and can be used as a sink (Hajer 1997). In less developed countries it is different, as pro-environmental behaviours mainly emerge from governments and, to a lesser extent, Non-Governmental Organisations (NGOs) rather than from the public at large (Rice 2006). Clearly, the resultant regulatory instruments and the active follow-up implementation efforts will differ to a large extent. Inevitably, such variations will have its impact on how seafarers frame marine pollution mitigation policies in general.

In this respect, Boehmer-Christiansen (1991) contends that the understanding of precautionary principles in relation to environmental pollution is different among the public and policy makers even within EU countries. In a study comparing the UK and Germany regarding 'acid rain' policies, she contends that such understandings are reliant on values embedded in language and culture. She contends that the English vocabulary for the environment and pollution control relies on Latin roots which conveys a greater sense of abstraction and distance between people and the world surrounding them. While in German, for example, the chosen word for environment 'Umwelt' literally means the surrounding world and refers specifically to air, water and soil which brings more of a sense of intimacy to the recipient of media resources. Regarding the precautionary principle, she contends that the equivalent word for precautionary in German 'vorsgae' when added to legal texts may elicit many forms of responses, for example; promoting research, setting-up liability and compensation regimes, mandating the use of cleaner technologies by law, and/or using economic measures such as pollution taxation (Boehmer-Christiansen 1994). Bearing in mind the internationalised structure of ships' crews in the contemporary shipping industry, and within the context of different interpretations to environmental protection, one could reasonably argue that seafarers will also have different conceptualisations of the precautionary approach as well. Hence, the interaction of this diverse professional group with the resultant techno-fixes is expected to be dependent on their established frames about technology solutions in general and frames about on-board pollution filtering devices in particular.

In this context, some scholars argue that shipping companies, being at the receiving end of ecological modernisation and its embedded 'precautionary principle' policies and technology solutions, focus on identification of cost-benefit risk-reducing measures and not on explicit reduction of individual or societal risks (Kim 2007; Vanderzwaag 2002). For example, the IMO, as a global regulatory body representing the abstract legal system, strives to have risk-based methodology widely accepted by member states that may have different approaches and conceptualisations to risk criteria, or may not have risk criteria at all (Trbojevic 2006). Being detached from the regulatory domain, seafarers in this study question the rationale behind precautionary environmental policies in what could be considered as further evidence of faceless mistrust in abstract systems (see chapter six). However, more important are the consequences of such conceptualisations on compliance practices with the precautionary-based marine environmental instruments (e.g. Marpol) when being implemented with different levels of rigor in various parts of the world.

2.5.3 The Technology Approach

Maritime policy makers, as well as policy makers in shore based industries, have attempted to satisfy the global environmental concerns by adopting an increasing number of new technology-based maritime environmental instruments in the last decade. However, on the global maritime front, they need to gain the consensus of all maritime nations in reaching the adoption and implementation stages of any international instrument. For example, the introduction of new techniques (see Chapter 3) by the Marpol convention to reduce the uptake of the marine environment from ship-based pollutants were meant to allow individual shipping companies to integrate into their overall environmental strategy calculations of cost and risk. These introduced technology solutions can be classified into the following: firstly, new ship construction technologies to manage and minimise the amount of waste oil generated on board (e.g. crude oil washing systems - SBTs). Secondly, the enforcement of mandatory (by the MARPOL convention) oil discharge monitoring and filtering devices which could be termed as a form of 'end of pipe' technology (e.g. OWSs and ODMEs). However, ship owners, taking advantage of flagging out and lenient regulations in many open register countries, were able to keep their ships on the edge of being compliant to MARPOL. They often install cheap, unreliable equipment that apparently fulfils the minimum requirements mandated but do not achieve the ultimate goal of the convention (DeSombre 2000).

On the international maritime legislative level, for an instrument to be adopted, the economic interests of many maritime nations (both traditional flags and open registers) have also to be satisfied before trying to adopt new costly technologies, a trend which is clearly in line with the EM approach in general. For example, the BATNEEC approach is usually on the top of the choice list when trying to present a new marine environmental instrument (e.g. ballast water treatment plants – exhausts filtering equipment for Marpol Annex VI). However, at the IMO, the economic ability of less developed countries usually triggers a heated debate whenever a new instrument is introduced that incurs extra cost to ship owners and consequently necessitate new monitoring, inspection skills, and investment by the flag state, port state, or coastal state (field observation notes MEPC 55,56 – IMO – London).

Consequently, most of the recently adopted marine environmental instruments are overtly attempting to balance economic and environmental interests by adopting the IMO's 'minimum requirements' approach. This approach requires flag states to implement the bare minimum measures to be compliant with the adopted legal instrument (Brookman 2002). This encourages different marine equipment manufacturers to produce cheaper devices for cost-conscious ship owners who are just seeking statutory recognition in order to operate. According to some seafarers in this study, such equipment initially passes the required statutory performance tests and may operate only for a short period of time after installation but deteriorates very quickly causing persistent daily operational problems as explained further on in the next chapter.

Following this theme, at shipboard level, some manufacturers, in order to gain more market shares, design sophisticated equipment that is not easy to operate without adequate training, claiming that these are innovative technologies. These 'innovative'- and - at times - cost-effective technology solutions for controlling marine pollution are not proving to be effective enough especially when looking at the compliance levels of seafarers worldwide which still stop short of being satisfactory (Bloor et al. 2006; Mattson 2006). However, and as reflected from the above discussion, this study needs to explore the tensions between seafarers in their daily face-work encounters with technology and agents of the abstract legal system on board the ship. It may be that such conflicting interpretations and application of the precautionary approaches confuse seafarers in terms of their 'risk' perceptions and in their search for 'ontological security' in their work place. The potential impacts on their decisions about using non-fault proof technology in various geographical settings and contributes to enhancing distrust in specific governments and certain shipping companies will be discussed further ahead in this thesis.

2.6   Concluding Remarks

In the context of policy making, the vision of ecological modernisation advocates that precautionary approaches and the resultant preventative end-of pipe technologies, although increase cost, increase efficiency and enhance competitiveness, thus ultimately producing both economic and environmental benefits (Lomborg 2001; Mol 2001). However, in the shipping sector, trying to convince shipping companies with ecological modernisation harnessed concepts such as 'pollution prevention pays' has not yielded – so far – much success (Mattson

2006). This may have led maritime policy makers to think about complimentary approaches to the more coercive type 'technological' solutions. The proposed approaches range between encompassing green marketing, environmental certification (e.g. green ship awards), and new, radical, environmentally-oriented training methodologies for current and potential seafarers (McConnell 2002) . However, none of these policies have yielded notable success to date.

In this respect, Mol (1995) contends that whilst this approach to ecological modernisation recognises the economic and environmental potential behind the adoption of end-of pipe technologies, it did not pay enough attention to the practical difficulties behind implementing this approach. The result is that the technological solution had the largest share of criticism among all other approaches to ecological modernisation (Mol 1995). For example, in the area of regulating greenhouse gases (GHGs) and other air polluting emissions from ships which is still in the discussion stage, there is still a sweeping reliance on new 'innovative' technologies to mitigate the allegedly globally imminent problem (Oberthur 2003; Pisani 2002). In the case of MARPOL, and despite the fact that technology solutions in general were implemented more than two decades ago, the level of prognostic conceptions about potential 'risks' from adopting such approaches is prominent among seafarers as I demonstrate further in chapters six and seven.

Taken together, the above two approaches (i.e. precautionary approach – technology solutions) to ecological modernisation provided insights that will aid in interpreting and analysing the data in this study. It is clear however, from the above brief review of the ecological modernisation literature in general that most policies were initially designed for land-based industry sectors. However, on the application side, maritime policy makers are no exception to their land-based peers. They, while having a 'precautionary' vision, especially after pollution disasters, coined the technology solution to a large extent in an attempt to pre-empt the anticipated adverse effects of marine pollution. The next chapter will discuss and exemplify how current and future marine environmental regulations - as an expert system - are largely based on the EM approach, and why seafarers are finding difficulties in complying with such a regulatory approach.

CHAPTER THREE - MARPOL 'An Expert System'

3.1 Introduction

One consequence of the eco-modernist thinking among maritime policy makers in the last two decades is that we progressively saw the introduction of a myriad of maritime safety and environmental regulatory instruments adopting many of the embedded principles of the EM concept. These principles were: the precautionary principle, the polluter pays principle, cost-benefit analysis, and risk analysis, recycling of waste and technology solutions. This chapter explains the operation of pollution regulation at sea within the maritime regulatory domain using the most prominent regulatory tool dealing with marine pollution (i.e. The MARPOL convention). Doing this, an evaluation to what extent are 'reflexive' seafarers able (or not) to maintain routine and sound daily environmental practice amidst the increasing bulk of marine environmental regulations is carried out.

In this context, I will attempt to introduce the different examples of environmental regulatory approaches focusing on what an active seafarer working in the current shipping industry atmosphere is subjected to on a daily basis. This task is done by exploring the rather limited maritime oriented literature on the implementation and compliance difficulties with the current marine environmental regulatory scheme focusing on the MARPOL convention as an 'expert system'. This convention is widely ratified by the vast majority of maritime states worldwide. My aim is to link the current marine environmental regulatory situation to the arguments discussed in previous chapters regarding reflexive and ecological modernisation concepts in order to chart the way forward in the thesis.

3.2   MARPOL Compliance Duties

MARPOL policy makers chose two types of technically driven actions to circumvent the issues of both accidental and intentional marine pollution; both of which have implications for the daily environmental practices of seafarers. Firstly, the progressive adoption of new ship-building criteria mandating on-board piping arrangement standards to segregate and separate the oil-based cargoes from ballast water and to separate oil from tank cleaning water (e.g.

segregated ballast tanks SBTs and COW systems). Upon implementation in the 80s, these requirements mostly affected the new buildings raising the cost incurred by ship owners and resulted in extra practical duties on the Chief Mate and Second Engineer of a typical tanker ship as discussed below. Secondly, there were mandatory requirements of installing what could be classified as 'end of pipe' oil discharge monitoring technology, namely oily water separators in the engine room (on all ships), and oil detector monitor systems (for Tankers only). In this case, the added daily tasks on the same ranks and other ratings on board a tanker were significantly increased as I briefly outline below.

Firstly, in the deck department the Chief Officer is the person responsible for the cargo operations on board any ship aided by other officers and dedicated well trained ratings (e.g. Bosun, Pump Man). On-board an oil tanker, for example, his regular cargo duties cover the safe transfer operations of the oil cargo from shore to ship and vice versa. Consequently, the environmental duties will vary between the loaded and the ballast passage of the ship. The duties that are directly related and/or causing potential marine pollution constitute but are not limited to the following:

First, clearing up the residual oil accumulated in the cargo manifold drip trays by transferring it to dedicated residual oil tanks on board in liaison with the ship's Second Engineer. This is a transitional stage until deciding whether it will be stored on board for discharging to a dedicated port reception facility or if it will be discharged to sea according to MARPOL's guidelines using the mandatory oil detector monitoring equipment (ODME) on board. Clearly, this decision depends on the trading area of the ship (inside or outside MARPOL's special areas), on the availability of the port reception facilities (PRFs) along the ship's route, and on the consent and willingness of the shipping company to use it.

On the loaded passage the chief officer will ensure the integrity of the cargo system and prepare, in liaison with the Second Engineer, the cargo pumping system in preparation for the discharging port. After the cargo is discharged, a comprehensive task awaits the Chief Officer in the ballast voyage. On crude carriers the cargo tanks are usually washed during the discharge operation using the crude oil washing (COW) system. However, if the next grade or cargo distribution is different than the last voyage, tank washing using seawater is inevitable. This is a lengthy operation that may consume several days on a large tanker and which results in a large amount of tank washing effluents (sea water mixed with oil residues). This accumulation of oily effluents is gathered in slop tanks to separate (oil remains on the top while water is separated at the bottom) and clear water is pumped from the bottom back to sea via the ODME which will re-circulate the water back to the tanks once the MARPOL oily content limits are exceeded. This whole operation is conducted by the Chief mate aided by the ship's pump man and other ratings during sea passage where he also has to keep up two navigational watches per day at the same time. It is important to note that during lengthy operations the Chief Officer can delegate some duties to another officer that he trusts, however, he will remain responsible for the operation. This clarifies the importance of maintaining such technology solutions to a high standard to aid in the smooth conduct of such vital compliance duties.

In the ship's engine room similar waste management duties are required. However, the oily waste is mainly generated by the daily operations of the main engine (i.e. waste from bunker purifiers) and auxiliary machinery (e.g. generators, pumps, boilers). This task in most companies is the responsibility of the Second Engineer aided by junior engineers and engine room ratings. The oily wastes are mainly gathered in a settling tank and, according to MARPOL guidelines regarding the oily content in the affluent, it could be discharged overboard in certain areas through the oily water separator (OWS).

3.2.1 New Instruments: Extra Duties

The MARPOL convention is also an example of an extremely dynamic convention. Seafarers thus have to cope with complying with a growing number of annexes, codes and protocols. To give examples of the more recent MARPOL instruments that necessarily impact on the daily practice of seafarers, table 2.1 provides a concise overview on the newly introduced environmental instruments and what is still forthcoming. The argument put forward in this thesis is that seafarers are evaluating the compliance levels of the long standing Annex I (in force since 1983) and questioning the ability of the shipping sector to comply with the growing pace of marine environmental instruments.

Table 2.1 MARPOL Requirements

IMO Instrument	Date of Entry into Force	Implications on Daily Practice
-**Annex IV** (sewage) To Marpol -The 2004 (April) Amendments	-23rd September 2003 -1st August 2005	-Engine staff and crew to operate and maintain the installed Sewage commuting and disinfecting system.
Annex V (Garbage) to Marpol	31st December 1988 (under Review -2006- for more Stringent Application) New requirements implemented 2013 prohibiting all types of garbage with very small exceptions.	-All crew to implement a garbage management plan on board and segregate different types of garbage. -Maintain and use incinerators.
-**Annex VI** (Air Pollution) to MARPOL and NOx Technical Code 2008 - SOx emissions control areas (SECAS) - Volatile Organic Compounds (VOCs) emissions control from Tankers -Implementation of and increasing number of GHG emissions control areas ECA	19th May 2005 -1st July 2010 (already in force in certain areas) - Enforced by certain ports -Adopted and translated so far in EEDI index for ships	-Monitoring engine exhaust NOx emissions (some areas coming into force soon) -Conducting fuel oil change-over before entering current emission control areas - Crew to control VOC emissions and connect to available vapour return lines. - Potential extra duties for operating and maintenance of emission filtering equipment, record keeping and maintaining equipment.

Source: data compiled from the IMO website (www.imo.org)

From the table above it is clear that each newly adopted instrument constitutes new duties for the crew of any ship. For example, seafarers need to establish knowledge of the contents of the annex to be able to carry out the added daily compliance requirements relating to the entry into force of MARPOL Annex IV concerning air pollution from ships. This relatively new Annex sets limits on sulphur oxide emissions (SOx) and nitrogen oxide emissions (NOx) from ships' exhausts and prohibits deliberate emissions of ozone depleting substances. The annex also contains provisions for special SOx Emission Control Areas (SECAS) to be established with more stringent controls on sulphur emissions. In these areas (e.g. North Sea, Baltic Sea), the sulphur content of fuel oil used on board ships must not exceed 1.5%. Alternatively, ships must fit an exhaust gas cleaning system or 'use any other technological method to limit the SOx emissions'. It is important to note that many ports in the world implemented this annex inside their port limits even before enforcing it internationally. Clearly, the equipment needed to monitor levels of prohibited materials or to clean the exhausts have to be operated and maintained by ships staff and crew during the ship's passage and also in port constituting another added duty for seafarers. The external problems identified, so far, relate to the availability of low sulphur bunker stations in most parts of the world or that the actual sulphur content in the fuel exceeds what is written in the bunker specification data sheet which may cause the ship's detention if a sample is taken.

In the process of dealing with the new technical devices installed on board, it is important to note that each of the above Annexes with their stipulated requirements needs extra record keeping and logging that seafarers often frame as added 'paper work'. Consequently, all such new areas of the ship's environmental practice will need to be audited and inspected by various audit and inspection entities as I explain further on in this chapter. However, what is at stake is the seafarers' scepticism as to whether the evolution of environmental instruments with its resultant extra duties would actually be reflected in reduced pollution levels. In this respect, one could argue that during such sensitive operations mutual trust must be maintained between senior ranks, junior ranks, officers and engineers, and even assisting ratings to ensure a more efficient daily operation. However, according to this study, that was not always the case especially with the enforcement of harsh prosecution and criminalisation measures by many coastal states in the aftermath of marine pollution incidents and accidents in the shipping sector.

More recently, in July 2011, The Marine Environmental Protection Committee (MEPC) at the IMO adopted the revised MARPOL Annex V which entered into force on the 1st. of January 2013. This brought more stringent conditions with the ban of almost all types of waste (previously allowed) to be discharged with very small exceptions. This was reinforced in March 2012 by an MEPC resolution with guidelines for the development pf garbage management plans (resolution MEPC.220(63)).

Regarding air pollution from ships (Marpol Annex VI), and as per Resolution MEPC. 202(62) THE United States Caribbean sea Emission Control Area (for SOx, NOx and PM) came into effect on the 1st. January 2014, bringing in stricter control on emissions of sulphur oxide (SOx), nitrogen oxide(NOX), and particulate matter for ships trading in certain waters adjacent to the coasts of Puerto Rico and the United States Virgin Islands. It is worth mentioning that there are now four designated emission control areas under MARPOL (ECAs) in effect globally: the United States Caribbean Sea ECA and the North American ECA, and the SOx ECA in the Baltic Sea area and the North Sea area. These ECAs necessitate that crew members on board prepare the vessel prior to the entry of such areas with certain types of fuels (e.g. low sulphur) and switch back to normal fuel after exiting. This procedure also adds to the daily duties of seafarers with the potential need of extending their working hours to be able to comply with such evolving and dynamic international legislations.

Moreover, for ship owners who are in the process of building new ships, Resolution MEPC.203 (62), ADOPTED ON 15th July 2011 regarding Energy Efficiency for ships (entered into force on the 1st. January 2013) adds a whole new chapter on energy efficiency for ships to MARPOL Annex VI, to make mandatory the Energy efficiency design Index (EEDI) for new ships and the Ship Energy Efficiency Management Plan (SEEMP) for all ships. Naturally, like all IMO regulations these new elements will require seafarers to deal with newly installed equipment, and spend more time on record keeping and monitoring compliance.

3.2.2 Sanctioning Violations

Pollution incidents are, by their very nature, emotive affairs and there will often be pressure on those entities responsible for administering justice to severely punish the offenders. In this respect, violations of the MARPOL convention are still considered by the regulators and public at large as frequent and unacceptable (Brookman 2002; Mattson 2006; Sahatjian 1998). As a result, the seafarer is subjected to a twofold type of sanctions if detected to be breaching the MARPOL convention. The first is personalised fines that many ports are imposing on the person responsible for the pollution and the second is the possibility of criminally prosecuting the seafarer for any act of pollution. The most troublesome type of breaches are what is called intentional spills, meaning that a crew member, for example, by-passed the OWS or the ODME on board and dumped pure oil or oily effluents overboard. These illicit practices may happen at high sea (i.e. outside the jurisdiction of a particular state) or inside the territorial waters or exclusive economic zone (EEZ) of a particular country or even inside any port (Anthony 2006;

Gallagher 2002). The first tier of potential sanctions are delegated by the MARPOL policy makers to the flag administration that the ship belongs to; this is clear from the provision of article four of the MARPOL convention stating:

'Any violation of the requirements of the present Convention shall be prohibited and sanctions shall be established therefore under the law of the Administration of the ship concerned wherever the violation occurs. If the Administration is informed of such a violation and is satisfied that sufficient evidence is available to enable proceedings to be brought in respect of the alleged violation, it shall cause such proceedings to be taken as soon as possible, in accordance with its law.'
(MARPOL 73/78 – Article four)

Hence the task of imposing certain monetary fines falls with each flag administration. However, due to the rising number of cases of violations by ships registered in open registers, and due to the problems arising from the loss of any genuine link between many ships and their respective flag states, most countries are sanctioning any spill violations under their own law (when occurring in their waters or ports) or under relatively new regimes such as the port state control (PSC). In the U.K., for example, under the Merchant Shipping Act 1995(c.21) – Section 131 – Discharge of oil from ships into certain United Kingdom waters:

'A person guilty of an offence under this section shall be liable – On summary conviction to a fine not exceeding £50,000.'
(This was subsequently increased to £250,000 by the Merchant Shipping and Maritime Security Act 1997)

In Canada, The law currently allows judgements of up to $500,000, but the most severe judgement to date has been no more than half that amount. In the United States, under new E.U. regulations, and in other parts of the world the penalties are even greater and include possible criminalisation and imprisonment of offenders. Clearly, such 'personalised' large monetary fines and strict criminal sanctions (see section 2.4.6) are a constant fear for seafarers from various ranks on board the world fleet. What adds to this fear is the recent rising trend of criminalisation of seafarers recently (see below) which deepens their distrust regarding the support of their companies in case they are prosecuted or unjustly criminalised for an accidental spill.

3.2.3 Fears of Ship Owners: Reflections on Seafarers

The largest fear of shipping companies is that their ships get detained in any port or terminal (Chen 2000). This incurs huge financial losses for the company, and the seafarers responsible on board are frequently blamed for ignorance to exercise adequate professional practice and then dismissed. In the case of environmental practices, in 2005 alone, PSC inspectors found over 220 MARPOL infringements among vessels classed with Lloyd's Register. The top 10 detention items related to oil filtering equipment (40), shipboard oil pollution emergency plan (SOPEP) (36), falsification of oil record book (27), 15 PPM (parts per million) alarm arrangements (23), retention of oil on board (22), other MARPOL Annex I (19), prevention of pollution by oil (IOPP Certificate) (18), garbage record book (17), garbage management plan (11) and oil discharge monitoring and control system (9) (Lumbers 2006). It is important to highlight that the detentions related to oil filtering equipment are the ones relating to the by-passing of OWSs and ODMEs. Clearly, most of the above violations, arguably, relate more to the environmental practice of seafarers than to the management policies of their respective companies. In this way, it is reasonable to understand why seafarers are fearful from being dismissed by their company if they get caught committing any such offences resulting in detention which usually incur large fines and delays to the ship. More generally, it is also clear that the highest rate of offences on the list relate to the by-passing of techno-fixes installed on board tankers. Hence, it is important to discuss the implications of using techno-fixes on board tanker ships on the daily compliance duties of seafarers. This is discussed in the following sub-section.

3.2.4 Best Available Techno-Fixes: The MARPOL Case

The above review of MARPOL mandatory requirements and associated infringements reveal that; for controlling the marine pollution problem on board ocean going vessels, the choice of science and technology is dominant as can clearly be seen especially when looking at MARPOL compliance requirements. In this respect, I argue that the influence of the 'ecological modernisation' harnessed concepts such as the 'precautionary principle' and 'best available technology' (BATNEEC) for mitigating the pollution caused by shipping is prominent within this global technical convention. Generally, however, recent studies have assumed that using BATNEECs in pollution abatement policies is hoped to improve the detection limits in order to influence the initial authorised limits through an iterative process (Barrieu and Sinclair-Desgagne 2006).

To manage pollution risks from the world fleet, the installation of discharge monitoring and filtering equipment became mandatory almost two decades ago (e.g. oily water separators OWSs for engine room effluents and oil detector monitoring systems ODMEs for cargo tanks tank cleaning effluents) as a requirement of Annex I of the MARPOL convention (i.e. the oil annex). However, as previously mentioned, criticism, persistent complaints, and the by-passing practices of these techno-fixes are still on the rise resulting in a significant number of prosecutions to seafarers in the last decade (Gallagher 2002; Grosso and Waldron 2005). The argument is whether seafarers frame such pollution mitigation technologies as 'the best available ones' or not is an issue for enquiry in this study. In other words, this paradoxical problem of framing preventative technologies, reflexively, as a source of high consequence environmental risk is discussed further ahead in this thesis.

Along similar lines, previous research in the UK focusing on the technical management of pollution to the marine environment from land based industries seems to be sceptical about the efficacy of such approaches. It contends that precautionary statutory principles such as the Best Available Techniques Not Entailing Excessive Cost (BATNEEC) and the Best Practicable Environmental Option (BEPO) are vague and ineffective (Richards et al. 2000). This study argues that the non-clarity of such concepts leaves the industry to define the standards of the best available technologies that does not essentially, for their own benefit, include excessive cost(s). In the case of the very competitive shipping industry, the result is that the technical equipment mandated and installed on-board ships observing the mere 'minimum requirements' prove to be problematic and in need of a comprehensive policy review. The use of this metaphoric 'minimum requirements' phrase in many of the IMO mandatory safety and environmental instruments opened the door for a myriad of manufacturers to compete in supplying cheap technology to cost conscious ship owners (Gray and Sims 1997) .

Along the same lines, previous studies about trusting technology draw a distinction between trusting existing technology and distrusting the people who manage the technology. One of the results of these studies is that individuals may be convinced that social systems are often more important, because technology can be by-passed and misused and it is only as good as its management (Bryan and Wondolleck 2003; Elliott 2005). In this respect, Tesh (1999) contends that citizens' framing of the relative risks of using various technologies may include value concerns, not accounted for by technical experts, such as equity, fairness, costs, and benefits (Tesh 1999). Clearly, this literature can be linked directly to the 'risk society' theory which identifies the paradox between the increasing role of science and technology in identifying risks and the growing scepticism of science and technology as a result of institutional failures to manage these risks (Adam and Van Loon 2000; Beck et al. 1994; Giddens 1990). To manage such risks and overcome the global implementation problems, maritime policy makers complimented the regulatory regime with comprehensive monitoring, auditing and inspection schemes that provide several portals of access between seafarers and numerous types of practitioners. For verifying the implications of interactions between seafarers and various agents of the abstract legal system, it is important to discuss briefly the various contemporary environmentally related audits and inspections that a seafarer may experience working on board a tanker ship.

3.3   Audit and Inspection Schemes

Alongside technology solutions, the second most prominent instrument used, within the regulatory regime in the maritime domain is the prominent 'audit culture' that targets safety and environmental performance of ships and crews. This prominence is triggered by the enforcement and implementation difficulties among different flag states which elicited various types and levels of auditing and monitoring regimes in the maritime and shipping sectors (Van Leeuwen 2004). For example, on a typical tanker's round trip she is very likely to be inspected by the 'port state control' at one port of call, go through a vetting inspection by an 'oil major' in another port, and be prepared for the ISM internal and/or external audits on returning to her home port (see below). This excludes any potential safety or unscheduled environmental inspections that may occur according to the local legislations of a particular country or in-house rules of a specific loading terminal. In this study, such interactions are considered 'access points' - using Giddens' terms - where seafarers interact with whom they perceive as 'experts' or agents of the abstract legal system (Giddens 1990). For this reason, it is necessary to clarify the nature, potentiality, legitimacy, and implications of such various audit regimes on the seafarer's framing of environmental compliance.

In this context, Power (1997) argues that an audit system requires a commitment to the auditing philosophy, its social norms, and an investment in this concrete technical practice. He observed that society is increasingly committed to evaluating itself through various kinds of audit practices. The rationale for this commitment is the notion that individuals must be accountable for their actions and this accountability must be verified. Related to the environment, internal auditing has evolved as a tool for companies to ensure their compliance with environmental regulations through a management based style of self-assessment emphasizing a self-informing notion (Power 1997) . However, in shipping, seafarers are subjected to several ties of external and internal audits; the main two external audit regimes are Port State Control inspections and the ISM audits, both of which are discussed below.

3.3.1 Port State Control Inspections

The audit approach was introduced in the maritime sector more than two decades ago by the port state control system (PSC). PSC is the ability to inspect foreign ships in one's own port, as an attempt to overcome the growing failures of flag state inspections to detect and sanction sub-standard ships (Bell 1993). There is a generally held belief that many flag states are unable to adequately perform their mandated duties of ensuring that ships flying their flag comply fully with international safety standards formulated under the auspices of the International Maritime Organization (IMO) and the International Labour Organization (ILO). This failure is usually due to the compliance track records of the open registry type of ship registration regime (i.e. FOCs), which rarely (if ever) visit its port of registry in its service life and incapacity - or unwillingness - of such maritime administrations to inspect their ships overseas (Haralambides and Yang 2003; Lillie 2004). In this context, the United Nations Convention on the Law of the Sea (UNCLOS 82) terms this state of lack of regulatory attachment between ships and their respective flag states 'lake of genuine link' (UNCLOS 1983). Because of this, the degree of enforcement of international standards can vary widely between national flagged ships and FOCs and even among the various open registries themselves (Cariou et al. 2007). While the more conscientious open register flag states may have an inspectorate system under which flag state surveyors and inspectors are stationed or appointed in strategic locations around the world to visit ships under their flags, there are many more ships that are effectively beyond the reach of surveyors and inspectors of the flag state (Alderton and Winchester 2002c; Knapp and Franses 2007). It was this irregularity that port state control was mainly designed to address.

The ships defined by the PSC inspections as non-compliant (i.e. with a major non-conformity rendering the vessel un-seaworthy) are detained by the port state until rectifying the deficiencies detected (Cariou et al. 2007; Li and Zheng 2008). Not only this, many PSC authorities contribute to a public access database to publicise the names and flags of the ships detained which is what many ship owners are trying to avoid (Equasis 2007). As a result, seafarers who are encouraged to promote a 'no blame' culture on-board to report near misses, incidents, and accidents (Bhattacharya 2007), became more sceptical about initiating such reporting. They feared that their actions might cause their company to be 'named and shamed' by these public databases thus risking their own job as a retributive action from their ship owner. Moreover, in the light of the recent criminalisation wave, seafarers also do not want to risk getting into legal complications as they fear that reporting may incur an element of self-incrimination (Hed 2005) (see section 3.6).

However, with the recent evaluation of the performance records of PSC authorities, auditors, and inspectors it became clear that the emphasis by the PSC on vessels' environmental records increased in the aftermath of major tanker spills in EU waters (e.g. Erika and Prestige in the Bay of Biscay) which caused devastating marine and coastal pollution to French, Spanish and Portuguese shores (Cariou et al. 2007; Lumbers 2006). Investigations revealed that these vessels were properly certified and inspected which raised many questions, especially by seafarers, regarding the effectiveness and limitations of the PSC as an inspection regime (Bahree et al. 2002; Bloor et al. 2006). In this context, it is worth noting that the PSC have no control neither on standards of design, construction, and equipment nor over standards of training, certification and qualifications of the crew of a ship, all of which are considered vital factors for sound environmental performance of any vessel (Bell 1993; Chircop 2002; Raftopoulos 2001). The argument is that seafarers, as situated professionals, are well aware that the PSC regime cannot influence these factors representing the root causes of the problem. Hence, they expect PSC inspectors, at least, to have expert knowledge enabling them to identify technical MARPOL violations as a vital condition to build 'trust' in the overarching PSC regime. However, as I discuss in this thesis, having such high expectations was not always met with professional 'expert' performance especially at 'encounters' (or access points) such as conducting the PSC inspections and /or the 'smarter' regulatory approach known as 'safety management' and its associated ISM audits.

3.3.2 The ISM Audits

Recognising the implementation difficulties of safety and environmental treaties in the maritime sector, a relatively new 'smarter' approach to regulation was introduced just over a decade ago. This is marked by the adoption of the ISM code as a mandatory chapter embedded in the SOLAS convention. The code urges shipping companies to establish a safety and environmental management policy that includes a commitment to comply with applicable laws and to work towards continual improvement of environmental awareness and pollution prevention (Anderson 2003). This code is twofold; one is implemented by ships and the other by their respective shipping companies. What is more, this code mandated internal and external audit procedures to be conducted on a ship's various safety and environmental management areas and performance. However, since its inception, it triggered an open debate in the maritime arena about whether the 'tick box' and check list type approach to auditing safety and environmental behaviours of seafarers is a viable strategy (Gray and Sims 1997).

The ISM'S main potential, similar to other shore-based safety case approaches, is to impose on shipping companies an obligation to demonstrate to the regulator their ability to identify hazards, assess risks, and implement controls (Gunningham 2007). This shifts the regulator's role from direct coercive regulation to monitoring and oversight. For the purpose of my arguments in this thesis, I will focus on the monitoring and audit side of the ISM code. This focus is to highlight the role of auditors of this scheme in enhancing or compromising the seafarers' trust in the abstract legal system through evaluating its embedded audit structure which is considered as a 'face work' interaction between seafarers and ISM auditors.

The ISM can be counted as a model for a 'process-based' regulatory approach that focuses on the organisational structure, roles and responsibilities of operators, and the identification of resources to maintain safety and environmental management systematically (Gunningham 2007). In other words, regulators rather than regulating prescriptively, may seek by adopting a mandatory instrument - such as the ISM code - to stimulate the design of self-regulatory approaches within an enterprise thus encouraging a notion of self-criticism about its internal safety and environmental management performance (Celik 2008). In shipping, the ISM code pursues this 'process-based' approach through identifying implementation gaps to regulatory instruments using two tiers of audit processes. First is the internal ISM audit process carried out by the shipping company internal auditors. Second - the external audits by independent audit groups (e.g. class societies delegated by flag states conducting statutory ISM audits) which should be designed to provide feedback about the status of safety and environmental management in a specific shipping company to reassure cargo owners, charterers and governing bodies and autonomously rectify any caveats. However, the multiplicity of audit agencies and auditing standards did not yield these aims as I discuss below.

3.3.3 Multiple Auditing Regimes

If we agree that the ISM code provided enough guidance to shipping companies on how to manage their safety and environmental risks, we can detect that it did not fulfil the same purpose on the audit standards side. The result is a clear non-uniformity in audit standards and auditors' competence levels across the shipping sector and maritime administrations in various parts of the world (Bloor et al. 2006; Knapp and Franses 2007; Tatman et al. 2005). Moreover, the shipping industry is subjected to external auditing by a myriad of audit agencies to ensure, more or less, the same purpose and/or to ascertain the same standards (Van Leeuwen 2004). For example, a tanker ship in addition to being internally audited by its own company management will be subjected to being audited and/or inspected by flag state, port state, vetting inspections by oil majors, and terminal safety inspectors in various parts of the world. Collectively, this results in further contrasts in audit standards that clearly exists cross-nationally and are manifested in the local character of enforcement practice and the level of competence of the delegated audit agent (Bloor et al. 2006). Consequently, seafarers are caught within these conflicting views and approaches to the audit process which results in ambivalence, more distrust in audit groups and loss of purpose, especially when they expect such audit practitioners to be 'experts'.

However, in this study, at the shipping companies' level, it is important to differentiate between the ability of major and medium sized and smaller shipping companies to implement the ISM and effectively perform the required auditing and monitoring tasks. For example, looking at land-based studies, a safety management system implementation study involving companies owning coal mines (as an example of a hazardous occupational atmosphere where a safety management system is vital) identified several difficulties for small and medium sized companies. The study concluded that small and medium sized companies were unable to grasp the complexities involved in a comprehensive safety management system and that the challenge for such companies is proving to be 'overwhelming' (Gunningham 2007). Although the literature suggests that there could be more diluted safety management models for smaller companies, this could prove very difficult with a globalised shipping industry that is, arguably, supposed to be regulated at international standards (Hopkins and Wilkinson 2005). Hence, we can predict that the application of a safety management system in shipping and especially its vital audit strand would not be a straight forward task.

In this context, seafarers in this study often complain about this multiplicity of audit groups, diversity of audit standards, and non-uniformity of conducting the audit process when comparing between various ports and different audit groups and types of audits. Further to this, some seafarers argue that what could be adding to the inconsistencies of the ISM audit process is the existence, in the code text, of many vague phrases such as 'satisfactory' and 'according to the discretion of the maritime administration' to define the ideal standards. To date, flag states, shipping companies, port authorities and ISM auditors have not seemed to arrive at any consensual agreement on the actual meaning of such phrases (Anderson 2003; Vanderzwaag 2002). The argument is that the pursuit of a worldwide harmonisation of audit standards in shipping is potentially compromised by numerous difficulties resulting from such vague texts appearing frequently in legal documents. Most of the above on board difficulties are integrated with several external factors as discussed below.

3.4   External Factors

In addition to internal and on board technical and administrative difficulties discussed above, another set of 'external' factors influence seafarers' ability to comply with MARPOL and several other environmentally related legal instruments on the national and international levels. I discuss below two main external stressors that reflect directly on the daily environmental practice of a typical seafarer.

3.4.1 Lack of Port Reception Facilities

MARPOL mandates that each country should provide 'adequate' reception facilities in its ports and terminals for receiving ships' oily wastes (Regulation 12 – Annex I). However, many governments delegate this task to the respective port authorities without properly following up on the actual building up of such infra-structure (Abou-Elkawam 2008; Ball 1999; Carpenter and Macgill 2000). For example, the IMO's online Global Integrated Shipping Database System (GISIS) has the option to search for the availability of Port Reception Facilities (PRFs) in any country in the world with different criterion. I used this database to verify the availability and 'adequacy' of PRFs in UK ports. I chose the UK as I interviewed almost half the respondents in this study inside UK ports. The criteria of my enquiry were to search for ports with available fixed PRFs around the UK that are able to receive tanker washing water (slops) and engine room bilge and sludge oils at any time of the day seven days a week. These are the normal and expected operational requirements of any conventional tanker entering a port or terminal after an average sea passage and are the minimum standard mandated by the MARPOL convention. Nevertheless, the search result with these three criteria was non-existent (i.e. no ports in the UK meet these three requirements at the same time). The ports, for example, which could receive slops could not receive sludge, other ports do not have any fixed installation, and some ports only operate during weekdays and/or working hours only (GISIS 2008). This result supports the seafarers' claims - in this study - that although the facility might exist in some ports, they are denied the use of it due to conditional operational limitations, thus, the existing facility is considered - according to MARPOL - 'inadequate' (see chapters five and six).

To understand more clearly the difficulties that seafarers experience regarding the lack of 'adequate' port reception facilities worldwide it is important to explain briefly the element of 'special areas' mandated by the MARPOL convention. In this respect, MARPOL defines certain areas as 'special areas' in which, for technical reasons relating to their oceanographical and ecological condition and to their sea traffic, the adoption of special mandatory methods for the prevention of marine pollution is required (IMO 2006b). Under the convention, these special areas are provided with a higher level of protection than other areas of the sea. Naturally, special areas were allocated for each Annex of MARPOL. Table 3.2 summarises the adoption, entry into force and the controversial aspect of 'taking effect' of MARPOL's special areas.

Table 3.2 MARPOL Special Areas

Special Areas	Adopted	Date of Enforcement	In Effect From
Annex I :Oil			
Mediterranean Sea	2nd Nov 1973	2nd Oct 1983	2nd Oct 1983
Baltic Sea	2nd Nov 1973	2nd Oct 1983	2nd Oct 1983
Black Sea	2nd Nov 1973	2nd Oct 1983	2nd Oct 1983
Red Sea	2nd Nov 1973	2nd Oct 1983	Not in effect
"Gulfs" area	2nd Nov 1973	2nd Oct 1983	1st Aug 2008
Gulf of Aden	1st Dec 1987	1st April 1989	Not in effect
North West European Waters	25th Sep 1997	1st Feb 1999	1st Aug 1999
Oman area of the Arabian Sea	15th Oct 2004	1st Jan 2007	Not in effect
Southern South African Waters	13th Oct 2006	1st March 2008	1st Aug 2008
Annex V : Garbage			
Mediterranean Sea	2nd Nov 1973	31st Dec 1988	1st May 2009
Baltic Sea	2nd Nov 1973	31st Dec 1988	1st Oct 1989
Black Sea	2nd Nov 1973	31st Dec 1988	Not in effect
Red Sea	2nd Nov 1973	31st Dec 1988	Not in effect
"Gulfs" area	2nd Nov 1973	31st Dec 1988	1st Aug 2008
North Sea	17th Oct 1989	18th Feb 1991	18th Feb 1991
Annex VI: Prevention of air pollution by ships (SOx Emission Control Areas)			
Baltic Sea	26th Sep 1997	19th May 2005	19th May 2006
North Sea	22nd July 2005	22nd Nov 2006	22nd Nov 2007

Source: compiled and modified from the IMO Website (www.imo.org)

From the table above we can see that in some areas of the world (e.g. Red sea, Gulf of Aden, and 'Gulf' area) there is a situation where the legal instrument entered into force but the IMO considers it to be not 'in effect' yet. This is due to the lack of notifications from MARPOL parties whose coastlines border the relevant special areas on the existence of 'adequate' reception facilities (according to regulations 38.6 of MARPOL Annex I and 5 (4) of MARPOL Annex V). The paradox for the seafarer on the one hand, is that specific coastal countries in these regions are not clear about implementing the enforced instrument leaving the seafarer ambivalent about whether the discharge requirements of special areas should be adhered to or not. Moreover, in this study, seafarers witnessing oil and garbage dumping activities taking place within such areas start to frame them as 'free to dump' thus distrusting these countries' governments and the legitimacy of their actions. On the other hand, seafarers in other areas where the 'special area' is 'in effect' (e.g. Northwest European Waters) are questioning the reasons behind being frequently denied access to the existing PRFs in place.

In summary, seafarers are directly affected by these 'inadequacies' and inconsistencies of implementing MARPOL at many ports of call, an experience which can be more stressful if the ship is on a short coastal route or trading solely inside a MARPOL special area (i.e. areas where effluent discharges are totally prohibited). They cannot guarantee that the sea passage of their ship passes outside MARPOL special areas to be able to discharge some of the accumulated oil waste legally at sea (i.e. discharge oily effluents according to the allowable limits). However, once they have the chance to use the oil filtering technical equipment on board, some seafarers will have to deal with old, non-user friendly, defective equipment while others may deal with the 'state of art' technology that they are not trained for properly (depending on the shipping company they work for). But when all such tensions intersect with different environmental policies in various coastal states, seafarers become more confused. For instance, while the UK is an example of one of the western countries that is considered as one of the most active states in promoting and pushing forward the environmental protection agenda in the IMO, the above example shows that the implementation of the issue of PRFs is still problematic. Hence, it is reasonable to expect that the situation will be worse in less developed countries around the world especially when they lack funding and infra-structure to provide the vitally needed port reception facilities. Such differences, disparities, and the resultant implication on 'trust' in abstract legal systems are discussed in chapters five and six.

3.4.2 The Criminalisation Race

Not only this, but what awaits seafarers regarding marine pollution, took a dramatic turn in recent years. Another major 'external' obstacle adding to compliance difficulties on the daily ship board level is the seafarers' fear of being criminalised in the aftermath of pollution incidents and/or accidents. In the last decade many countries have followed the 'criminalisation' model of the USA for accidental, intentional, and operational spills (Gallagher

2002). They impose criminal sanctions on seafarers in cases of detected oil spills in their territorial waters or port areas without considering whether the detected pollution was intentional or done wilfully. Consequently, seafarers are extremely fearful of the non-distinction between intentional and accidental spills when prosecuting any detected case of pollution arguing that professional mistakes can happen but do not necessarily have to lead to imprisonment. Arguably, this adds to the problem of compromised trust between seafarers and maritime policy makers as discussed in chapter six.

In this respect, criminal investigations into violations of MARPOL usually focus on the crew and rarely have any criminal implications for the company's corporate managers. For example, the United States federal law allows creating a financial rewarding system for 'whistle blowers' to implicate their seniors on board upon detection of MARPOL infringements. This is a process which involves putting the screws on the lowest ranking crew member in an attempt aiming to eventually identify perpetrators at the highest level. Again, the argument is, on the shipboard level; seafarers see this as compromising trust relations between peers on board a ship in relation to environmental practice resulting in lack of co-operation and communication on board regarding environmental duties and practice.

Recognising the negative implications of the criminalisation issue on seafarers' environmental practice, the limited literature on this subject calls for a clear distinction that needs to be made between acts that inherently contain an intentional element and those that are purely accidental (Hed 2005). The argument is that the latter cannot be dealt with as a criminal offence but as a technical offence liable to a proportionate form of penalty without the need to prove intent (Anthony 2006). Furthermore, considering some recent criminalisation cases it is questionable whether the punishment fits the alleged offence and if indeed the environment takes precedence over what are widely perceived by seafarers as 'political reasons'.

Generally, however, in many cases, criminalisation of seafarers appears to be a backward door for political and revenue compromises in some countries (i.e. clean up costs after spills and restoration of the affected environment) or even scapegoats for the failings of legal enforcement regimes (Hed 2005; Morris 2002) . As a remedy, the literature suggests that such political and financial agendas would be more efficiently served by pursuing better control of some of the flag of convenience (FOC) vessel standards as well as the quality standards of training and education of seafarers on pollution mitigation new technologies (Anthony 2006). This pursuit could be a better approach rather than making seafarers reluctant to challenge pollution activities for fear of criminal prosecution.

The criminalisation trend has also significant implications on breaching the MARPOL convention reporting of pollution requirement. As per the MARPOL convention, incidents of pollution should be reported (despite the reason) and all parties involved should actively co-operate in the combating of pollution and overall management of the situation. If seafarers are personally intimidated and decide not to report mistakes made, or take appropriate action in the pollution cases for fear of criminal prosecution, this will, obviously, have detrimental and direct negative effects on the environmental decision making processes (Grosso and Waldron 2005). In the same context, it should be empathised that seafarers are entrusted with controlling and managing vessels which are increasingly expensive and technically sophisticated requiring high standards of training. Inducing such resident 'fear' is not a motivator of quality environmental performance and policy makers need to review these criminalisation actions promptly (Anthony 2006; Hed 2005).

3.5 Concluding Remarks

However, the above example of an international ratified 'expert system' such as the MARPOL convention highlights the external and internal operational and compliance difficulties that seafarers encounter on an almost daily basis are not in isolation from the growing global environmental concerns. This convention is applying the precautionary principle concept and the end of pipe technology solutions. The data chapters in this thesis will discuss the perceptions and reaction of seafarers regarding the mandated daily compliance tasks as per this overarching 'expert system'. As reflexive citizens living in a contemporary society and clearly aware of the consequences of their actions, seafarers also feel the pressure to perform on the environmental side more responsibly. Being employed in different professional settings and trading in different parts of the world their framing of the compliance tasks could be different dictating the resultant actions. In this sense, the next chapter introduces the relevance of the global environmental framing concept to this study.

CHAPTER FOUR - The Research Methodology

4.1 Introduction

When choosing among research methods, one has to think of better ways to reach the aim of the research and within this consider the time, personnel, and financial means available. My starting point was a pilot study at the bottom level of the compliance hierarchy (i.e. seafarers), which triggered the research design, conduct, and strategy. The literature revolving around the domains of risk and framing of intractable environmental problems had also, to a great extent, determined the methodology and methods employed in this research. Other factors which had a bearing on the methodology were: the research questions and purpose of the research (i.e. exploring perceptions and constructions), the relative novelty of researching environmental frames in a nomadic professional group, the rapid development in the area of marine pollution legislation (i.e. technical, social, regulatory), and last but not least, the constructionist perspective adopted in this project. For these reasons I decided to employ established multiple methodological and analytical approaches to reflect the different research sites and diverse hierarchical levels in the maritime regulatory and compliance spheres.

This chapter begins by discussing the main methodologies employed in this research project. Section one explains the importance of the established 'frame analysis' concept and how it underpins the more contemporary approach of 'reflexive framing' presented earlier. This is followed in section two by a demonstration of the utilisation of the framing concept in this research's pilot study highlighting the significance and influence of the pilot on the whole research design and conduct. Section three explains how I benefited from using a framing-based coding approach for analysis of the data collected at the seafarers' level of enquiry. Section four displays the tailored design and the road map for the conduct of the research process - based on the outcomes of the pilot study - followed in section five by a display and justification briefing of the practical data collection methods. Section six discuss the intellectual, philosophical, and theoretical underpinnings of this research and finally present the ethical considerations employed in this study.

4.2 Main Methodological Approaches

This research is informed by the two established methodologies of 'Frame Analysis' - coining the modern concept of reflexive framing which largely aided in the coding of the rich qualitative data set in this study. On one hand. the data on the seafarers' level of enquiry would be analysed utilising coding techniques highlighted by framing theorists to identify major or 'master' frames and to build up coding categories and tables. However, this leads to a second level of analysis to locate the 'reflexive frames' within the seafarers' interview material which proved to serve the aims of this qualitative enquiry. The following three sections highlight the reasons for these choices and explore the implications for this research.

4.3 Framing and Frame Analysis

Framing has been a key approach in dealing with intractable environmental debates (Bickerstaff and Walker 2003; Demeritt 2001; Gray 2003; Lewicki et al. 2003; Taylor 2000). It is important because it allows us to explore environmental problems as seen through the eyes of the parties involved by capturing the diverse interpretations that create the conflicts or problems themselves (Lewicki et al. 2003). Frames in this research act as lenses through which various parties interpret the dynamics of the marine pollution issues and construct the problem as more or less tractable. Framing is also sought to aid in moulding a wide view of individual interpretations into a comprehensive picture in order to identify opportunities for trade-offs based on clearly understood differences (Kaufman et al. 2003).

My use of 'frame analysis' was primarily inductive, although I developed the process of detection and analysis of 'master frames' from extant literature (Gamson 1992, 1995; Goffman 1974; Snow et al. 1986), However, in more mature stages of data analysis I coined the 'reflexive framing' concept to interpret the seafarers' accounts as I explain below (Chesters and Welsh 2002, 2006a). In this endeavour, my chosen initial unit of analysis is the 'concept unit', that is the words, sentences, paragraphs, or story lines used to express identifiable concepts. The use of 'frame analysis' in this research has the following general aims:

- To reconsider patterns of relationships among stakeholders in order to examine potential processes for managing the marine pollution problem more productively.

67

- To clarify or refresh the perception of MARPOL compliance issues, in order to promote information change and listening to ideas not previously considered.

- To identify how involved parties view the pollution problem differently in order to more fully appreciate the compliance dynamics and to seek ways to address them (Fineman and Sturdy 1999; Kaufman et al. 2003; Lewicki et al. 2003).

4.3.1 The Importance of Frames in This Research

Framing is seen as a means of exploring how different stake holders in the maritime industry can intelligibly have quite different understandings of the same problem (i.e. the marine pollution problem). Frame analysis would also aid in unravelling the social basis for both plurality and viability of opinions. In this context, Goffman (1974) focuses on unconventional subject matters, exploring details of individual identity, group relations, the impact of the environment, and the movement and interactive meaning of information (Manning 1977). In such a trans-boundary problem all of the fore mentioned are potential areas of qualitative inquiry in this research.

Frames are seen to organise peoples' experiences; that is to say they enable lay or expert people to recognise what is going on, providing boundaries and defining what counts as an event or feature, consequently frames define what really should attract attention and assessment (Perri 2005). Moreover, frames could also be seen to bias action and call for particular styles of decisions or of behavioural response. This point raises the importance of coining the concept of 'reflexive framing' which looks further into how research participants frame the issue of marine pollution and compliance to MARPOL. These reflexive frames, could affect their interpretation, decisions, aspirations, and behaviours towards the growing body of marine environmental conventions.

Classically, Goffman often uses the term 'frame' to refer to the set of rules governing a given type of activity. In his view, people can easily adjust to any perceived appropriate frame and operate within it, without even recognising any principles involved (Goffman 1974). He argued that people are able to adjust 'frames' or even exercise a 'frame transformation'. Since such 'adjustments' or 'transformations' may resemble the original 'untransformed activity' in many respects, they invite analytical comparisons that may generate insights regarding the activity being investigated (Gamson 1975). In this research, the 'untransformed' activities of polluting the marine environment and compliance actions (or non-actions) to the marine environmental conventions are the 'strips' of activities that need to be unravelled. In the pilot interviews, some participants showed signs of frame adjustments or transformations. However, the full data set clarifies that seafarers move on from recognition of marine environmental problems towards the identification of the actions needed to mitigate the problem influenced by their reflexive frames. Whether they succeed in this endeavour or not is clarified in subsequent data chapters of this thesis.

For analytical purposes the search for frames was carried out in at least four locations in the communication process; the communicator, the text, the receiver, and the occupational culture and practice (Entman 1993). In this research, there is an eminent need for defining how participants are 'framing' some aspects of the marine pollution problem making them more salient in a communicating text either verbally or written (e.g. interview transcripts – environmental conventions such as MARPOL - shipping companies' published environmental policies and reports). For example, in the pilot study interview transcripts, seafarers are explicitly demonstrating their own framing of the marine pollution problem by defining the problem, diagnosing causes, identifying the power relations creating such a problem, and suggesting remedies (Gamson 1992).

Along similar lines, Gamson (1992) contends that frames can be adequately analysed by focusing on three components namely: moral stance towards the subject matter, conceptions about the possibility of collective action, and conceptions of collective identity with some shared interests or values. These conceptions may aid in analysing different stakeholder's portfolios of themselves depending on the roles they play (Goffman 1974). Applying this focused analytical stance to data collected from seafarers will serve to answer the main research question relating to perceptions of the issue of marine pollution and compliance problems in general.

The measurement of frames in this research is carried out in three steps:
- First, the interpretive detection of frames;
- Second, the whole data set is then coded for the presence or absence of the identified frames;

- Third, validation of frames: this was done either by connecting the coding matrices to some chunks of data containing detected frames with the larger theoretical framework of the research project (Koenig 2006).

Seafarers interviewed in this pilot study demonstrate some detectable forms of 'transforming' from individual to collective frames. Within this context, it is argued that the 'established uses of frame analysis require significant modification to address micro-transformation processes' (Welsh and Chesters 2001). The introduction of the more contemporary approach of 'reflexive framing' provided, for my purposes, a more viable approach for understanding of the 'sense making capacities of individuals and collectives' in relation to Goffman's strips of activity (Chesters and Welsh 2002). One of the 'strips' of activity (or batch of occurrences) that was in need of investigation in this research is the continuity of illicit polluting actions in the marine environment attributed to shipping despite the latest stringent regulatory instruments, consequential audits, and stringent enforcement measures. However, it should be empathised that the utilisation of the 'reflexive framing' approach would still be limited to the realms of textual analysis as it is practically difficult to record participants' non-textual signs (e.g. tone – rhythm – facial expression) in this research's data collection settings.

4.3.2 Limitations of 'Frame Analysis'

Researchers using the framing paradigm are cautioned not to try to prioritize secondary components in the analytical process and try to interpret them in ways that may oppose the dominant meaning. It is argued that if the text frame emphasises one point of view, the evidence of social science usually suggests that relatively few people will conclude the contrary (Entman 1993). Hence Goffman's arguments pivoting on 'transformations' are sometimes seen to freeze social interactions into one single frame ignoring the multiple realities of different individuals in a given situation, moreover self-reflexive and self-aware individuals do and experience more than one thing at the same time (Denzin and Keller 1981). For instance, in this research, seafarers, while expressing their perceptions regarding compliance with environmental regulations may, at the same time, maintain a frame of 'caring' about the beauty of nature (i.e. a 'value' frame). To avoid confusion, it was decided that I conduct a pilot study to explore the main themes that emerge from a sample of seafarers to help decide the way ahead in the study.

4.4   The Pilot Study

The importance of a pilot study in qualitative research is often overlooked. However, in this project I developed a carefully designed pilot study which resulted in a beneficial data set that enlightened the whole research design and conduct. The experience gained in this pilot study was used to re-frame some of the research questions, re-collect background information about the compliance to MARPOL difficulties expressed by seafarers and encouraged me to explore new areas in the literature concerning work place, audit culture, corporate social responsibility, and environmental ethics. This exploration aided me in the further understanding of the dynamics of compliance to environmental legislation by shipping companies and seafarers worldwide. Moreover this pilot study helped in adopting the research approach (Hammersley 1984; Sampson 2004).

Upon reaching the design stage of this project, I was able to evaluate what a pilot could contribute to the research in terms of temporal and spatial planning. The lessons I learned in the preparation of the pilot interview setting, managing the flow of qualitative interviews and keeping my respondents in context, were not necessarily anticipated. Nevertheless, such lessons proved extremely beneficial during the conduct of the main field study. The pilot data also helped in refining my research tools. This has reflected into the re-formulation of my interview schedule by adding sections asking respondents to report back on how they experienced the detected rise (or lack) of 'environmental justice' among their peers. Additionally, the pilot study provided a set of usable data which will be reflected upon in the following sub-sections. It is important to give the reader a sense of the selection of the pilot sample, highlight my aims, and present the initial analytical outcomes from the pilot interview transcripts.

4.4.1 The Pilot Study Sample

A total of six participants were interviewed during the period between 14th and 27th June 2006 in the Arab Academy for Science, Technology and Maritime Transport (AASTMT) in Alexandria, Egypt. The interview period was approximately one hour for each participant. The trading pattern of the tanker ships they recently sailed on ranged between world-wide trade and coastal trade, representing two totally different working patterns on board such ships. On the one hand, the worldwide trading ships usually give the crew a good chance for a wider window of opportunity to deal with the ship's oily wastes resulting either from tank cleaning operations or from engine room residues. There is a probability that the ship will be sailing outside of MARPOL special areas where the discharge of oily effluents is allowed with specific limitations (MARPOL Annex I). This allows the use of the Oil Detector Monitoring Equipment (ODME's) fitted as per MARPOL's technical requirements to be used in discharging the oily waste to sea. On the other hand, the coastal trading pattern (in our case the Red Sea area) does not allow the crew to use this equipment as the discharge of oily waste originating from cargo is totally prohibited. Alternatively, the ship must retain any amount of oily waste on board and discharge it in a 'reception facility' in the ports or terminals upon arrival. These facilities are supposed to exist in every port as per MARPOL requirements; however, this may not be the case in some countries as seafarers argue further ahead in this study.

Participants were all certified officers (four deck officers, one engineer officer and one captain). At this pilot stage it was anticipated that the focus would be on the views and perceptions of decision makers rather than enhancing the sample to include ratings and un-certified crew members. This could be justified by the fact that the ship's officers and captain are the ones bearing the direct responsibility of complying with international conventions, local requirements and company instructions (including MARPOL). Moreover, in case any breach or violation of MARPOL is detected, they are the ones that may be subjected to arrest and criminal prosecution. The sea-going experience among participants ranged between 31 years and a few months (i.e. newly graduated officers), representing a diverse span of temporal engagement with the marine pollution problem and providing a reflection of the evolution of the compliance requirements across time and different generation of seafarers. All participants are active seafarers employed by certain shipping companies (at the time of the interview) and were recruited while attending some of the mandatory short courses in the AASTMT (e.g. ship handling, firefighting, personal survival...etc.).

4.4.2 Analysis of Pilot Interview Transcripts

'Frame analysis' was employed to analyse the 120 page of interview transcripts resulting from the pilot interviews. The analysis started with an interpretive detection of frames attempting to locate the major or 'master' frames (Koenig 2006). At this early stage of my intellectual journey, I need to emphasise that interpretations offered here for the pilot study should of course, be treated with caution, as being no more than suggestive of the dominant frames, constructions of seafarers of the marine pollution problem in general, and certainly not as constituting a definitive test.

My focus in this initial stage of pilot data analysis has been very much focused on the ways in which seafarers frame their daily troubles, aims, and goals in relation to compliance to marine environmental regulations in general, and MARPOL in particular. Three master frames dominated the seafarers' accounts while talking about the marine pollution problem which I named at that time, influenced by substantive classic framing literature; the 'injustice frame', the related 'indignity frame', and the unexpected 'harmony with nature frame' (Gamson 1992). However, seeking the presence of such frames and grievances in seafarers' accounts was not my only goal, but I needed to identify the manner in which such grievances are constructed and the generation and diffusion of those constructions (Snow et al. 1986). A coding table was created listing the accounts of participants in relation to each master frame in the whole data set to aid the analysis process. At this stage it was done manually, however, at later stages, qualitative data analysis software was used.

4.4.3 Pilot Study Findings and limitations

Participants in the pilot study clearly identified the marine pollution and compliance problems, assigning blame to peers, shipping companies, and governing bodies. They also offered suggestions and solutions to the problems, proposed specific pollution mitigation strategies, tactics, and set up objectives by which these solutions may be achieved. In other words, they were socially constructing the problem in their own ways.

In addition to the location of the above mentioned three master frames in the pilot study data, participants expressed many diagnostic and prognostic sub-frames along with the master frames in a clear demonstration of 'frame alignment' processes (Goffman 1974; Snow et al. 1986). Two kinds of frame alignment processes have been identified in the pilot data; 'frame bridging' and 'frame amplification'. On one hand, 'frame bridging' is the act of linking two compatible but separate frames that relate to the same issue, such as bridging individual identities or grievances with those of general society. Participants were clearly bridging

73

between their personal grievances in the 'indignity' frame and their helplessness in caring about the marine environment in the 'harmony' frame. On the other hand, 'frame amplification' refers to the process whereby the meanings and interpretive framework of an issue are clarified such that people can see how the issue is connected to their lives (Taylor 2000). In this context, participants also link the adverse effects of marine pollution to their personal lives in many areas of the data (e.g. polluted beaches that they go to, potential health problems for their children, seafood contamination… etc.). Moreover, pilot participants seemed to be reconstructing their perceived injustices by focusing their anger on the technical difficulties based on the mastery of 'science and technology' over the MARPOL compliance requirements and procedures. However, as I anticipated, further analysis and enquiry into this issue revealed more latent reasons for such reconstructions which helped me understand why seafarers and policy makers act the way they do (see chapter six).

Another very helpful issue was the locating of the quite emotional 'indignity' and 'harmony with nature' frames in the pilot data which raised some serious questions not only relating to the source of such emotions but also to their rational basis. To aid this enquiry, I needed at some stage of data analysis to move beyond the identification of structural frames by counting the appearance of key words and phrases, or specific metaphorical structures. Instead, as framing scholars contend, one must look for story lines or 'cultural frames' about what could be comprehended from the whole data set (Fisher 1997). It is worth noting here that the data collected on the seafarers' level at the main field study stage will be analysed independently utilising the coding practices derived from the framing analysis techniques for further validation of the results (see section 4.5.2). It is worth mentioning that employing the reflexive framing approach, there is no claim that the interpretive themes generated through the process of coding are generated independently from the researcher.

4.5   The Research Design Overview

Following the pilot data analysis, one of my main concerns while thinking about the research design was how I could balance between giving prominence to the respondents' individual views and constructions of the problem and at the same time attend to the more wider organisational, social and political issues involved. Trying to maintain a continuous link between all these aspects, I ultimately arrived at a basic design tailored to the situation in hand influenced mainly by the risk, trust and reflexive framing literatures, research questions, and inevitably, the pilot findings. On the seafarers and their respective shipping companies' front, the inter-group rivalry, demoralisation, and competition issues were considered in designing interviews and the choice of analytical methods.

On the organisational level, contact was established with the IMO information services staff and external relations office; they provide much- needed documentary information as well as act as gate keepers for various other divisions (e.g. legal drafting staff). This facilitated my access to the IMO's library services and allowed me to attend various MEPC committee meetings during 2006 and 2007 as an observer which proved very beneficial to the whole research process.

4.5.1 Sample Choice Criteria

On the seafarers' level, as previously mentioned, the pilot interviews were conducted in the "Arab Academy for Science, Technology and Maritime Transport" (AASTMT) in Alexandria - Egypt during June 2006. Regarding the main field interviews, they started by interviewing seafarers in two British ports (Cardiff and Milford Haven) during the spring and early summer of 2007 aided by the "Mission to Seamen" whom I established contact with the help of the SIRC staff. The second half of the main field interviews were conducted again at the AASTMT in Alexandria, Egypt. As in the pilot sample, the interviewees were recruited while attending various short courses during the summer of 2007 which totalled the number of respondents to 40. The AASTMT in Alexandria, where seafarers from most Arab and African countries join to either study for their Certificates of competency (COCs) or to attend mandatory short courses (as per the STCW95 requirements, e.g. firefighting , personal survival, … etc.). The researcher, being a lecturer - at that time - in this particular Maritime Education and Training (MET) institution was able to recruit seafarers from various ranks willing to participate in the research with relative ease (providing adequate preparation beforehand). This fulfilled the required sample of Middle Eastern and African seafarers. As for the sample from Asian and European nationalities; the interviews took place with seafarers while their ships called at ports in Cardiff and Milford haven during cargo transfer operations. Doing this, I was satisfied that the sample of seafarers interviewed using this strategy is an adequate representation of the wide diversity of this unique professional and social group.

However, bearing in mind the outcomes of the pilot study, it was important for me to explore the dynamics of the rule making process at the IMO to verify many of the seafarers' grievances regarding compliance to MARPOL and other environmental instruments. Fortunately, the (IMO) headquarters is in London, which is quite convenient from the access and financial expenses points of view. Contacts were established within the organisation with some of the information officers who act as environmental and legal staff that would be interviewed in the research's main data collection stage. However, collecting documentary data (draft amendments, working papers of environmental issues) from the IMO has already started since March 2006 while attending the Marine Environmental Protection Committee (MEPC) meetings and continued throughout the year (MEPC54 and MEPC55 meetings were attended in March 2006 and October 2006 respectively). It is worth noting that the attendance of the plenary session discussions in those meetings highlighted to me the dynamics behind the dominant theme of science and technology in drafting and amending marine environmental conventions. My interaction and discussions with the environmental policy makers from various member states in IMO and the legal drafting staff helped to verify the priorities that the former group circumvents to the latter and how they transform such priorities into a consensual legal text (i.e. a maritime convention) representative of all the power relations involved.

Concerning respondents' backgrounds, a diverse sample of tanker staff representing a mix between the decision making sector on board the ship and junior staff members (officers and engineers) was selected. The choice of this type of ships (i.e. tankers) was due to the fact that they have a dual compliance duty towards the MARPOL convention; one relating to oily residues from the engine room (as most ships do) and another relating to oily effluents resulting from cargo and tank cleaning operations. This makes the compliance duty more comprehensive for crew and staff, and it is most likely that participants working on board tankers will have more to say about the marine pollution problem.

The sampling process also considered two working patterns for tanker staff and crews; the first being the long international voyages and the second was the pattern represented by short coastal voyages confined to one area or a specific geographical region. These two types of trading and working patterns relate directly to MARPOL compliance duties exerted on the seafarers interviewed in relation to the environmental and waste disposal strategy employed on board the ship. The sample also considered including very experienced staff as well as newly graduated officers to be able to compare the frames and views of two different generations of professional seafarers about the marine pollution problem. The older staff members were thought to reflect a picture about the era before and early implementation stages of MARPOL and compare it (in their own accounts) with the contemporary compliance dynamics where there are multiple marine environmental conventions in hand. All these criteria were considered in the main field study with special care to include a more diverse sample representing different nationalities and maritime training backgrounds.

4.5.2 The Controlling Factors and Potential problems

The long standing regulatory problem of 'how clean is clean' and "how safe is safe' applies also to the marine pollution problem. In this research, seafarers were encouraged to express their own perceptions about 'pollution' and 'polluted places' in relation to marine and coastal environments. However, for analytical purposes a standard or a control point is needed for measuring what is considered 'clean' and what is 'polluted' (Weinberg and Kleinman 2003). It was decided that the MARPOL convention standards (expressed in MARPOL Annex I) would be the standard for measurement in this research between what is 'clean' and what is considered to be 'polluted'.

A potential design problem that emerged while analysing the pilot interview transcripts was how I could verify the reasons behind the detected moral stress and distress levels in participants' accounts. At that point, frame analysis techniques were used to isolate the detected 'moral stress' and 'helplessness' frames which are usually the early signs for moral distress (Lutzen et al. 2003). These frames were prominent in some of the pilot study interview transcripts. However, at a later stage of this project I had to scale-back this basic design eliminating components that prove to be un-beneficial to answering the research questions. The advantages of employing such a flexible approach to design were due to the need that the researcher should be explicit about the decisions which were made.

4.6   Practical Data Gathering

As reflected from the above discussion, the key practical methods for collecting data in this research was a set of semi-structured interviews with a sample of seafarers working on board tanker vessels trading world-wide. This set would be complemented by a further set of non-formal brief interviews with policy makers and legal drafting staff in the IMO and analysis of various shipping companies' environmental policies with data being triangulated to produce an in depth qualitative data set.

4.6.1 Semi-Structured Interviews

By choosing to conduct semi-structured interviews, I was thinking about generating data relating to my main research question, bearing in mind time and practical constraints at some interview settings (e.g. interviewing ship's officers in port during cargo operations). In this type of interview, this is done by introducing the topic and then guiding the discussion by asking specific questions. Scholars argue that with this choice, the potential generated data would - more or less - reflect a reality jointly constructed by the interviewer and the interviewee (Rapley 2004). Silverman (2001) suggests that qualitative researchers may have a better chance of reaching the solutions if they try to build a close relationship with the respondents by engaging personally with them (Silverman 2001). However, it should be born in mind that on many occasions, interviews rely on people's accounts of their actions as representing something beyond the interview situation (May, 2001:144).

4.6.2 Environmental policy texts: Content Analysis

At an advanced stage of the study, I needed to carry out 'content analysis' for some of the texts representing, for instance, one of the shipping companies' published 'Environmental Policy'. In relation to 'content analysis', scholars stress that the text of such documents should not be treated as true or false in terms of correspondence to 'reality' and question what actually happens. Atkinson and Coffey (1997) warned of this approach when analysing text in terms of apparently 'objective' standards. They suggested that what should be analysed is how the texts work to achieve particular effects (e.g. better attitude towards the marine environment) in parallel to identifying the elements used and the functions they play (Silverman 2001:122).

Clearly, this confirms the declared aims of this research as I need to verify whether such published policy texts achieve their goals among seafarers or not.

In this context, Gray (2004:128) stipulates that one key issue in analysing a specific case is the definition of the 'unit of analysis' then ensuring that this 'unit' fits with the research objectives. He mentions also that this unit could be a 'process', either developmental or relating to implementation of a system (Gray 2004). Linking the latter to my research, I would aim to use the 'MARPOL implementation process' as a single holistic 'unit' of analysis, and under this umbrella I shall look at how these regulations are reflected in the policy texts of a number of shipping companies. The aim here is to have a more systematic approach when looking at the shipping companies' environmental policy texts (Meyer 2001; Yin 2003) .

4.6.3 Categorisation of Shipping Companies

Segregating between different types of shipping companies was not thought of at the onset of this study; however, this hierarchy emerged clearly from the data set and was difficult to ignore especially when seafarers working in each category provided a different experience regarding environmental compliance (see data chapters). Not only this, but seafarers' accounts and feedback regarding their own company's environmental policies also were very much attached to the same categories identified at the earlier stages of data analysis. Hence, for a more coherent data presentation, it was beneficial to categorise the shipping companies that the seafarers responding to this research worked for and these were divided into three categories; Category 1 refers to shipping companies flying national flags and owned by a European owner or owned by a national or multinational oil giant. This category was characterised by dominant good feedback in relation to living and working conditions. Category 2 shipping companies are medium sized companies (in relation to the overall tonnage of their fleets), usually fly their national flag or an established open register, are owned by a national owner and have fairly good feedback regarding working and living conditions. Category 3 ships mainly fly a 'flag of convenience' (i.e. New open registers - see Chapter One) with an international or national owner and signified by fairly negative feedback regarding living and working conditions on board their vessels. However, it is important to note that category three companies were usually operational in certain geographic areas that lack stringent monitoring regimes, an issue which will be elaborated upon in data chapters.

Once the three categories were clear from the data set, it was important to try tracing some of the published environmental policy texts by these companies or similar ones. This was done using multiple sources of data; first, the publicised annual reports of the companies stipulating the environmental performance of their fleets. Second, collecting the declared environmental policy texts of the chosen shipping companies; this usually contains the company aims, visions and practical steps towards protecting the marine environment. Third, collecting news clippings and other articles published in specialised maritime journals and magazines (e.g. Fairplay - Lloyd's list) that relates to the corporate image of these shipping companies or their environmental performance.

At the analytical stage, qualitative content analysis was utilised as an interpretation method for analysing this documentary evidence (Mayring 2004). The main aim of this analysis process was to verify how compliance to the MARPOL convention is translated into policy text or internal rules, norms, and commitments. Moreover, an attempt was made to verify the reason(s) for the shipping companies' need to maintain or construct a specific corporate image and how this appears in their annual reports. Arguably, many shipping companies have good corporate images despite being unaccountable to a certain community, country or even the end customer (e.g. companies flying flags of convenience on their ships). This was a cause of concern for many respondents in this study and the reasons behind such concerns were also investigated.

To achieve these analytical aims, not only the manifest content of the material was analysed, but also the so-called latent content. This is done by developing a category system which is developed right from the material, following systematic procedures. The start point is to devise the material into content analytical units (e.g. compliance aspects, monitoring aspects, establishing internal norms, provoking loyalty, polishing corporate image, incentives, …etc.). This is followed by summarising the outcome of this categorisation and coding processes into a concise form ready for the final interpretation and extraction of results, which was included in a final 'case report' for each company (Kohlbacher 2006). The advantage of this approach is that one can replicate the findings from one case study to another (Meyer 2001). However, on reaching the stage of analysing the main interview data I needed a more established and systematic approach to extract the seafarers' frames regarding marine pollution and compliance practices.

4.7   Reflexive Framing

My decision to approach the main interview data analysis stage coining the 'reflexive framing' approach was not an easy task. It took me some time - and engagement with my data - to read and comprehend this relatively new framing approach and become convinced that it is ideal for interpreting the seafarers' accounts in this study. This decision became final when it was clear from the data that seafarers were not only influenced by the global environmental movements and media discourses (i.e. the global environmental frame GEF – see chapter seven), but also aspired to better environmental practices on both personal and professional levels. This was consistent with the relatively recent work on global social movements has extended these uses by developing a reflexive framing approach (Chesters and Welsh 2006). Reflexive framing thus applies to both the interpretation of environmental disputes and assessing the sense making devices activists use to orientate themselves in relation to contentious issues. In this study aspects of these approaches are used to interpret the seafarers' relationships with wider environmental stakes, marine pollution and their working practices.

It is important to draw the distinctions / key differences between traditional frame analysis and reflexive framing and the relevance of such differences to this study. Firstly, reflexive framing recognises the new developments in technological means of disseminating information and communications and how these could be mediated to shed more - or less - light on specific environmental issues / disputes. The evolution of communication technologies and their effect of the seafarers' framing of marine pollution is argued in this study (see chapter seven).

Secondly, the reflexive framing approach refers to how people can record, recall, retrieve, and rehearse the particular events, pictures, videos that contributed to their framing of environmental issues. The pilot study flagged the existence of such activities among respondents which will be further investigated in this study. Thirdly, reflexive framing focus on sense-making practices of individuals that are developed over a longer period of time and not reliant on one interaction / observation or 'strip of activity'. Again, the pilot study highlighted the development of frames over an extended period of time with respondents comparing between what used to happen in the past and current practices in relation to environmental compliance practices. The main data set reinforced these frames through numerous accounts of experienced seafarers (see data chapters).

Fourthly, reflexive framing, whilst recognising the importance of aesthetic primacy of individuals, highlights the transformation of such aesthetic registers to expressions of identity, an element that proved to be beneficial for interpreting the accounts of seafarers when talking about their professional identities with regards to understanding marine pollution. Last but not least, reflexive framing serve my purpose of integrating individual experiences and collective narratives about marine pollution. In this study, the lines of qualitative enquiry will span personal experiences, professional practices and will investigate, any potential resistance strategies on the personal or collective level (Chesters and Welsh 2006).

To sum up, the reflexive framing approach with the above mentioned marked departures from traditional framing practices is seen to strengthen the argument presented throughout this thesis. This argument is regarding how a professional and 'nomadic' group such as seafarers, who roam the world on board ships and being subjected to diverse mediated resources about marine pollution, are reflexively framing this information when integrated with their own sense-making of the problem. Moreover, how professional settings (i.e. Different shipping companies) and even multiple geographic settings (i.e. coastal areas / ports of different countries) can contribute to their framings not only of the marine pollution problem but also to the means of mitigating it (Chesters and Welsh 2005a).

As I argue in the following data chapters, seafarers are striving to arrive to a state which can be termed 'ontological security' regarding environmental practice, but on a rather more personal and professional level. Whilst the above account was mainly referring to social movements, the emphasis on the individual experiences, frames, and actions clearly served my interpretive purposes to underpin my data analysis and explain why seafarers do what they do and why are they expressing such grievances about environmental practices observed at different work settings (i.e. shipping companies) and/or in different parts of the world.

Nevertheless, having settled on the reflexive framing approach, I was still concerned with the issue of producing a systematic coding routine to be able to extract such reflexive frames from the data gathered from seafarers. It was very important to me to approach the data with clear systematic steps when utilising the framing approach.

Since settling on the reflexive framing approach to deal with the data generated from interviewing seafarers, the regular use of memoing was conducted as a reflexive tool to record own abstract thinking about the data. Using this habit helped me in reconstructing the data by reflecting on both participants' stories as well as own interpretation (Mills et al. 2006). Along similar lines, constructivist theorists advocate the importance of the researchers identifiable presence and voice rather than dealing with the data as a 'distant expert' (Charmaz 2000). This is an approach that Reflexive framing theorists openly acknowledge as well (i.e. researcher attributes the frames), which is methodologically important for this study (Chesters and Welsh 2006).

4.7.1 Sampling and Analysis

This research project started (at the pilot study level) with selective sampling of officers working on board tanker ships to verify views of such decision making personnel about the marine pollution problem and how they represent the different views and opinions about compliance to marine environmental conventions. The next stage of inquiry (i.e. main field interviews) with seafarers took into account the theoretical sampling strategy in parallel to the process of the data already gathered. For example, seafarers from developed countries were interviewed to be able to compare their views with Middle Eastern and Asian seafarers about marine pollution.

4.7.2 The Coding Process

At the data coding stage I decided to apply the frame analysis approach in the coding process:
- Level one coding: starting by desegregating the data into categorical units (categories and sub-categories);
- Level two coding: trying to locate inter-relations between categories;
- Level three coding: the integration of categories to locate 'reflexive frames'.

The initial categorization of the data in this coding process triggered more insightful questions about the marine pollution and compliance problems. For instance, what are the conditions behind compliance hardships expressed by seafarers and what are the actions/interactions resulting from such hardships? The coding revealed that there are micro and macro conditions

83

resulting in the construction of such problems. On the one hand, micro conditions in this data relate to the shipboard work culture (e.g. hierarchal decisions, peer pressure, working hours, fatigue, etc...). On the other hand, macro conditions relate to company economic pressures, regulatory monitoring and auditing procedures, and misinterpretation of regulatory language. These initial observations are vital to my interpretation of the whole data set and allowed me to focus more on the interweaving of events causing the continuing marine pollution phenomenon.

Moving towards the second coding stage (i.e. establishing causal and relational connections between categories), the data revealed that seafarers were likely to use different and alternative tactics to either comply with or bypass the MARPOL requirements. Doing this, the global environmental frame seems to be the means through which they dispense information about their views, suggestions, demands and solutions to the marine pollution and compliance problems expressed in their accounts. This reflexive frame is what seafarers use as a justification vehicle for their aspirations to arrive to a much needed state of 'ontological security' as discussed further ahead in this thesis.

Once levelled coding is accomplished, the data is to be re-interpreted and systematically explored to generate meaning. For instance, the story line from the initial categorisation of codes in this study could be formed around an essence of 'interest' and 'value' frames. My choice of this more flexible analytical approach is justified by the research questions I need to tackle which revolve around diverse opinions and processes through which seafarers apply their knowledge and training in dealing with the marine pollution problem, what goes on within their interactions, and how individual interactions relate to each other (Jeon 2004). Such a diversified enquiry process is better approached with more systematic and well defined analytical steps. At the final coding stage of data analysis, the integration of categories was vital to locate the relevant reflexive frames among seafarers which directly relate to my research questions. However, in this rather rich data set, this was also a stressful process as I had to select which themes would serve to achieve the overall aims and objectives of this thesis. It is important that 'frame analysis' does not claim that the interpretative themes are generated in isolation from the researcher, rather the researcher attribute the frames (Chesters and Welsh, 2002). The coding process was largely aided by the qualitative data software package Nvivo and complimented by my own tabulations and segregation of key frames emerging from the data set (see appendix three).

4.8   Philosophical Perspective

Deciding on social constructionism (SC) as an underpinning philosophical perspective became clear only upon realising that it allows me to deal with the reflexive frames of seafarers regarding marine pollution in a more dynamic and open minded mode. Doing this, I need to acknowledge that my experience as a social constructionist researcher created both credibility within the research process and granted me an invaluable experiential base from which to interpret respondents' contributions. However, I will begin with a discussion of the philosophical underpinnings of my constructionist argument. This discussion is necessary for broadly defining what I believe to be the construction of the marine pollution problem. I draw my forthcoming arguments on my experience as a seafarer for over 15 years and on various social studies of environmental problems (e.g. Demeritt 1998, 2001, 2002 - Collins and Yearly 1992 - Bickerstaff and Walker, 2003). As a result of such an approach, for example, this research would help to highlight how the constructed technical regulatory instruments resulting from science application represent the problem of "marine pollution" materially and politically to seafarers in different ways.

Within this context, a major gap was identified in social research attention towards the understanding of seafarers' positions as a global professional group regarding the issue of marine pollution and compliance to marine environmental regulations. Within the maritime regulatory domain, it is quite clear that scientific and technological solutions have dominated the structure of marine environmental regulations, protocols, and even future and recent legal instruments (e.g. MARPOL annex six, Ballast water invasive species convention, anti-fouling convention, ship recycling convention) without detectable involvement of social factors. However, some sociologists of science contend that nature and environment are 'epiphenomenal' and that scientific knowledge of them is entirely explicable by how they are socially constructed (Collins and Yearley 1992). This research endeavors to explore, among other issues, how the sole reliance on science and technology for mitigating the marine pollution problem is affecting representations and constructions of various seafarers occupying the end link in the marine environmental compliance chain.

4.8.1 The Social Constructionism Application

At this point I need to stress, yet again, that social constructionism as it will be applied in this research, does not refer directly to the materiality of existence of marine pollution, but to the complex interactions between the human and non-human agents involved with this problem (Bickerstaff and Walker 2003). For instance, it is hard to imagine that seafarers' concerns about the marine environment could be developed independent of wider socio-environmental and global issues. In such regulatory domains, questions about environmental risks may be asked to science but not answered definitively by it. The detection and exploration of such interactions between people, ideas and institutions are essential to answer most of the research questions (Hacking 2000). In this context, many scholars already acknowledge that contingent social relations exist in all scientific studies even among the so called 'hard' sciences (Bickerstaff and Walker 2003; Demeritt 2001; May et al. 2001; Woodgate and Redclift 1998).

In conclusion to my justification of using the magnifying lens of social constructionism and given my own interest in exploring the seafarers' framing of marine pollution and their consequences, it is important to reflect on where I anticipate this framework will lead me conceptually. The use of social constructionism (SC) was anticipated to be as a heuristic device to raise some questions about the meanings of 'marine pollution' and 'compliance' and to suggest possible means of investigation. However, once I started to locate the diversified reflexive frames of seafarers regarding marine pollution and compliance dynamics, I became more confident that SC was the most appropriate approach that could help me to interpret and analyse my data.

4.9 Ethical Considerations in the Research Process

The research proposal was presented to the School Research Ethics Committee (SREC) in February 2006 and approved in May 2006 (Ref. SREC/74/2006). This approval includes the assurance of the confidentiality and anonymity of respondents during the research process. In this section, I shall first note some relevant ethical principles that are taken from official guidelines, and then consider how my research relates to these.

4.9.1 Confidentiality and Anonymity

The research conforms to the BSA ethical guidelines. All names of shipping companies, regulators and seafarers participating in the research were coded for anonymity reasons; pseudo names will be used instead (Kimmel 1988) where needed. The access to real identities is strictly kept between the researcher and his supervisors. These guidelines were downloaded from the BSA website, read thoroughly and the researcher is committed to comply with all the guidelines listed in the BSA code of conduct (BPS 2004). Particular care should be directed to the following: (extracts from the BSA ethical guidelines posted on their website – accessed Nov. 2007)

> - The anonymity and privacy of those who participate in the research process should be respected. Personal information concerning research participants should be kept confidential.
> - Where possible, threats to the confidentiality and anonymity of research data should be anticipated by researchers. The identities and research records of those participating in research should be kept confidential whether or not an explicit pledge of confidentiality has been agreed.
> - Appropriate measures should be taken to store research data in a secure manner.
> - Members should have regard to their obligations under the Data Protection Acts.
> - Where appropriate and practicable, methods for preserving anonymity should be used including the removal of identifiers, the use of pseudonyms and other technical means for breaking the link between data and identifiable individuals.

4.9.2 Recruitment

In addition to the BSA guidelines stipulated above, the doctrines of "valid consent" and "no harm to respondents" are the ones primarily guiding my conduct of the collection of data for my research project (Hopf 2004). I made every effort to clarify this in the project information sheet given to respondents (it should be clear to respondents what they are agreeing to and be willingly able to participate). The issue of anonymity and confidentiality was highlighted very clearly to respondents before they decided whether to participate or not (Punch 1986).

Care was taken when preparing the project information sheet to include:

- Brief self-presentation (about the researcher).
- Invitation to participate in the project.
- Clear information about the issues that would be asked in the interview.
- That participation is entirely voluntary.
- Arrangements concerning confidentiality and access to information.
- A statement assuring respondents that all names of persons and companies or organisations would be kept strictly confident.
- Own contact details (researcher) in case the respondent needed to re-contact me for any reason.
- Contact details of the chair of the school's ethics committee.

It should be noted that the participant kept a copy of the 'information sheet' form for his/her further reference or if he wished to withdraw. The last step before conducting the interview was to present the 'Consent Form' to the participant after allowing sufficient time for reading and asking any questions about the research project. This was practiced with all respondents participating in the study and all additional enquiries were answered prior to conducting the interviews. Most interviews lasted for around 45 minutes to one hour and interview data were transcribed by me over a 3 month period (see appendix two).

4.9.3 Potential sensitivities

Participant seafarers may feel that certain acts such as the daily compliance duties to MARPOL requirements belong to their private sphere, preferring not to discuss such issues in depth. On the one hand, this problem was largely eliminated upon presenting myself to respondents as an ex-seafarer/ Master mariner and a current researcher as they might consider me 'one of them'(Guillemin and Gillam 2004) especially when stressing the strict anonymity and confidentiality elements. On the other hand, a new concern arose from such duality as other seafarers may have perceived the interview as a personality test especially because of the interview questions relating to attitudes and practices regarding the marine environment which is nowadays considered by many as a moral issue. Here, I tried to carefully design the wording of the interview questions and manage my impressions during the interview so as not to let my wordings be misinterpreted reflecting on the respondents or the outcome of the study (Fletcher

1990; Obando-Rojas et al. 2004). This problem may have a fairly different form especially when interviewing ships' senior staff members (i.e. Captains and senior officers) who may present different levels of self-esteem during the interviews. The best approach to handle such ethical and practical problems is to try to steer the interviewing process towards reflecting on the concepts being measured rather than questions that encourage respondents' self-esteem (Schaeffer and Maynard 2001). By doing this, the identification of reflexive frames discussed earlier was largely facilitated while analysing the seafarers' interview transcripts.

4.9.4 Key Frames

In what follows the key frames detected among this study's respondents are listed to briefly introduce the reader to what is expected in subsequent data chapters:

- Trust and Distrust Frames

  This frame takes several forms and depicts trust or distrust in expert systems, shipping companies, technology solutions and / or peers on board.

- Professional Frames

  This frame is detected also in several forms and could take the form of 'ability to perform' or 'inability' due to various workplace and geographical variables.

- Characterisation Frames

  This is mainly linked to how respondents characterise policy makers, auditors and inspectors in relation to environmental practices bearing on the rigor and efficiency of different regulatory verification and monitoring procedures and practices.

- Global Environmental Frame

  This important frame is detected among respondents in this study as a result of various contemporary mediated resources available for modern seafarers. A comprehensive discussion around the sources and effects of this frame is in chapter seven of this thesis.

- Conflict Management Frames

This frame is employed by seafarers in their attempts to balance between personal and professional compliance demands to Marpol and also takes several forms as discussed in chapter eight.

4.10 Concluding Remarks

The theoretical and methodological concepts presented in this chapter are selected on the criteria of whether they provide useful insights in relation to the research questions, aims and objectives. After reviewing the initial outcomes of my pilot study and thinking about internal validity I was more concerned about my ability to pinpoint the relationships between the detected moral stress expressed by seafarers and the inherent reasons for such constructions. At this point, I need to stress that in order to establish such relationships, one has to understand how these constructions are continually produced and reproduced by 'persons acting in specific local settings at a micro level' (Barness 1995; Giddens 1984). It is worth noting that this thesis does not only aim at discovering perceptions, and frames expressed by various strands of seafarers, but also aims to identify consequences of such framings on environmental practice to be able to suggest remedies, propose solutions to reform behaviours, and recommend policy solutions to such problems. Finally, if my study could contribute to integrating social, legal, and technological inputs to reform the wider marine environmental policies, my endeavours will have been worthwhile.

CHAPTER FIVE - Seafarers' Mobile Identities: The Need for 'Faceless' Trust

5.1 Introduction

This chapter reports on my tracking, in this study, of the mobility and multiplicity of seafarers' identities in their journey from a normality of 'dumping' practices to more responsible environmental behaviours. The chapter evaluates the value of Gidden's conceptualisations of identity and trust in abstract and expert systems and the limitations of such concepts on the development of a 'reflexive' seafarer. This reflexive seafarer who, as this study suggests, has to interact with new and increasing sets of environmental regulations coupled with his ability to use and gain access to new information and communication technologies.

In my quest, I propose to assess the extent to which the theorisation of the 'identity' and 'trust' concepts contribute to a better understanding of environmental perceptions and practices by this professional group. Doing this, I also recognise the relevance of the 'reflexive framing' concept and explore the reasons behind seafarers' aspirations of becoming better citizens and professionals. In other words, how they are not only striving to 'be' better regarding their current environmental practice but also their need to ensure that environmental compliance situation 'becomes' better in the near future. This recognition opens the door for a discussion around how both concepts have something to contribute to my arguments. In this study seafarers are engaged in a continuous evaluation process of environmental policy and agents of these abstract policy domains. In this chapter I focus on - using Giddens' term - the 'faceless' type of interactions that may promote or undermine trust in the policy making process and contribute to creating established reflexive frames among seafarers from different backgrounds.

To achieve this aim, I shall proceed on two fronts. First, I start by an analysis of research data highlighting the experiences of seafarers as they acknowledge the transitions in their daily environmental actions and practices. The point I make here, however, is that relatively little attention has been paid to the dynamic processes by which particular environmental frames emerge or change among professionals rather than lay public. As argued in this chapter, it is this dynamic processes of identity reframing and frame changes that can not only influence how seafarers come to understand pollution risks but also to trust or distrust appropriate policy responses as well. Second, I evaluate the cogency of 'trust' as a concept to the seafarers' framing of pollution risks at three levels; different regulatory agencies, shipping companies, and other seafarers at a 'faceless' level (based at times on preconceptions and stereotypes of different nationalities and/or training backgrounds). A central question I propose in this chapter is: how, then, do seafarers' dynamic self-identities impact on 'framing' of institutional and expected personal performances (i.e. without or prior to direct interactions) on the three above mentioned levels and how does this influence the ways in which they view the allocation of roles and responsibilities for the management of such risks?

One of the most frequent arguments regarding people's perceptions around environmental issues is the concept of 'reflexivity' in contemporary society. Giddens stresses that humans have the capacity for 'reflexivity'. They can monitor their own actions and review them in the light of new information and knowledge. This capacity led him to define self-identity as: 'the self as reflexively understood by the individual in terms of his or her biography' (Giddens 1991:224). He contends that 'self-identity' is one of the distinguishing features of late modernity that individuals have to work at in recreating their own reflexive activities (Giddens 1994b). In this context, the need to recreate a reflexive 'environmental' identity is an important theme that I explore among seafarers considering the new wave of environmental responsibilities that are added to their traditional professional duties. A central problematic element I address in this chapter is therefore how seafarers' constructed identities may respond to this particular reframing of policy (i.e. marine environmental policies). In doing so, I am concerned with the identities seafarers employ for framing risk managers' intent and practice and their practical daily responses to such framing processes.

Before proceeding to explore the emergence and dynamics of various identity frames employed by seafarers in this study, and for the sake of clarity, it is important to explain what I mean by various non-individual identity terms that I frequently use below. On the one hand, by 'organisational identity' I refer to the shared meaning that an organisational entity is understood (e.g. a certain shipping company) which arise from its members' awareness of belonging to it. On the other hand, by 'corporate identity' I mean the distinctive public image a corporate entity communicates and projects that structures people's engagement with it (Cornelissen et al.

2007). It is worth highlighting also that the different identity frames I discuss below are employed by respondents both at individual and collective levels. What my analysis also points to is that these levels are not separated by an iron curtain as the person could shift between both levels or even employ an integrated identity as I discuss below. In what follows, I argue that the identity frames detected fulfil the conditions of being 'reflexive frames' as they encourage seafarers towards seeking improved environmental practices. Whether these frames are successful or not in their endeavours is dependent on multiple factors, as I discuss throughout this chapter.

5.2   The building of an 'Environmental' Identity Frame

Despite the fact that this study is not a longitudinal one, respondents often compared between what they used to do in the past and the current situation regarding environmental practices. Having pollution 'risks' centre-staged in their accounts, I argue that such comparisons are a key contributor to the building-up of 'environmental identities' among seafarers. From this perspective, such 'environmental' identities were observed to largely contribute to the building up of a faceless or impersonal trust or distrust relationships with regulatory agencies and maritime policy makers as I demonstrate further below in this chapter.

By 'environmental' identity frame I refer to the dominant frames of care towards the marine environment and willingness for action to prevent further pollution presented by almost all seafarers interviewed in this research (Stets and Biga 2003). For a reflexive individual/seafarer, it is plausible to say that such an identity constitutes a part of the overall social identity in contemporary society (Giddens 1991; Webb 2004). However, among seafarers in this study, this frame seems to have shaped and strengthened only in the last 'few years' as reported by many respondents in resonance with the wave of environmentalism and the calls for a 'greener' shipping industry (Oberthür 2003; Pisani 2002). Progressively, this obviously led to a perceived improvement in the general attitudes of some 'reflexive' seafarers towards the marine environment as reported by the following respondents:

'Yes, it is improving, I notice myself, in relation to environmental issues, when I was a cadet, junior officer, third officer, and it differs. Maybe this progress relates to

experience or enhanced awareness or God knows but I am different now from me when I was a cadet.'
(Respondent D23C/C3)

'Some time ago, I was only operating the oil monitoring equipment at inspection time. In other times I don't. Sometimes I throw (dump) it away overboard, but now there is nothing of the sort completely.'
(Respondent E29R/C3)

The above accounts clarify how both respondents 'reflexively' sense progress in the environmental practices on board ships in recent years which, I argue, contributes to building up a new form of re-framed (or re-appraised) 'professional' identities that integrates the resultant added 'environmental' duties as an inherent part of the daily duties on board a ship. In this context, seafarers are mobilising such reflexive identities in the face of environmental 'risks' such as marine pollution in an attempt to contribute actively to the prevention, and mitigation of this risk and reach out to a state of 'professional satisfaction' or 'ontological security'. However, this general feeling of actual improvement is the prime mover for demanding more coherent policies and action among this study's respondents despite the difficulties they may face on the implementation level. This state, to borrow from Giddens (1990, 1991), is one step towards the quest of most respondents towards a more comprehensive form of 'ontological security' needed by individuals in late modern society. Along similar lines, it could be argued that this form of 'reflexivity' detected among seafarers in this study is also supported by Beck's arguments that reflexive citizens are in a state of continuous re-appraisal of one's risk position in the contemporary 'risky' society (Beck 1992).

Following this theme, these ongoing re-appraisal processes and the building up of 'environmental identities' among this work group have also contributed to feelings of guilt and shame when recalling the normality of previous dumping habits that seafarers used to exercise some years ago. These feelings of guilt can be sensed in the account of a Filipino Second Engineer comparing between his current 'reflexive framing' of environmental issues and his memories of the practices that he used to conduct some years ago:

'I've been in the 80s on the cruise ships. I was then a garbage manager. I threw a lot of rubbish; it's a mistake so I saw it is very upsetting. I recently saw some documentaries, in which birds and fish entangled with this plastic rubber...'
(Respondent E10/RO)

The above account clarifies, in relation to past and present framing of pollution risk(s), that this seafarer, as a reflexive individual and a professional, needed to break with his dumping habits of the past and to 'contemplate novel courses of action that cannot simply be guided by established habits' (Giddens1991:73). He clearly re-framed his past environmental practices as being wrong and a disturbance to a needed state of 'ontological security' in current circumstances especially after being exposed to a multiplicity of media resources highlighting adverse effects of pollution on wild life (see chapter six). However, this re-framing of the 'mistakes' of the past goes along with anticipation of the future for many other seafarers as seen from the following accounts:

'The more talk out there about the environment, the more you feel the pressure to apply and you don't want to do things that will result in pollution. You want to behave as good as you can.'
(Respondent D4RO/C2)

'I do wish that one day I don't see such things and our waters to be clean same like European Countries' waters, and I can be able to eat edible fish.'
(Respondent E29/C3)

It is clear from the above accounts that 'ontological security' is not given but something that needs to be created and sustained. Neither respondent seemed to draw lines between professional environmental compliance practice and normative environmental attitudes of themselves and of their fellow seafarers. The empirical data is laden with clear aspirations by seafarers to 'become' better on the environmental practice side. The notion of 'reflexive framing' (Chesters and Welsh 2006a) is very helpful for data analysis here as it deals with 'ontology' as a process of 'becoming' rather than 'being' thus integrating the changing conditions arising from the individual's experiences and progressive framing of environmental issues in latest years. The above respondents are not only aiming to behave better on the environmental practice side but are also looking forward to an improvement in the future based on their sense of a progressive improvement in recent years. Hence, one could argue that this sort of 'ontological dualism' (i.e. to 'be' better now and also 'become' better in future) is a key factor in building up the very conspicuous environmental identity frames that seafarers are employing.

5.3   The 'National' Reflexive Frame

Many seafarers in this study are posing with a 'national' identity frame when asked about compliance levels to marine environmental regulations. On the one hand, most European respondents claim that the salience of their environmental identity frame is due to their nationalities and how they were brought up in their countries and taught how to preserve the environment. By employing this identity frame these European respondents, for example, are acknowledging their countries' efforts in environmental protection in general and showing their national superiority in environmental protection issues. This trust in one's own country's environmental policies and distrust in others from different nationalities can be seen from the explicit account of a Swedish Chief Officer highlighting his country's superiority in environmental protection:

> 'For example in Sweden we divide our garbage to glass, paper etc. what do nine million people do? We do our best, but you think what 1.5 billion people in China are doing?! Nothing. So putting it in perspective you can be a little bit angry.' (Respondent D9RO/C2)

From the above account, one could expect that this Chief Officer would be sceptical about the environmental behaviour of Chinese crew members - when and if they exist on board - as a result of framing that their country is doing 'nothing' to protect the environment in general. This theme could be detected in the data among European nationals who often perceived their own countries as more considerate regarding environmental protection in general than most developing countries. This distrust was clearly extended to flag of convenience states (FOCs) as seen from the following account of a Swedish Chief Engineer explaining his views about some developing countries running an open register system:

'There is always a ship owner who wants to make a lot of money in as short time as possible [...] then it is very hard to fly the Swedish flag, UK flag, French flag or any reasonable country flag in the aft of the ship. They take Panama or Marshall Islands or something like that; they find some cheap management company that can supply cheap crew and they just run it like they want...'
(Respondent: E8RO/C2)

Whilst not all open registers are running sub-standard ships (Alderton and Winchester 2002c), the above account shows how this respondent assumed that shipping companies choosing to fly a flag of convenience (FOC) would recruit cheap unqualified crew to run their ships. The point I make here relates to the trust relations between European crew members and crews recruited from developing labour supply nations. Such European seafarers - who usually hold more senior rank than nationals of developing countries - frequently frame crew members from developing nations as careless and in need of close monitoring and continuous advice regarding environmental practice. Not surprisingly, some of the senior ranked staff accept this task as part of their job responsibilities on board while others see it as an added burden leading them to either complacency or despair when facing non-responsible environmental practices.

In this context, a fairly recent study strongly suggests that the above detected pre-suppositions of respondents in this study regarding FOC recruiting policies are questionable. The study contends, after analysing the flag market, that treating the FOC flagged ships homogeneously may not be the right approach. This study also detected distinct differences within the FOC system itself contending that more established FOC states are willing to bear and actually bearing many of their implementation and enforcement responsibilities (Alderton and Winchester 2002c). While this process is still far from being ideal, it suggests that the above mentioned conceptualisations of this study's respondents may have been a reasonably accurate presentation of the flag system a number of years ago. The point I want to make here is that the tensions between national identity frames and characterisation of other flag states within the analysis of the flag market may serve to undermine the 'basic' trust of seafarers in certain countries. Consequently, there is sufficient evidence in the data that this distrust could be extended to these countries' nationals as well. Clearly in the multi-national crewing atmosphere in shipping, this cannot be considered a healthy sign.

Many seafarers, especially the younger generation, acknowledge and complain that their countries are still lagging behind in dealing with environmental issues in many ways. This is clear from the following accounts of two newly graduated Saudi officers comparing Arab and European countries regarding the promotion of environmental culture among different nationalities employed by a major established shipping company:

'They have better awareness and they care more about the environment. We don't have the vision for environmental pollution consequences or we don't see it, or we see it but close our eyes. They have committees that talk, we don't have that [...] we lack such things in our society.'
(Respondent D33O/C1)

'They are concerned with such environmental issues a long time ago, we don't have books, we don't have organisations taking care of such issues, and we don't even have the right legislations to interfere with environmental issues.'
(Respondent D36O/C1)

The above accounts suggest that some seafarers from Arab countries identified the problem which creates the lagging of their countries in dealing with environmental issues to be multi-faceted (i.e. at cultural, educational, and legislative levels). Having higher expectations from their wealthy oil-rich nations, they accused them of neglecting environmental education and is 'turning a blind eye' to signs of environmental degradation. Drawing on the data analysis, it is difficult to establish that both respondents have based their opinions on accumulated experiences as they are still newly graduated officers who have never visited European ports during their very short career at sea (working in coastal trade in the Arabian Gulf). Hence, it is reasonable to argue, in this case, that the comparisons they are making are not based on actual face-work experiences but on general beliefs and prejudices that European countries are better equipped legally and practically to tackle environmental issues. In the following chapter, I will consider how the initial trust and distrust may be maintained, strengthened, or compromised upon reaching the stage of face-work interactions. Equally important are the consequences of the intersection and/or confrontation between the seafarers' national and professional identities as I discuss below.

5.4 The 'Professional' Reflexive Frame

Another prominent frame detected among seafarers in this study is the professional reflexive frame. This is a frame that is very prominent especially when seafarers talk about their relationships with various shipping companies they currently work for or worked for in the past and what they expect in the near future. The professional frame is often employed as a form of consensus with or as a form of resistance to corporate environmental strategies and/or demands. In this study, accounts starting with phrases like '*I am an officer*' or '*I am an engineer*' reflect not only their occupational affiliation but also the seafarers' will and aspirations to confront the difficulties to reach to 'better' environmental practices which, I argue, is yet further evidence of their strive to self-fulfilment or 'ontological security' as previously explained (Giddens 1990). However, the salience of this frame is very much attached to the category of shipping company that a seafarer works for which clearly influences the emergence and mobilisation of this professional frame as I discuss below.

It is clear from this study's data that all categories of shipping companies are engaged in what could be termed 'professional identity regulation' each in its own way (Alvesson and Willmott 2002; Webb 2004). Category one and two companies are focused on the promotion of a certain sense of belonging and loyalty among their employees which helps in integrating the environmental and economic elements of their professional practice. In other words, some of these companies have succeeded - to some extent - in convincing seafarers to balance between corporate economic concerns and building up their 'environmental' identities thus reaching out to a stage of commitment to both goals even at a faceless level. As a sign of the partial success of such policies, many respondents in these two groups show a good level of consensus with their company's idealistic 'environmental policy' texts at a 'faceless level' and acknowledge that what is written in such texts is actually being done.

In this context, many seafarers working for category one and two companies (see appendix one) felt more comfortable on the professional side especially in relation to professional daily compliance tasks to MARPOL. For example, they reported that their company would respond to their demands to use port reception facilities (PRFs) when needed and would supply spare parts for critical oil discharge monitoring equipment (ODMEs) when requested. Such prompt responses resulted in maintaining a relationship based on mutual trust between seagoing staff and shore based managers in the company. However, these loyalty expressions and trust relations could not be detected in all respondents due to the diverse backgrounds of seafarers on board a ship and their different framings of the marine pollution and compliance problems, especially if they shifted between several categories of shipping companies during their seafaring careers, carrying over their established frames. Examples of these consensual views are the following accounts of a Filipino Chief Engineer and a Swedish Chief Officer depicting their positions regarding their shipping companies' policies in relation to MARPOL compliance requirements:

> 'I have been working for this company for only one year and I can see the structure of the company. It is a very good company. They have been modifying all the equipment to comply with environmental issues, the waste oil incinerators, OWSs has been changed in 2003 and they have been spending lots of money in trying to upgrade their equipment to maintain compliance with the regulations.'
> (Respondent E14O/C2)

> 'I am not concerned about the money, I have to clean the ship and I have to do my job. The company understands, because we want to load so we do it, and we want to protect the environment also, so we do it the right way. In this company it's no problem.'
> (Respondent D9RO/C2)

Regarding the first account, whilst most of the company's actions are clearly a response to amendments of mandatory instruments, its sound compliance policy reflected on this senior engineer in the form of a clear sense of professional security and satisfaction. This respondent perceived the equipment upgrading process as an action contributing to the protection of the marine environment and being compliant with MARPOL which provides a clear value similarity with his own company. In the second account, this chief officer working on another ship owned by the same company responded to these policies which clearly created a sense of professional autonomy, which at the same time, does not neglect the commercial aspect. This senior officer concluded that in general, compliance tasks are going to be carried out in the 'right way' in this company. In other words, this respondent has established a frame that this is a 'good' company with 'no problem' based on what could be termed 'faceless' communication process with its management policies.

We can expect that this frame is going to be communicated when handing over to the next Chief mate and may even remain salient when joining another ship owned by the same company as long as it was not compromised by any disqualifying 'face-work' experience (see chapter six). This was evidenced by the accounts of respondents working for the same shipping company for several years who expressed their satisfaction with their company's environmental performance which clearly reflected on their individual practices. Importantly for my purposes, such feelings of professional security were crucial to maintaining trust relations between 'reflexive' seafarers and the company even on a 'faceless' level without the need for direct interaction with management staff and/or internal auditors. In other words, they established that their company is trustworthy regarding protection of the environment on a more 'abstract' level and it can be relied upon when needed.

In contrast, most category three respondents reported their dissatisfaction with the coercive dumping strategies imposed by their companies to save port reception facilities fees. They felt that, despite being well trained and well educated, corporate strategies were overriding their professional demands and aspirations to practice sound compliance with MARPOL. This is clear from the account of an Egyptian Master working for more than a decade for a category three company:

> 'Ok I am a seafarer, if my company tells me when you go to the port ask for a garbage barge and give them your garbage and then I come before entering the port and throw my garbage overboard ok I deserve to be hanged frankly. But if my company is telling me, for saving the cost, try to get rid of it outside. Well what should I do? […] yes these orders could lead me to a disaster or imprisonment, but this is my bread generator my way of earning my living if I say no to the company, they will reply: ok you can't handle the situation Captain, and in the first port I find my substitute waiting for me.'
> (Respondent D30C/C3)

It is clear from the above account that in category three shipping companies the process of professional identity regulation takes quite a different form. The above respondent is ready to comply but cannot act unilaterally and he is clearly in need of his company's support. Not surprisingly, such companies build a skewed form of professional identity among their staff especially when threatening them with issues relating to the diminishing job security in today's volatile global labour market. Based on several similar accounts in the data, such policies left this Master - and other senior ranked respondents in this category - with little choice regarding which action is deemed to be professionally and socially appropriate.

In this respect, it is reasonable to argue that maintaining a professional identity frame among seafarers working on-board these ships is problematic does not contribute to a sense of 'ontological security' in the work place. On the empirical side, the case of category three shipping companies could be an example that targeting the seafarers' vulnerabilities proves to be more economically feasible than renewing old and defective equipment on board their aging fleets or paying for the use of port reception facilities (PRFs). This argument is based on the multiple accounts of seafarers in this category in which there are clear assumptions and expectations rather than actions from their respective shipping companies (e.g. expectations by seafarers of getting fired and replaced if they refuse company's orders).

Put more simply, it is clear from the seafarers' accounts that many of these companies decided that environmental compliance is costly and it is more economical to work on putting pressure on seafarers to operate with minimum costs. The point I make here is that such corporate strategies undermine commitment towards the more abstract notion of environmental protection in general and do not help in maintaining a trust relationship between seafarers and their corporate managers. In this light it is clear that, in the shipping sector, these corporate policies compel the seafarers to classify shipping companies as 'good' or 'bad' companies in relation to their perceived or reported environmental policies (i.e. their corporate identities). Based on my data, the spread of this sort of company's 'good' and 'bad' classification results in undermining seafarers' expectations in sound compliance with environmental conventions from and within such 'bad' companies, their ships, and their crews. As evidenced from the data, this also results in more feelings of despair and helplessness among seafarers working for these companies especially when most of them provide accounts full of strong aspirations to have an active role in the wider issue of environmental protection in general.

Having discussed the relevance of framing shipping companies for seafarers, it is important to highlight that, a reflexive and environmentally aware seafarer is attempting, among these tensions, to reach to a state of 'ontological' security but finding this increasingly difficult. It is clear, however, that these dynamics create different types and levels of 'trust' and trust relations between seafarers and regulatory agencies. Along the same lines, Giddens (1991) refers to this form of trust as 'basic trust' identifying the concept as 'a screening off device in relation to risks and dangers in the surrounding settings of action and interaction' (Giddens 1991:40). The dynamics of various levels and types of trust relations between seafarers and various regulatory agencies, companies and crew members are discussed in more detail in the next section.

5.5   Reflexive Frames and Trust Relations

To reach to the state of 'ontological security' among reflexive seafarers regarding the mitigation of pollution risks, various reflexive frames were generated and mobilised among seafarers as discussed above. However, it is inevitable that maintaining any established frame needs to be based on trust between seafarers and various stake holders perceived to have a role either in environmental governance or the implementation and enforcement of environmental conventions. In what follows, I argue that such vested 'trust' and trust relations starts at a 'faceless' level between seafarers and various stake holders perceived to have a role in managing pollution risks long before direct 'face work' interactions. It is also important to note that some of these stake holders are perceived by seafarers as 'expert systems' in relation to environmental protection issues in general.

In this section I explore the detected set of trust and distrust perceptions about regulatory agencies, shipping companies, and fellow seafarers and demonstrate how these conceptions are a consequence of the formation of the observed multiplicity of reflexive frames employed by seafarers when confronted with pollution risks. This observation is supported, theoretically, by Giddens' (1990, 1994) arguments that citizens would have high expectation from such 'expert laden' institutions (e.g. the IMO). In this context, and drawing on recent empirical studies, trust is considered a crucial concept in studying citizen's perceptions and reactions to technological risks (e.g. chemical and marine pollution) especially ones surrounded by social controversy (Poortinga and Pidgeon 2005). In this light, and based on the interview data, I explore to what extent the seafarers' multiple identities contributed to the formation of 'initial' trust relations with regulatory agencies on the faceless level. By 'initial' trust, I mean the status of trust generated by the seafarer's established frames that starts at a 'faceless' level and further develops through face-work interactions (see next chapter). Hence, I will explain how the 'initial' or 'basic' trust is generated among seafarers when interacting with the requirements of the risk management sphere at the 'faceless' level.

In this context, there are multiple signs in the data that by the time the seafarer joins a new ship or a new company, a certain level of initial trust -or distrust- would have already existed based on the reputation of this ship or shipping company, or even depending on the flag of the ship (i.e. national or FOC). In this study's data, the input of framing is clear and reflects various levels of trust and/or distrust in regulatory agencies, shipping companies and other crew members. In what follows, I identify the different levels of trust located among respondents from the different shipping company categories in this study. Before doing so, it is important to classify and highlight the different types and/or levels of trust as described by previous studies.

5.5.1 Typologies of 'Trust'

This study provides qualitative evidence for the simultaneous co-existence, of more than one trust degree between seafarers and various risk managers (i.e. experts). The table below stipulates three types of institutional trust identified by previous researchers with relevant similarities to the type of data collected in this study (Poortinga and Pidgeon 2003). This typology proves to be helpful to the analysis of this study's data as it is attuned to the different trust levels detected among seafarers from the three allocated categories of shipping companies.

Table 4.1 Typology of Institutional 'faceless' Trust Modified from (Poortinga and Pidgeon 2003, 2005)

Trust	Critical Trust	Distrust
- High degree of 'general trust' and not sceptical about a certain institution.	- Relatively high level of scepticism that can co-exist with a high degree of general trust.	- A state of low level of general trust and high level of scepticism.
- Accepts decisions and communications from this particular organisation.	- One relies on information but still somewhat sceptical and may still question the correctness of the received information.	- This state could deteriorate deeper to cynicism which is not only distrusting an institution but also being sceptical about its intentions.

In what follows, I demonstrate the different levels/types of trust vested by seafarers in this study towards regulatory agencies and countries, shipping companies, and fellow seafarers on board at the faceless level. This is done bearing in mind the influence of the seafarers' social, professional, or environmental reflexive frames employed while creating and negotiating such trust relations.

5.5.2 Trust in Regulatory Institutions

Seafarers identified two primary factors that are seen to affect their 'faceless' trust in regulatory agencies. These are termed by scholars as 'value similarity', and 'familiarity with institutional goals' (Cvetkovich et al. 2002; Poortinga and Pidgeon 2003, 2006). By regulatory institutions, I refer to global maritime regulatory agencies (e.g. the IMO), flag states, and coastal states, all of which are perceived by seafarers as the 'expert systems' governing marine pollution issues.

5.5.3 Value Similarity

Seafarers in this study employing their reflexive frames needed to maintain a high level of trust in the regulatory institution(s) managing marine pollution risks. In this context, previous research contends that regulatees need to feel mutual 'value' interests along with regulatory institutions managing environmental and public health agendas (Munnichs 2004; Poortinga and Pidgeon 2006). In other words, for example, if seafarers perceive regulatory institutions as sharing the same 'value' interests (e.g. environmental protection) rather than pursuing political agendas, they are more likely to trust the regulatory institution, its staff, and more importantly, the rationale behind the legal instruments adopted by this particular institution (e.g. the IMO). This research identified a directly proportional relationship between these two elements and traced the implications on practice among this diverse professional group. The account of this Kuwaiti Second Engineer exemplifies the distrust in various regulatory stake holders when perceived to pursue goals carrying different 'values' other than protecting the marine environment;

'By Marpol they are trying to reach zero pollution, but they can't. As I said: company, economic pressures, and political pressures. These are a lot of issues; is the company ready to pay? Is the country going to accept it politically? [...] Europeans asked the US to reduce pollution, and a lot of demonstrations against George Bush going to Europe because he refused to reduce the pollution from his factories and that is because it is a political issue (sarcastic giggle) so what applies on these factories, the shipping industry will be the same. So political... yes, so you're talking about money and politics is money.'

(Respondent E21O/C1)

This respondent argues that mitigating pollution risk(s) is the ultimate goal of the MARPOL convention. However, he is sceptical about the ability to achieve this goal due to what is perceived as an array of global economic and political pressures confronting shipping companies and governments. While his perceptions are still considered to be on the 'faceless' level, he is clearly influenced by the ways in which many countries prioritise political and economic revenue agendas over environmental protection contending that the shipping industry case will be no exception. The point I make here is that such perceived incompatibility of values and goals compromise the trust of seafarers in regulatory institutions even before being engaged in any form of face-work interactions. The outcome of such distrust is a seafarer who needs to comply with a growing set of environmental regulations that are adopted by a regulatory agency that he may be unsure of, or sceptical about its true intentions, leading to reflexively framing the whole regulatory regime as ineffective.

From this perspective, many coastal states visited by seafarers may be implementing 'ecological modernisation' inspired policies such as precautionary approaches, and as previously discussed, may be attempting to balance between environmental protection and economic revenues. However, according to this study's data, these policies are 'framed' by seafarers according to their initial trust or distrust in each specific country (i.e. coastal states). Not surprisingly, respondents tend to doubt the intentions of any coastal state that is portrayed by the media as prioritising national economic agendas over enforcing environmental protection legislations (e.g. promoting offshore oil production and offshore terminals without monitoring or prosecuting polluting activities). In this study, this distrust could be extended also to one's own country or own region as we can see from the account of a Swedish Master distrusting western industrial states collectively for prioritising economic interests over environmental interests:

'In our countries here we neglected the environment because we want to work and we want to put the industry first and things like that [...] in this industrial world we are heading in the direction of destroying the environment and actually have done so in certain areas already.'
(Respondent D4RO/C2)

In light of the above account, I argue that if an individual (especially a professional) reaches such level of scepticism in his country's intent and priorities regarding environmental protection, the result will be not be in the direction of better compliance practices to what this country (or regional group) is adopting or implementing. In this context, Giddens (1991) contends that even the most reliable authorities can be trusted only until further notice and that 'the abstract systems that penetrate so much of day-to-day life normally offer multiple possibilities rather than fixed guidelines or recipes for action'(Giddens 1991:84). In this light, we can see how this senior ranked seafarer re-framed the policies of a group of western industrial countries due to realising that economic revenues takes precedence over environmental protection issues which contradicts his own values and initial expectations. For seafarers in particular, what makes the issue more problematic is that they often have to comply not only with international legal instruments adopted by a global regulatory institution, but also with regional and local environmental codes enforced by some countries that may already be distrusted.

5.5.4 Familiarity with institutional goals

In the maritime legislative domain, and when adopting a new environmental instrument, maritime policy makers are frequently accused of not properly communicating the ultimate goals of this particular piece of legislation (Bloor et al. 2006). Often the aims and goals are lost amidst very legal or detailed technical jargon allowing for different interpretations for the same instrument. Recognising this for the MARPOL convention, for example, the IMO included in its latest consolidated edition of the MARPOL convention text a section called 'unified interpretations to MARPOL' in an attempt to explain the aims and goals behind the technical and legally oriented text of the convention (IMO 2006b). However, in this study, it is clear that seafarers are unaware of such facilitation tools and are not familiar with the updated versions of maritime regulations in a timely manner (i.e. it takes a long time for them become aware of a new maritime legislation). Moreover, the technical or legal language of the convention text provides another barrier - at times - especially with predominantly busy seafarers who need to extract practical compliance elements from the convention. This can be seen from the contrasting and diversified accounts of respondents when asked about their perceptions of the ultimate goals of MARPOL which demonstrate a fundamental non-familiarity with the content and goals of this established convention as the account of this British Chief Officer demonstrates:

'Sometimes I find it difficult to understand. It is a bit like a legal document, I mean I am English and I have to read it for a few times to try to understand exactly what is it they are saying. There is no easy version of it; it is very very difficult to understand.' (Respondent D6C/C2)

This British respondent (as an example of a native English speaker), is clearly struggling to understand the content of the MARPOL convention which resulted in being ambivalent about the goals of the convention and consequently the aims of the regulatory body adopting such conventions (i.e. the IMO). However, by viewing this account and linking it to other multiple similar accounts in the data set emanating from senior experienced staff, it became clear that this British senior ranked officer implies that his inability is in grasping the objectives and goals of the legal or technical text rather than not comprehending the English text itself in terms of what the actual aims and objectives of the MARPOL convention are.

This ambivalence was widely detected in the data especially when reviewing the different and diversified answers of respondents regarding their perceptions about the ultimate goal of the MARPOL convention. While some respondents refer to MARPOL as a legal document that needs a lawyer to understand its goals, others refer to it as a complex technical document that should be directed to naval architects and shipyards. As a result of such diverse interpretations, some very experienced and highly ranked staff even resorted to reliance on the more compact and brief 'company regulations' instead of reading and trying to understand the MARPOL text. The following account of this experienced Iraqi Chief Engineer demonstrates this trend:

'Frankly I didn't read a lot in MARPOL, but it is not simple. You need to read carefully and concentrate to understand. Well, I depend on the company circular letters and briefings as they are using a more understandable language for me, so I follow them.'
(Respondent E25O/C3)

This trend was also very clear from the account of an Egyptian Master working for more than twenty years for the same major category one shipping company:

'It is not easy, it's complicated, regarding myself I didn't read the MARPOL, I read the environmental practice booklets coming from the company and that's it. [...] many of these technical regulations are not needed by me, maybe for the shipyard, but for me, I need simple things, here I should discharge so and so, here no discharge, very simple things, I am not a specialist.'
(Respondent D27O/C1)

It is clear from these two accounts that both respondents are trying to extract information relevant to their own environmental practice amidst what they frame as a very complicated set of legal and technical requirements that is meant to address multiple stake holders (i.e. ship yards - surveyors - port authorities – shipping companies - seafarers). However, finding this extremely difficult, they granted their trust to the more brief and straight forward company instructions in order to satisfy themselves that they have fulfilled their statutory obligations. In this context, I argue that taking this short cut choice may not always prove beneficial as most company regulations rely upon and refer to the current status of legal documents in force and cannot act as a substitute to reading and implementing the prescriptive requirements of the convention unless they are timely amended and updated following the dynamic maritime conventions trend. Not only can this, but the non-comprehension of MARPOL content and goals also be reflected on distrusting policy makers as the following account demonstrates:

'In the end, I don't know who wrote these rules? What are their backgrounds? They may not be like us people. They are all intellectuals [...] some of them haven't even been on board a ship (sarcastic laugh) so it is not a perfect regulation.'
(Respondent E14O/C2)

What this respondent ended-up with is clearly a form of distrust in the legal system adopting maritime conventions characterising the people behind the system as very detached from the dynamics of life at sea. This respondent demands that people involved in maritime policy making preferably have a maritime background rather than a purely intellectual one which results in a set of legal instruments that are 'detached' from the realities of everyday life at sea. While these perceptions could be evidence of the respondents' lack of information regarding the specific dynamics of drafting or amending a maritime instrument, it is very influential on their eventual framing of policy makers especially with the new array of environmental instruments being adopted recently.

Along the same lines, some recent studies suggest that levels of trust may vary according to the function of familiarity with the actual goals of different regulatory and monitoring processes of a specific institution (Poortinga and Pidgeon 2005; Poortinga and Pidgeon 2006). In this light, and based on my study's data, it is reasonable to argue that seafarers may have had more trust in regulatory agencies if the goals and objectives of the regulatory processes were clearly announced and well communicated especially through the widely ratified written regulatory instruments (e.g. MARPOL).

5.5.5 Trust in shipping companies

This study identified that seafarers' trust in shipping companies on the 'faceless' level is based on two main factors. The first is the general trustworthiness of this particular shipping company based on its name, flags flown by their fleets, and reputation (seafarers often employed trust and distrust frames regarding specific shipping companies without working for them). The second is the perceived competence of shore-based and sea-going staff employed by the company and their Maritime Education and Training (MET) backgrounds (i.e. being certified by an EU or a developing country).

The first factor is detected among respondents from all three categories of shipping companies while talking about oil majors (i.e. major oil MNCs that operate their own shipping fleets). They framed such companies to be 'trustworthy' regarding environmental protection without working for them at any stage of their career while framing some 'other' companies as regular polluters. Surprisingly, on the one hand, the level of trust in these large multinational companies seemed very high with no detected signs of sceptical accounts even without any direct interactions with such companies (i.e. no respondent in this study was working or had worked in the past for any of these highly trusted companies with well-known names). On the other hand, the level of distrust in 'bad' companies was taken for granted as the following account demonstrates:

> 'They say Greek ships are pumping anywhere, Indian ships (a sign of throwing away), but what about 'Shell'? They don't do it this why? Because the head office, they are more concerned about the environment and they want a standard for the ship, an international one. So they educate the Chief, the chief is very much educated and you could feel it.'
>
> (Respondent E21O/C1)

This respondent, who has worked for two national companies owned by a rich Gulf state all his seafaring career, framed that a large multinational 'oil major' was essentially very considerate towards environmental issues and invests in raising the standards of their ships and crews. He remotely 'felt' that crew members especially senior ranks working for this 'oil major' are properly educated and well trained. This assumption existed without direct face-work interaction and was based on a general belief that such companies – as often publicised in their highly funded campaigns – do care about the 'environment' in general (i.e. as an abstract notion) thus keeping very high and stringent crew training standards that are guaranteed to ensure sound environmental practices.

The same could be applied to the general belief among many seafarers that Greek shipping companies - among some other national companies - are an example of polluters and they generally pump oily effluents overboard 'anywhere'. The issue of general beliefs permeating the perceptions of seafarers regarding environmental pollution issues was observed in many instances in the data as providing a sort of filter between 'civilised' attitudes and the widely publicised by-pass infringements of discharge monitoring technical devices such as oil detector monitoring equipment (ODMEs) and oily water separators (OWSs) (Grosso and Waldron 2005). The demarcation between dumping practices and sound compliance can be seen in the following account from an Egyptian Third officer:

'Well I visited some of my former colleagues while moored at a terminal in their ship. I was pleased with their working standards, very civilised people indeed!! They have no problem discharging the ballast in reception facilities in port, no problems operating ODMEs and OWSs, these are 'good' companies. Other people will just fit the by-pass line and keep the record in shape that's it.'
(Respondent D23C/C3)

This young Third officer who had the chance to visit some of his former class mates on board a ship owned by an oil major moored in the same terminal concluded from his short visit that they are 'very civilised people'. This opinion was based on a short discussion and some feedback from his former colleagues regarding their company positive policies in dealing with waste disposal and using PRFs. The point I make here is that he was ready to trust a company only from a short interaction without being engaged in working for this particular company due to an established frame that oil majors should be - using the respondent term - 'good' companies. At the same time, this respondent reported that some 'other' company crew members would have by-passed the technical monitoring devices and dumped the pollutants overboard. In this case, it is reasonable to argue that this is still an example of 'faceless' trust and distrust in different strands of shipping companies. These frames frequently emerge from the data regarding not only certain shipping companies but also some flag states that are not necessarily open register countries (e.g. Greek ships). The argument is that when a seafarer joins a ship with such pre-established trust or distrust in the managing company, this will reflect on his choice of which version of professional practice to employ (i.e. sound compliance or dumping) in dealing with environmental compliance practice(s) on the daily face-work level. This is discussed in more detail in the next chapter.

Clearly, from the discussion above, it could be argued that today's reflexive seafarer joins a certain shipping company with an initial aspiration to fulfil his professional obligations regarding environmental compliance practices. In this respect, this overall task will not be easy if this company is contributing - through its projected image and practical dumping policies - to compromising the mutual trust relations between management and seagoing staff. Nonetheless, the latest account provides evidence that a one-time narrated positive experience could have a significant positive impact on a distrustful seafarer who is desperate about his own company's environmental practice. However, this mutual 'trust' situation becomes more difficult if trust is compromised regarding the competence level of seagoing staff that a certain company employs, as I discuss below.

5.5.6 Trust in Crew Competence

Respondents divided crew competences according to their training backgrounds, from which country they obtained their certification, and even - at times - by the salaries they are prepared to accept when joining a certain company, categorising them at times as 'cheap' or 'expensive' crew members. This was often done, as the data suggests, without any current or previous direct interaction with these crew members on board any ship (i.e. to be able to assess competence). In some instances, these framing characterisations and divisions could be directly linked to framing of certain nationalities in the seafaring labour force as incompetent and 'cheap'. For example, some staff members perceived the competence of crew members from a certain nationality to be deficient only because of the multiplicity of Maritime Education and Training (MET) institutions in this specific country which could not possibly be monitored and regulated properly by the respective authorities. Along similar lines, other respondents perceived that their colleagues on board who have had their education in a developing country's MET institution to be less 'knowledgeable' regarding environmental issues as the following accounts demonstrate:

'We have only one maritime academy. Go to the Philippines and see how many MET institutions they have, or to India, you don't know from where they've got their certificates...'
(Respondent D26/C3)

'So both of us will get our COCs (certificates of competency) and will work in the same large company, but if we compare between his environmental awareness and knowledge about issues relating to marine pollution with mine, he will only have 10% to 20 % of what I know.'
(Respondent D34O/C1)

The first respondent above, although interacting solely with crew members from Bangladesh and Pakistan in his current and only company, had obvious doubts about the authenticity of certificates issued by the Philippines due to the large number of MET institutions in this country. This led him to doubt the authenticity of the certificates issued by this country in general even when this particular country is currently the largest labour supply nation for seafarers in the world (i.e. the Philippines). The second respondent, a Saudi junior officer certified from the UK, is comparing his 'environmental' knowledge with his colleagues certified from Egypt's sole MET institution. He concludes that there is a vast difference in awareness and/or knowledge essential to deal with marine pollution issues between graduates from both countries. His opinion was based on the non-existence of 'enough' environmental content in the syllabi of the Egyptian MET regarding environmental protection in general. Clearly, for this junior officer who is just starting his career at sea, it is difficult to assume that his opinion was based on comprehensive experiential knowledge and/or sufficient interaction with fellow crew members from different training backgrounds. I argue that these anecdotal types of data results in the building up of reflexive frames that could be difficult to change among seafarers and continue to dictate many of their actions throughout their careers.

In the light of the discussion above, it is clear that 'reflexive' seafarers are starting with a certain level of trust or distrust in their fellow crew members even before reaching the actual daily face-to-face interaction level. Here, it is important to highlight that respondents characterising their fellow crew members as incompetent, contend that this incompetence constitutes a prominent 'risk' to the marine environment as it will inevitably reflect on their daily compliance practice. Hence, the framing of 'others' as constituting a potential threat to the environment is a sign for the prioritisation of environmental risk by this study's respondents as citizens living in contemporary society, an issue stressed upon by many prominent risk theorists in the last two decades (Beck 1992, 2000; Giddens 1990, 1991). In the context of environmental compliance, it could be argued that these characterisation frames could change the level of the acceptability of pollution risks emanating from the practices of certain seafarers (e.g. from seafarers who come from a certain country or are educated under a certain MET system).

Another clear consequence of these framings is that seafarers who perceive themselves as more educated and/or competent in environmental aspects anticipate that working with incompetent - or environmentally ignorant - crews, would create an additional role in educating 'others' who are seen to be in need of being continuously mentored and monitored. This was perceived by some senior ranks (especially Europeans) as an added task that needs investing more time in an on board awareness raising process. Naturally, this could pose practical difficulties given the already stressful and growing daily environmental tasks the average seafarer needs to perform, especially senior ranks in relation to cargo care and transfer operations. In this respect, if the daily face-work interactions prove stressful or if seafarers encountered any form of resistance, they often reach a level of total distrust and despair as I demonstrate in the next chapter.

5.6   Concluding Remarks

Corporate and management environmental strategies in some shipping companies compel concentrated and stressful frames and actions among seafarers. We were able to explore how preoccupations with certain perceptions and trust levels clearly disrupt the basic individual and collective frames of seafarers as humans and as professionals. On the other hand, we were also able to explore the mechanisms and consequences of the construction of these reflexive frames at different work settings (i.e. different shipping companies) and the ways in which seafarers perceive their environmental protection responsibilities as result of such frames.

In this context, most respondents attempt to ground their professional compliance demands into the organisational identity of their companies in a quest, I argue, to reach to a state of

115

professional satisfaction that may eventually lead to a much needed state of 'ontological security'. However, the data evidences clearly that there are inherent institutional difficulties in mobilising environmental practice in various shipping companies. For example, respondents in category one and two are less willing to accept environmental compromises (e.g. dumping pollutants at sea) that may lead to polluting the marine environment. Having adequate trust in their companies, they manage this by integrating their environmental practice with the organisational identity of their company aided - at times - by the perceived 'value similarity' and readiness / willingness of many of these companies to spend over environmental compliance.

In contrast, category three respondents contend that accepting environmental practice compromises is their only means of keeping their jobs in a globalised shipping industry. Lacking trust in their companies, they argue companies are taking advantage of the globalisation of seafarers' labour market and they cannot guarantee that any resistance to such compromises will enable them to keep their jobs. However, this trend did not hamper the prioritisation of risk to the marine environment among this category's respondents. They are equally concerned with the potential consequences of their own dumping activities on biological resources, their children's health, and the integrity of the environment in general.

The analysis outlined above gains many insights into the dynamics of framing and construction of environmental debates in a globalised multi-cultural setting. It is quite obvious how globalised economic pressures created growing compliance demands on individuals and highlighted how these pressures are getting harder to face pressure in the latest few years. For a global professional group such as seafarers, they are faced with growing environmental compliance demands in their workplace; however, their attempts to fulfil their 'reflexive' demands were not always successful as per this study's data. Nevertheless, we have seen how these reflexive demands were created, managed, and developed in a fast changing maritime regulatory atmosphere with more emphasis on the environmental protection agenda.

Finally, it is clear from the data analysis presented that what seafarers face, therefore, is not simply the potential for failure in relation to the framing of responsibilities on the part of regulatory institutions upon which they are dependent for managing pollution risks. Rather, what is at stake is a more complex situation in which relations of responsibility – both on the individual and institutional levels – are constantly being contested and re-framed in a litigious atmosphere charged with more 'environmental' responsibilities. Seafarers are continually attempting to define and tune their environmental practices accordingly to conform to their reflexive frames in order to understand their environmental, professional, and societal responsibilities in relation to managing pollution risks. However, the picture would not be complete without a more in depth discussion of their relationships with the human and technology elements of the equation through 'face-work' interactions with their fellow crew members, company management staff, new and old technology solutions, and agents of the 'expert systems'. This is discussed in detail in the next chapter.

CHAPTER SIX - Face-work Interactions: Maintaining or Compromising Trust

6.1 Introduction

Seafarers, in their daily interactions with environmental compliance practices, need to balance between conflicting interests, priorities, values, and assessments of risks in the face of a growing 'environmental' litigious atmosphere and an extremely fluid maritime labour market. From this comes the importance of the identification of the impacts of 'face-work' interactions in order to understand the generation of reflexive frames embraced by seafarers in relation to such conflicting interests. This chapter will look at how respondents characterise their peers, shipping companies, and agents of the overarching governance regimes leading eventually to the establishment of salient reflexive frames as discussed earlier. Such characterisations were detected in the data when respondents interact either with people or technology solutions in the context of mitigating marine pollution and compliance to the MARPOL convention. In this chapter, I argue that tracing the generation of such characterisation frames helps in better understanding trust and distrust perceptions among seafarers towards the more abstract legal sphere of governance of pollution by shipping activities.

It is important to note that the coding of characterisation frames was partially textual but mostly contextual. In many stages of the analysis process the characterisation frames were evoked in the same breath as identity frames (see previous chapter) and in some cases were inseparable (Bryan and Wondolleck 2003). Characterisation frames as described throughout this chapter, are often generalisations or assumptions that seafarers make about the characteristics of 'other' stake holders or about certain pollution mitigation strategies (e.g. technology solutions) and policies (Gray 2003; Gray and Putnam 2005) utilised in the maritime legislative sphere in order to mitigate ship-based pollution.

6.2 'Face-Work' Interactions: Trusting 'Experts'

Most of the characterisation frames generated by seafarers in this study are based on their face-work interactions with people they perceive as 'experts' and the trust or distrust emanating from such intimate interactions. These are termed by Giddens (1991) as 'access points' or 'portals of access' and are described as crucial in accounting such experts as trustworthy or not. Once an expert is framed by a seafarer as competent (or incompetent), this clearly impacts on the trust relations developed between professional seafarers and their expectations on how this 'expert' will perform in a certain field (e.g. auditing the environmental aspects of the ship's performance). However, my argument around this point is that the resultant trust or distrust described in this chapter is based, not on a lay-expert version of relationships, but on a more complex professional-expert version of relations. Such complex tensions of developing established characterisation frames about certain people and pollution mitigation policies (e.g. techno-fixes) is discussed throughout this chapter.

6.2.1 Trusting Auditors

Several respondents in this study expressed a form of initial trust in auditors and inspectors representing various regulatory and audit agencies based on reputation, origin, or even anecdotal feedback. This could be accounted as a form of faceless trust in agents representing the abstract legal system governing maritime issues as discussed in the previous chapter. From this perspective, and based on this initial trust, seafarers expected individuals representing such highly trusted and reputable institutions who are tasked with ensuring compliance to possess and demonstrate sufficient knowledge and expertise when dealing with the areas they are assigned and tasked to audit on board a ship. For example, whilst inspecting the environmental aspects of the ship's performance, seafarers expected inspectors to have sufficient technical expertise in the operation and testing of various on-board technical devices such as OWSs and ODMEs (i.e. the sensitive over-board discharge monitoring devices mandated by MARPOL) that leads to a standardised inspection procedure. However, in many cases, 'face-work' interactions with inspectors did not seem to provide enough support to back-up such initial trust as the following account exemplifies:

'…but external auditors from these major oil companies, yes, they are fine, because at least they check on the conditions of the vessels but what I don't like about them is their different opinions. I don't think they have these actual guidelines on what to check on board. The way I look at it is that it is based on their own opinions […] so

119

this makes us confused, we don't know which to follow and how to follow, they should have guidelines. They should have a standard.'
(Respondent D5RO/C2)

This experienced respondent, while still maintaining some trust that the inspection process is legitimate, clearly had less trust in inspectors due to the inconsistency of the inspection standards they applied which was detected at a face-work interaction level during the conduct of various ship inspections. Focusing on the environmental aspects of the inspection, the respondent perceived that with a lack of standard or harmonised audit guidelines the inspector was reliant on their personal judgments which were clearly not sufficient to sustain the detected initial trust in the inspection process. Not only this, but the reported lack of consistent and harmonised inspection standards led the inspectors to rely on their professional judgments which could differ among different audit / inspection agencies (e.g. class societies – vetting inspections – port states – flag states etc.). The following account of a very experienced Norwegian Master (40 years at sea – 26 years as Captain) depicts his reasons for distrusting the vetting inspectors more clearly:

'All the oil companies have their own vetting inspections, their own rules, some inspectors say this you can do, others come on board and say this is wrong, so I think the best thing is to have a big inspection once a year or maybe half a year, that's good enough, but not all these different rules and regulations from the oil companies...'
(Respondent D13O/C2)

The important point to highlight from this account is that this very experienced seafarer, while acknowledging the rights of different oil majors to inspect the ships they charter for transporting their invaluable cargoes, contends that the process is conducted in an inconsistent manner. His repetitive interactions with what he perceived as 'expert' agents representing – in this case – major oil companies undermined his trust, especially when the issue of conflicting standards and interests emerged to the surface at various inspections. Consequently, he characterised inspectors conducting the so called 'vetting inspections' on behalf of oil majors as lacking standard guidelines and consistency.

In this context, it is also important to highlight that the case above is very common as most respondents showed clear signs of scepticism and distrust in the whole 'abstract' legal system after repetitive negative experiences, especially on the face-work level with auditors and inspectors in various ports worldwide. Equally important is to highlight that respondents in this study have a high level of acceptance to the audit process in principal. My argument is that this acceptance could be attributed to a reflexive professional aspiration for this legal enforcement and monitoring process to 'become' effective. This is yet another example of a reflexive framing process that deals with the 'ontological' aspect based on face-work experiences and an aspiration of 'becoming' better (Chesters and Welsh 2006a) regarding environmental practice (see Methodology chapter). Hence, the reference to the striving of seafarers, in this study, to reach to a state of 'ontological security' incorporates the reflexive framing notion of a quest of not only 'being' but also 'becoming' better on the environmental protection side. Some aspects of this notion can be seen from the account of this experienced Iraqi chief engineer who, despite working for a relatively small company, aspires for a better inspection process by ensuring the follow-up actions in the aftermath of an inspection as this account demonstrates:

'What an inspector can see, I can see better, so I have no objection to these inspection procedures. In fact I favour these checks and audits, but I need to say that when a vetting inspector issues some remarks, he should be checking if it was rectified in the next vetting inspection, I mean to see if it was done or not.'
(Respondent E25O/C3)

Drawing on the above account, it is clear that certain communication / procedural characteristics can result in greater distrust in the legitimacy of the whole inspection process due to another sign of detected incompetence of certain auditors who do not follow up on previous recorded deficiencies identified by them or by their colleagues during previous audits. In this light, one could argue that seafarers in their reflexive quest need to re-assure themselves that the audit process yields the desired results. However, in many instances, the incompetent and inconsistent practices of personnel perceived as expert professionals could undermine this re-assurance process.

In this context, it is important to note that this respondent - and other experienced respondents working at sea for many decades - is acknowledging the shift from the normality of dumping practices, to what they framed as a better situation. However, the accounts evidencing high levels of distrust always referred to the 'vetting inspections' conducted by various oil majors on tanker ships while internal audits and inspections done by in-house management staff (known as internal audits) enjoyed a higher level of trust. Some respondents clarify the reasons behind this difference which are two fold; first, internal audits were not seen as a threat on the personal level (i.e. job stability) as internal auditors are seen to share mutual interests with seagoing staff - these staff being, predominantly, former seagoing staff at the same company. The second reason related directly to the clear aspiration of seafarers to improve on their environmental performance, an issue perceived to be promoted by identifying 'non-conformities' - using ISM audit terms - with the aid of experienced company staff who provide valuable advice to improve shipboard environmental practice. This can be as seen from the following account referring to company 'internal audits':

'The auditing process effect can be that it encourages the crew to follow the different rules, and it can also encourage the crew in the sense that they see that the shore personnel of the company are trying to help in this area because these are people who know this more specifically and have knowledge in these areas that we may not have here on board.'
(Respondent D4RO/C2)

Not surprisingly, the above account - and similar ones - is common among respondents from categories one and two companies (see appendix one) as they still maintain a trust-based relationship with their management staff ashore. However, from the data analysis, there is much to suggest that seafarers' characterisation of company audit staff as 'in group' personnel have contributed to this level of trust, especially as they have an advisory role and do not represent a threat to their job security or to their professional identities. Within the environmental audit context, the above respondent trust in internal auditors originates from perceiving shore staff as 'experts' - or at least expecting them to be so - in certain technical issues that seagoing staff may lack sufficient knowledge about. This trust results in high expectations about the performance of such auditors while conducting the audit process on-board as explained earlier. In contrast, external auditors from major oil companies (e.g. auditors conducting vetting inspections) are framed as 'out group' which also contributes - alongside potential perceived incompetence and evidence of audit standards inconsistence - to deepening distrust of the external 'experts'.

Along similar lines, scholars identified the out-group distrust frame as a classic frame often expressed by respondents in many aspects of social science and human resource management studies (Chiasson et al. 1996; Granitz and Ward 2001; Reynolds et al. 2000; Schwarzwald et al. 2005; Willemyns et al. 2003). In this context, and due to the diverse structure of crew members on board ships in the contemporary shipping industry, different levels of trust and distrust were detected between seafarers working on-board the same ship in relation to environmental compliance practices. The point I make here is that such trust relations on board the same ship significantly contributes to maintaining or compromising trust in the 'abstract' legal system because such personnel are seen as representing the integrity and the rigor of the overarching governance system. However, in this study, trust relations and resultant frames were also dependant on on-board professional relations and tensions, as I discuss below.

6.2.2 Trusting Senior Ranks

In an established profession like seafaring, senior ranked personnel on board a ship are always seen by junior staff as very experienced and their practices in all professional tasks are expected to be exemplary. In other words, the Captain, Chief Engineer, and other senior officers are regarded, especially by new junior staff and ratings, as having enough 'expertise' to perform their duties in an efficient and reliable manner. In this study, most newly graduated officers expected exemplary environmental practice from their seniors especially when working for a renowned shipping company. Being newly graduated and as new entrants to the seafaring profession, they aimed at learning exemplary professional practice from senior ranks in all professional aspects on-board especially in relation to protecting the marine environment from pollution. Many junior officers recalled the emphasis on environmental protection during their latest studies and were expecting to practice the sound environmental compliance measures upon joining their first ship. However, many junior ranked seafarers in this study reported witnessing 'very disturbing' and shocking dumping activities carried out by senior ranked individuals on board as seen from the following account:

'It happened to me, I saw when I was a cadet, after discharging in the Mexican gulf we went out of port with a large quantity of oil 'remaining on board' (ROB). The chief officer washed the tanks and discharged the washing oily affluent at sea several times in a special area. Although this was done through the ODME but the idea is not by-passing the device, it is the large amount which was really discharged to the marine environment. The whole idea is to satisfy the company and cast some good reports.'

(RespondentD34O/C1)

This young Saudi third officer who was just starting his career at sea witnessed these dumping practices carried out by a senior ranked officer when he was a training cadet on board one of the largest and renowned shipping companies in the world. The senior officer ignored the fact of being in a MARPOL special area and also ignored the quantity per mile restrictions of the convention upon using the ODME. This 'face-work' experience, on the one hand, contradicted with what he expected from senior ranks in such a company which is owned and flagged by his own country. Clearly, this experience compromised the trust vested by this young officer in his superiors on board and opened the door for more scepticism around the compliance practice of certain nationalities and training backgrounds of fellow seafarers as discussed in the previous chapter.

On the other hand, we can also see from this account that this respondent is reflexively framing this high quantity dumping practice as 'risky' to the marine environment even when being discharged through the mandatory filtering system (i.e. the ODME). It is clear that the risk emanating from the high quantity of oil dumped at sea is at the fore front of this reflexive young seafarer's priorities as he expresses his concern about how much is dumped rather than the clear breach of the MARPOL rules. This is clearly in line with Beck's (2000) arguments that the perception of threatening risks determines thoughts and actions of individuals in the risk society. The argument is that if we agree that such prominent perceptions of risk could act as a catalyst to deepen the distrust in the implementation of a specific environmental convention (i.e. MARPOL), we also need to consider that - as Giddens (1991) contends - the actual repository of trust usually reflects back to the abstract system (i.e. the legal system of governing marine pollution).

In this light, one could argue that most seafarers, especially young officers employing their 'fresh' and relatively immature professional identities, assume that when joining a ship owned by a reputable shipping company in such an extremely litigious environmental atmosphere, all environmental practices employed by senior ranks would be - using respondents' expressions - 'per the book'. However, contradicting practical experiences such as witnessing oil dumping at sea - if witnessed or forced to be involved in - evoked various forms of distrust and attribution of blame to the 'incompetence' of senior ranks on board. For example, seafarers working in category three companies attribute similar dumping activities by any member of the crew to the lack of exemplary environmental attitudes and missing exemplary practice by senior ranks on board as we can see from the following account:

'All these mistakes comes from the senior staff, if the leader is good everybody will follow him, there is no way he will ever tell you one day: throw away this to the sea. You have to build-up this by educating the leaders. If you fix the head the whole body will work.'
(Respondent D24R/C1)

This Egyptian Master witnessed several dumping incidents from senior ranks when he was still a junior officer in his previous company. Clearly, in this account he is attributing a 'collective' blame to decision making staff on board contending that educating senior staff regarding environmental issues is the way ahead. He metaphorically describes the ship as a coherent body and believes that the whole ship's crew's environmental practice will be rectified once the senior ranks are well trained and educated regarding environmental issues. However, whilst this respondent (category one company) envisages some hope in enhancing environmental knowledge, other respondents (category three company) seem to have completely lost trust in their senior ranks as seen from the following account:

'I need to tell you that the majority of people don't comply, I can see that every day, even the senior ranks, and sometimes the company is the reason for that. They don't follow up and check after the chief officers and chief engineers; where did the sludge and bilges go? They usually don't comply and escape from this and by-pass the lines [...] I am one of them, if for example I have some garbage, I will throw it at sea, a

plastic bag I throw it overboard instead of going to the dedicated pin. I did that many times, what happened to me nothing.'
(Respondent D23C/C3)

It is clear form this account that environmental practices of crew members of this category have deteriorated as a result of distrusting experienced senior ranks. This junior ranked officer reported witnessing dumping practices conducted on a daily basis by crew members including senior ranks. Consequently, he blamed the senior ranks on board and framed the issue as a form of collusion between senior ranks and company management to minimise cost. The collusion, as the respondent contends, was by shutting an eye to the waste disposal records of the fleet which would clearly show that the vessel did not use any form of reception facility as per MARPOL requirements. In the process, it is important to sense how on-board dumping habits seems to have dominated on this ship among junior crew members which went, in this case, un-detected and/or un-punished. It is also important to highlight that this respondent's ship is only trading in the Red Sea and Gulf areas on coastal trade basis. Hence, we can deduce that all these reported daily infringements are committed inside a MARPOL special area and within the territorial waters of several states and, obviously, went undetected.

The point made here is that distrusting senior ranks as a result of face-work interactions have contributed to the build-up of a dominant dumping culture on board this ship that has gone undetected or unpunished as a direct result of the perceived ineffectiveness or non-existence of pollution surveillance activities in the trading areas of this particular tanker. I argue that this culture could be easily extended from one ship to another in the fleet (especially in the same company) due to the 'handing over' of these practices between off-signing and on-signing crew members who roam between different ships in the company's fleet. These dumping activities are also very likely to be observed by other seafarers (especially visible oil dumping activities) trading in this geographic area and recounted as evidence of being a lawless place that is free for dumping which eventually leads to framing certain countries - by seafarers - as environmental pariahs. Nevertheless, most of the excuses reported by respondents in this study when attempting to justify the reasons behind resorting to dumping assign blame to other difficulties and hardships such as inefficient technology solutions. This is discussed in detail in the following section.

6.3 Face-work Interactions: Trusting or Distrusting Technology

One of the main tools utilised by maritime policy makers to mitigate marine pollution is the high reliance on technology solutions (see chapter three). On the daily environmental practice level, a typical seafarer needs to interact and operate several technical devices on board to store, dispose, or clean the ship of waste materials (e.g. oily effluents, garbage, slops, and bilges). Technology is seen by seafarers in this study as the end product of a negotiation process among policy makers who may be framed by seafarers as pursuing political rather than environmental goals. The argument presented in this section is based on widespread antagonistic complaints from respondents about the efficiency of technical devices on board and the problems they encounter when trying to keep these devices in an operable condition. It is important to note that such grievances dominated the data and were not dependant on company categories, nationality, areas of trade, or training background. In this context, it is clear that the attribution of blame and distrust in techno-fixes has clearly extended from the technology to its creators and managers in a clear example of perceiving pollution mitigation technology as a 'risk' in its own. Crucially, this unique transformation of risk perception is impacting on trusting regulators and inevitably on the environmental practice of regulatees. Generally, however, it also raises questions regarding the efficacy of using precautionary approaches as an overarching strategy in the maritime legislative domain as I discuss below.

As a consequence of witnessing the dumping activities from ships in various parts of the world, many respondents are engaged in characterising technology as a hurdle rather than a facilitator in mitigating the marine pollution and compliance problems. The most prominent complaints are focused on ODMEs and OWSs as both devices could be used on a daily basis by ship's officers and engineers respectively. The argument I bring forward in this section relates to the attribution of technology failures to its managers by this study's respondents. In other words, seafarers failing to deal with technical devices on board are blaming policy makers for their failure to enforce standardised design features on manufacturers of such devices leading to such prominent and repetitive technical failures. This clearly contributes to further undermining trust in 'expert' policy makers and, more importantly, in the abstract legal system governing marine environmental issues.

6.3.1 Techno-fixes on Board

Technology solutions are seen by respondents in this study as the end product of 'expert' negotiations at global regulatory institutions (i.e. the IMO). As reflexive citizens and professionals assessing risk to the marine environment, they expect that such experts would develop techno-tools that are considerate of the special circumstances of working at sea and the daily tensions that a typical seafarer is subjected to. In this study, we can see how seafarers started with high expectations in technology solutions (i.e. faceless trust) as a viable - and much needed - marine pollution mitigation strategy. However, the initial trust in the technology solutions was compromised at 'portals of access' - using Giddens' term - as demonstrated by the accounts below.

The vast majority of respondents characterised the general approach of using techno-fixes for monitoring waste disposal on board as either 'ineffective', 'dangerous', 'in need to improve' or, more importantly, 'easy to by-pass'. This prominent distrust contains a widely spread level of predictability that future technical solutions for other environmental problems in the shipping sector (e.g. ballast water invasive species proposed technologies - air pollution filtering equipment) will fail to work. As proposals to environmental regulatory instruments are being discussed in order to adopt new marine environmental conventions relying on scientific and technological solutions (e.g. carbon emissions from shipping, ballast water treatment plants) seafarers are becoming more distrustful of technology solutions in general. In this study, the seafarers' techno-failure predictions are clearly based on past experiences or current face-work experiences (i.e. observations whilst interacting with technical discharge monitoring equipment on-board ships). In this chapter, I examine the reasons behind such daily hardships when interacting with pollution mitigation technology on board ships while trying to verify how this may have led seafarers to distrusting the technology-based solutions in general.

6.3.2 Ineffective Technology

The first feature that respondents complained about was the ineffectiveness of installing discharge monitoring equipment due to the persistent technical difficulties they experience with this equipment on a daily basis. For example, some brands of these devices are reported to stop short of carrying out the task of separating oil from water when the viscosity of the effluent

128

mixture significantly changes. This technically 'ineffective' example is clear from the account of a Swedish Chief Engineer who has spent his entire career working for the same category two shipping company (national flagged):

> 'The person who can show me an OWS that is working perfectly, I will give him a prize of one million pounds, this is very hard, they are very good when they are brand new, but then when you start using it with heavy oil, really heavy oil, then it doesn't work anymore.'
>
> (Respondent E8RO/C2)

Face-work daily experiences of this chief engineer (20 years at sea) who has been working on board Swedish flagged tankers for two decades with these techno-fixes were clearly - as he describes - 'very hard'. Narrating his experience with technology solutions, this respondent, further to the account above, contends that oily water separators (OWSs) in the engine room may work without operational problems only when they are newly replaced or installed on a new ship. Nevertheless, when the engine room 'heavy' (i.e. highly viscous) oily waste is pumped through the system it seizes frequently. This respondent has roamed many ships in his company's medium sized fleet and reports that he was subjected to many brands of oily water separating equipment. However, after lengthy and repetitive face-work encounters with these techno-tools mandated by the 'expert systems' we can detect clear signs of losing trust in such equipment.

6.3.3 Dangerous Technology

The second feature reported by respondents is the most prominent complaint and relates to the repetition of 'self-shutting down' of such equipment even when it is in normal operation mode. This usually requires the responsible officer/engineer to re-start the lining up of the whole operation from the beginning to ensure the device is able to record the overboard discharge activity (which is usually a prime area of inspection). This is clearly a time consuming operation which results in extra working hours for a responsible officer and may lead to fatigue and errors in operation and recording of discharge data, an element posing danger to ships if inspectors become suspicious. An example of this can be seen in the following account:

'It has been taken out of certification, not required now, but the few experiences I've had with it hasn't been very good I'm afraid, they tend to shut on you, which is a bit dangerous.'
(Respondent D6C/C2)

This respondent, despite his limited interaction with such devices (mainly trading on a coastal trade route), highlights that the use of such equipment required staff members to be patient as the equipment shuts down occasionally which results in the extension of working hours for the responsible officer potentially leading to fatigue. Most auditors and inspectors ask to check the records of the ODME to evaluate the environmental performance of the ship. Hence, this respondent rightly considers the frequent shutting down of the device as a potential danger as the auditor may assume that the oily effluents on board were dumped and may detain or delay the vessel in port for further investigation.

In the same context, it is important to note that some shipping companies operating in European waters where any small pollution may incur very high financial fines have decided to remove the device entirely from their ships. This was reported by several respondents working in coastal trading companies. The above account by a British Chief Officer working for a category two company in European waters reports that the management decided to stop using the oil discharge monitoring equipment (ODME) on the entire fleet due to the repetition of failures and malfunctions reported by crew members. He stated that the company decided to remove the device from the statutory certification of the ship (could be done on coastal trade ships only) as the risk of miss-operation or malfunction may cause the company to incur huge fines. Clearly, if the company evaluated the technology solution to be a risk, we can expect that this may be propagated to staff and crew members in its fleet.

On the daily practice level, the removal of the distrusted technical devices leaves seafarers with very limited choices. They either have to incinerate all the oily waste accumulated on board or deliver it to a shore facility (PRF). However, the incineration option is subject to new air pollution legislations (e.g. MARPOL annex VI) which are already enforced in some parts of the world (e.g. the Baltic Sea region). Whilst these alternative waste disposal scenarios may be available for some respondents in category one and two shipping companies, it is increasingly difficult for seafarers in category three companies. For example, the account of a Syrian Chief

Officer working on-board a ship trading worldwide clarifies how failure of this equipment could lead to extra working hours added to the daily duties of senior ranks responsible for the operation, testing, and maintenance of the equipment:

'I had to discharge at sea by the rules from Singapore to the Gulf; I am entitled to do it. I tried but a fault that kept making the valve close on me every two minutes, many attempts failed. I am trying to satisfy everyone, including the company.'
(Respondent D40O/C2)

This respondent, being on a cross-oceanic passage, had ample opportunity to discharge the oily effluents overboard using the ODME out in the open sea as per MARPOL allowances. He is describing a familiar pattern of operational difficulties which led him to fail to carry out his daily professional duties efficiently due to the repeated shutting down of the device. Pursuing incompatible goals, he is clearly attempting to avoid the cost of using PRFs by using the legitimate right to discharge through such technical filtering devices in the open sea but was not able to satisfy neither his Captain on board nor the company ashore. This is why I argue that these feelings of helplessness and despair, especially among senior ranks directly responsible for these operations, lead to attempts to by-pass such equipment when and if possible. These attempts develop through time and transform into a dominant culture on board especially when there is a perception that this will go un-detected and/or unpunished. Based on the empirical evidence in this study, one could argue that the persistence of these problems over a long time span in the maritime industry resulted in the creation of an established frame about the high 'risk' of using technology solutions to the long-standing marine pollution problem. This argument could be supported by the account of a British Chief Officer working on-board a category two ship. The account summarises many reasons for the emergence of the 'dangerous' or risky image of overboard monitoring technology on board tanker ships:

'It is a bit disappointing really, with crew numbers dropping and dropping. They are giving you a piece of equipment that is supposed to make your life easier and of course it is not doing that, because it does fail, then it causes you more work, and you have to get someone out to have a look at it, or may be keep it on-board which causes a headache.'
(Respondent D15O/C2)

The assumption brought forward by this respondent is that mandating these devices on board ships will aid in reducing the work load for seafarers with the shrinking number of crew members on board a typical tanker ship. However, as the equipment is failing to fulfil what it was designed for, this trust is clearly compromised. With losing trust in the equipment, this respondent is bringing into question the very need to retain such equipment on board when they are seen as adding more 'risky' job burdens rather than facilitating the waste disposal tasks on board. Looking at this in a more holistic way, this account highlights the failure of one of the normative assumptions that policy makers and seafarers share regarding the implementation of new techno-fixes on board ships. This initial assumption is primarily based on trust in expert generated technology solutions which - as this study demonstrates - is proving to be an incorrect assumption in the maritime regulatory sphere.

6.3.4 Easy to by-Pass

Many respondents reported that resorting to by-passing the discharge monitoring equipment was not their first choice. Respondents who reported being forced to go through such an experience contend that they attempted several courses of action including negotiating with their shipping companies before resorting to this very 'risky' choice. For example, some respondents working on-board category one or two companies opted to highlight to the company that the accumulated oily waste in the slop tanks (tanks dedicated for retaining the tank cleaning oily effluents on board a conventional tanker ship) would reduce the amount of the lifted cargo thus resulting in loss of freight. This convincing strategy was occasionally successful with category two respondents despite some minor difficulties. However, others in category three companies had no choice but to communicate clearly to the company the high possibility of detention of the ship with this lack of proper records of waste disposal (i.e. as a result of dumping – no disposal records are kept) if detected during the statutory inspection process (Chen 2000; Lumbers 2006). However, respondents in category three contend that the negotiation process with the company usually reached an abrupt end with either an explicit or implicit threat of replacing the disobedient staff member with another in the next port of call if he continued refusing to by-pass the equipment. This is illustrated in the account of an Egyptian Master talking about his experiences while working for a Greek owned company in the past:

'The company was telling me 'handle it', don't tell me this or that, don't ask me. So being in a special area I had to by-pass the monitoring device and throw it (i.e. the oil effluents) in the sea, but if I said no, they would have sent me home [...] but now (i.e. in his current company) I can say no, it is better to be sent home than to prison...'
(Respondent D24R/C1)

This account suggests the relative ease (technically) of taking the decision to by-pass the technical devices on board. However, the problem is twofold as reported by this respondent. Firstly, the inability and /or fear of using the devices due to being in a MARPOL special area where discharges of cargo related effluents is totally prohibited from tankers. Secondly, the fear from being detected along with the threat of contract termination by the company (the device automatically records the dates of operation and quantities discharged - newer versions also record the position coordinates). Needless to say that there is a fear of criminalisation culminated among seafarers in the aftermath of numerous high profile jailing and prosecutions for ship's Masters and officers (Hed 2005).

In the same context, an experienced Iraqi Chief Engineer (30 years at sea- category two) explains that the reasons for his distrust in technology solutions started with the inception of this approach (i.e. using technology solutions) many years ago. We can see this from the following account in which he recalls his memory of the first installation of a technical monitoring device on-board his ship:

'I remember the French technician when he installed the device he gave us the trick how to by-pass it, so he knows that you can deceive the equipment, this also applies to all technical equipment.'
(Respondent E25O/C2)

It is clear that the face-work interaction with the technical 'expert' who installed the device on board also contributed to establishing the general belief that such equipment is easy to by-pass. From the above account we can see how the shore technician volunteered to provide the ship's staff with the trick of by-passing the newly installed waste monitoring technical device that is designed and manufactured by his own company. This encounter opened the door for this engineer to coin a frame that generalises this experience to 'all technical equipment'.

One of main consequences of these frames is discounting the whole technology solution as providing an effective role in mitigating marine pollution. This is an issue which is clearly vital for a reflexive seafarer attempting to fulfil his personal and professional aspirations of a cleaner marine environment. As a result of framing technology solutions as ineffective, most respondents reported a high level of distrust in technical devices upon joining a new ship or a new company. Such frames are clearly based on previous and current face-work experiences and/or handed over by their predecessors on board as evidenced from the above accounts and discussion. However, at times, the distrust in technology is clearly strong enough to be able to trigger accounts of disbelief when the technology does work (e.g. on newly built ships). The following account by a Swedish chief engineer clarifies how he - and his staff - were very impressed to find a MARPOL technical filtration device in an operable condition:

'They have to find a device that works, that is the only way. We on-board this ship, we have a device that actually works good, I am really impressed, all the engineers I have also on-board have been seafarers for a long time, they also say they are impressed, really impressed.'
(Respondent E8RO/C2)

The implied scepticism in this respondent's account emanates from his twenty years of persistent hardship with such equipment (according to his extended interview account). Nonetheless, reviewing his previous account (see section 6.2.1 above) it is clear that one experience with operable techno-fixes on board this newly delivered ship was not enough to re-gain the lost trust in technological solution to the marine pollution problem.

From the above data and discussion, it is reasonable to argue that most respondents have reached a level of established distrust in techno-fixes on board especially after face-work interactions with such equipment. As a consequence of this distrust, some respondents reported that many seafarers abandoned thinking about rectifying the problem and instead focused on how to override and by-pass these technologies without being detected by relevant authorities in a quest to keep their corporate masters content or as one respondent expressed to 'please everybody'. These attempts and strategies were observed among seafarers from all categories but are more significant among category three respondents. For example, some seafarers working at category three companies reported witnessing what could be termed as 'innovative' by-passing practices to technical devices on board. Not surprisingly, these newly introduced forms of by-passing practices were always coupled with the reluctance of the company's management to allow their seagoing staff to use PRFs, a move leaving the seafarer with the sole choice of using technology solutions as per MARPOL. An example of the new 'innovative' strategies resulting from established distrust in techno-fixes is represented by the following account:

> 'The issue of discharge monitoring equipment is not a guarantee either, some can have a bucket and bail the tanks out overboard, or even have a submersible pump and a hose and throw all overboard without coming near any monitoring devices at all, so it is an awareness issue. After the awareness there must be incentives for people to comply...'
>
> (Respondent E29R/C3)

This category three chief engineer talks about witnessing a by-passing practice that can easily go undetected as it does not require fitting any additional piping arrangements (e.g. magic pipes). The 'innovation' lies in using some equipment that already exists on board for tank cleaning purposes and the pumping operation takes place manually on the ship's deck away from the recording devices installed in the cargo control room and the ship's pump room. The data is laden with similar attempts by seafarers who have totally lost faith in techno-fixes on board and decided to pursue other courses of action to solve the problem of waste (i.e. oily effluents) accumulation on-board. Consequently, such 'face-work' interactions lead this respondent to prioritise other factors such as increasing environmental awareness over the use of technology which he perceived as 'ineffective' and 'easy to by-pass'. Along very similar lines, Giddens, in his description of lay-expert relationships, contends that an individual may decide to opt out of the relationship when discovering that the technical skills in question are relatively low levelled (Giddens 1994b). In our case, as a result of framing technology as the main mitigation tool used by 'expert' policy makers, seafarers accused the 'experts' of failing to enforce standard specifications on manufacturers of these techno-fixes.

Following this theme, it is important to examine how respondents, as a consequence of face-work interactions with techno-fixes, distinguished between 'new' and 'old' ones. According to the data, the availability of such 'new' functional devices was limited to some new ships in category one or two shipping companies only. However, the argument is that such new technologies were not free from respondents' criticism and scepticism which could be attributed to an existing distrust of technical devices and technical-based solutions in general. In this context, the account of an Egyptian Master who recently worked on the newly built tankers in his major tanker shipping company clarifies how previous daily interactions with techno-fixes are dominant among seafarers due to many years of hardships in dealing with such equipment:

'In the past the equipment were very bad, so people were by-passing it. It was not giving correct readings and you want to discharge the waste, so we were doing these things [...] but the new technology now is helping. When I saw these new beautiful ships, we do the decanting (i.e. discharging thru the ODME) very smoothly, oh my goodness, everything is really ok, this is a relief, not like the old equipment.' (Respondent D22R/C1)

'On-board the new (company name) ships we have static and dynamic OWSs, so the main concern is about people and their proficiency in operating the devices not the equipment. I think there is no much difficulty with it. It is just about how to make people feel the responsibility...' (Respondent E21O/C1)

It is clear from this account that the emergence of 'new techno-fixes' are regarded as a relief for both respondents who had a long history of hardship with the 'old equipment'. This category one major shipping company, by installing the new generation of OWSs and ODMEs, seems to have partially succeeded in changing the established frames that 'technology does not work' among its seagoing staff. The first respondent, who is an experienced Master, is clearly relieved with the arrival of new ODME equipment that allows his staff to carry out waste disposal duties more smoothly. Similarly, the second respondent, while acknowledging the improved quality of new equipment, is still sceptical about the attitudes of people operating such equipment especially after many years of distrust in technology solutions. However, it is important to highlight that the above cases of two senior ranked staff working for such affluent major shipping company represent a small fraction of seafarers who were lucky enough to be employed by affluent companies capable of installing - wilfully - such updated technology solutions. In this study, for example, many category two and almost all category three respondents are either sceptical or distrustful of both the existing and the forthcoming technology solutions.

The above accounts raise many doubts about the effectiveness and/or efficiency of the employment of the economically inspired option of BATNEEC (the best available techniques not entailing excessive costs) in the shipping industry (Biermann 2003; Tarui and Polasky 2005). The approach of applying precautionary principles to the maritime industry by using technology solutions are clearly still problematic despite being implemented more than 25 years ago (e.g. MARPOL). The point I make here is that despite the recent partial improvement of the quality of technology solutions to the marine pollution problem, this technology is still only available to a marginal portion of ships and seafarers worldwide, a status quo for many years ahead. Hence, most shipping companies and seafarers in the foreseen future still need to deal with existing ships and techno-fixes that are already distrusted by its operators. However, in this study seafarers extended their distrust beyond maritime policy makers or 'experts' to coastal states especially when their face-work interactions with port officials and pollution avoidance policies of such states were below their initial expectations. Doing this, they started talking about the notion of 'risk' to the environment and to human health more prominently as discussed below.

6.4   Trusting or Distrusting Coastal States

With a bird's eye view, this study's data shows clearly that seafarers, as reflexive individuals, have extended their risk framing to the potential devastating effects of trans-boundary marine pollution. They are also engaged in a continuous risk assessment process of the impact of their on-board environmental practices on the cleanliness of the coastal environment in various coastal states that they visit (including their own), impacts on their families' health, and the impact of these practices on the economy and reputation of their countries. In this light, it is important to highlight that risk perceptions by seafarers were directly linked with the face-work interactions with pollution such as sightings of visible pollution inside ports of certain countries and attitudes of port and terminal representatives of some countries that evidence a policy of tolerance towards polluting activities to open the door for more economic revenue (e.g. some rich Gulf states). The main two processes in which the risk concept was prominent among seafarers in this study were their personal risk evaluations to visible pollution within coastal areas in different countries and their interactions with port and terminal authorities regarding the crucial requirement of port reception facilities (PRFs).

To be more precise, on the face-work level, respondents evaluate what is 'risky' to the marine environment using two main parameters. The first is their own observation of the water quality in coastal areas and inside ports of various countries they visit. The second parameter depends on the existence and availability of port reception facilities in these coastal states in relation to MARPOL compliance requirements. In the process, we can detect the notion of transforming marine pollution risks to economic, health, and political risks (Beck et al. 1994). In what follows, I examine the development of these concepts and evaluate their impact on trusting (or distrusting) various countries as a result of actual interactions and observations of respondents of this study.

6.4.1 Visible Pollution, Risk Frames and Trust

Despite stressful 'face-work' experiences with many coastal states, reflexive seafarers are still clearly engaged in an autonomous environmental risk assessment process of the potential dangers arising from marine pollution. The data analysis points to how implicitly and explicitly respondents reject the scenes of pollution and attempt to respond to the problem in various ways (see chapter eight). Naturally, the roaming nature of the seafarers' job pattern facilitated the capacity to observe and monitor the water quality and compare these visual observations between various parts of the world. This process involved a prominent comparison process between different countries (coastal states) as seen from the following accounts:

'With this vessel, she is trading only in the Baltic, North Sea and down to the Canary Islands, I am still seeing some ports in Russia, in 'Kaliningrad' they are not strict. For example there is this thing that is getting stricter in the western European countries which is the vapour return, well in Russia and even in eastern Baltic States; you can load without anyone giving a dam, just blow-up.'
(Respondent D1R/C2)

138

'In the East Asia region we saw a lot of oil pollution many times especially when approaching Singapore from both sides, so obviously in these areas there is no surveillance but when you go to Europe, no you don't see this…'
(Respondent D37O/C1)

'This pollution issue is a culture, I've gone to Nigeria, inside the river, you see it is full of oil, but if you see this happening here in Europe, a big problem.' (Respondent D19O/C2)

Collectively, the above accounts show the concern of respondents with the marine pollution problem and the on-going comparison between coastal states they visit whilst on-board. It is important to highlight that the comparison processes usually consider Europe as a perceived reference point for exemplary environmental practice on a regional level. These perceptions are clearly based not only on established frames about certain countries but are also backed-up with actual water quality observations and - at times - feedback from more experienced staff or crew members. Naturally, the resultant trust frame is supported or diluted by actual face-work interaction if the trading pattern of the vessel permits.

My argument is that when some coastal states or regions are eventually framed by seafarers as lacking the political will and/or adequate surveillance and enforcement measures for pollution mitigation, this may encourage some seafarers to characterise these areas as dump-free zones. Following this, the unique hand over culture on board ships (i.e. the usual briefing that the off-signing staff member provides to his on-signing colleague) contributes to the build-up of a growing 'dumping' culture aboard a specific ship or even in the whole fleet of a company especially when facing problems with techno-fixes as explained earlier. For example, seafarers trading on liner routes (i.e. fixed routes between two or more ports) may 'hand over' to their successors the areas that are free to dump along the ship's route in which surveillance is perceived to be non-existent. It is clear from the data that this culture can be handed-over and spread among the fleet of a certain company especially when the ship is navigating through some coastal waters perceived as lawless.

However, when respondents observe visible oil pollution in their own country's territorial or coastal waters the problem takes a different dimension. Respondents observing visibly high pollution levels in their own country's territorial waters and/or inside ports are clearly more concerned, stigmatised, and ambivalent about the attribution of blame and/ or assigning responsibility regarding what they consider as 'lenient environmental policies'. These grievances can be clearly sensed in the following accounts:

> 'I feel great pain about our seas and waters. But when I enter Rotterdam or any port in the US I see the water is crystal clear, why the ships when coming to our waters don't respect the environment? ...'
>
> (Respondent E28O/C3)

> 'I am working in the Gulf area, yes the garbage is less but I can see the bilge and tank cleaning water everywhere around me. In the 'Jubail' area (northern Arabian gulf) the chemical tankers sail about 20 miles offshore, not very far though and wash their tanks and throw the tank washings at sea, you can see it everywhere, who is checking this? Who is responsible for that? ...'
>
> (Respondent D30C/C3)

The above accounts show that the resultant distrust was not limited to seafarers' own country's policies only but was extended to distrusting international shipping activities in coastal and territorial waters under the jurisdiction of their own countries. This clearly pushed the notion of 'risk' emanating from such activities to the fore-front of seafarers' perceptions as evident by transforming such risks in their extended accounts to family health problems, intergenerational equity arguments, and quantification of economic damages to their countries. In this respect, I argue that the framing own country as an environmental pariah paves the way for the transformation of environmental risk to health, wellbeing, and economic contexts.

Not surprisingly, the accounts reporting feelings of injustice and stigma are detected more among category three respondents regarding such visible pollution observations. This is due to the enhanced feelings of helplessness in this category of shipping companies which do not support their seagoing staff towards sound environmental practice as previously discussed. However, the detection of visible pollution inside a certain country's ports or territorial waters was not the only factor in maintaining or compromising trust in certain countries. The port segment of compliance to MARPOL requirements which is to provide 'adequate' reception facilities and the face-work experiences of seafarers regarding this issue was crucial to establishing trust in coastal states they visit.

6.4.2 Adequacy of PRFs: 'Face-work' Interactions

The issue of the lack of - using MARPOL's terms - 'adequate' reception facilities as mandated by the MARPOL convention in many ports of the world (frequently reported by respondents) is a prominent cause of trusting or distrusting a coastal state on the statutory compliance side. The initial assumption - at the beginning of the field work - was that affluent western nations ratifying MARPOL would have no reasons not to implement the port segment of commitments as per the convention requirements (i.e. building, installing, or providing adequate port reception facilities for receiving oil waste from ships). However, most respondents, including seafarers trading solely between EU ports, described a very different and unexpected picture as the following accounts show:

> 'Once they implement MARPOL, they should do it, I mean make sure they are ready to apply the rule, so they should put up these port reception facilities if they are really ready to implement the rule.'
> (Respondent E10RO/C2)

> 'Under the MARPOL regulations, they don't accept what they are supposed to accept (i.e. the ports) this waste, they should have facilities in place.'
> (Respondent E14R/C2)

The above accounts are from Filipino Second and Chief Engineers (trading mostly in European waters) respectively, when asked about their views of the compliance by member states with the requirement of providing PRFs. They reported that countries ratifying the MARPOL convention are not 'properly' implementing the convention leaving seafarers on coastal trade routes in a difficult practical situation. However, the 'inadequacy' problem reported by this study's respondents is more complex than the mere existence or non-existence of such facilities in certain ports or certain parts of the world. Again, in what follows, we can see how the performance of port authorities in managing and operating the existent PRFs contribute to framing a country as a 'good' and 'compliant' country thus facilitating the on-board compliance tasks for seafarers and another country as 'bad' with undesirable consequences.

6.4.3 Non-existent facilities

A common complaint among most respondents is the total lack of PRFs in many ports and oil terminals they visit in their areas of trade whether these are in developed or developing nations as stated by this respondent:

> 'I don't know why in big refineries there are no reception facilities? So they put the rule and they don't implement it (sarcastic tone) I don't know, it is very common, and it is written that every refinery should, and you know that, but you're in port and you have sludge or waste, no facility.'
> (Respondent E12R/C2)

This Filipino second engineer sailing in European waters complains about the non-existence of PRFs in large oil terminals operated either by the relevant port authorities or by major oil Multi-National Corporations (MNCs). What adds to this respondent's ambivalence is the fact that many terminals lacking the facility are owned or operated by these renowned affluent oil MNCs that - in his view - cannot claim any lack of financial resources. Adding to this, the mere non-existence of the reception facility in a well-developed affluent western nation contributed to more distrust in the validity of the abstract legal system governing marine pollution issues. Consequently, this respondent is questioning the reasons behind the wide spreading of this problem across many European ports despite the fact that all western countries have already ratified the MARPOL convention for many years.

6.4.4 Denial of access

Another form of the PRFs problem occurs when the facility exists in a certain port simply to fulfil the statutory requirement but ships are denied permission to discharge their oily effluents at the facility without acceptable excuses as reported by the following respondent:

'Suppose I go to a port and I have 600 barrels of slops (i.e. oily effluents) then they tell me that our facility is full and we can't take it, so I lost the equivalent quantity of cargo. My personal experience is that sometimes they say no, economically speaking. If I stay in a special area for long keeping the slops and nobody want to take it, I lose the equivalent freight.'
(Respondent D24R/C1)

This Egyptian Master reports another pattern of difficulties with PRFs. He describes how often he is denied access to using the existent facility due to what he perceived as 'excuses' such as the facility being declared full. He is clearly under pressure from his company to offload the oily waste on board to be able to load the full parcel of cargo nominated for his ship. Clearly, failing to achieve what is considered by respondents as a professional and statutory compliance goal resulted in compromising the trust in the enforcement of MARPOL statutory requirements by ports and terminals. Many respondents compare the strong enforcement sanctions imposed on ships and crews in cases of MARPOL infringements (including criminalisation) with what they consider as a 'lenient' enforcement atmosphere on the shore facilities. More importantly, it opens up a questioning process among seafarers experiencing such face-work interactions about the persistence of maritime policy makers, flag and port states to monitor, inspect, and audit the shipping segment leaving the port segment without similar scrutiny.

6.4.5 Operational requirements

The third form of the problem is stipulated in the accounts of seafarers who declared their inability to use the PRF (either a shore facility or floating barge) due to unexpected operational and effluent viscosity requirements demanded by the terminal operators as seen from the following account:

'I am very disappointed [...] I am trading all the time around here in Europe. For example the sludge, we have to burn the sludge because no facility is able to take it, I think it is not good enough. If you come to Antwerp for example it is very expensive, it shouldn't be like that...'
(Respondent D13R/C2)

This very experienced Norwegian master expected PRFs to be more efficient and capable of receiving different types - and various viscosities - of typical oily waste on board his ship. However, he reports that he is often denied the opportunity to discharge the high viscous types of oily effluents (e.g. sludge) due to pumping and operational difficulties ashore. While the alternative choice of incinerating this sludge is diminishing due to the implementation of MARPOL's air pollution annex in the Baltic region (where his ship occasionally trades), this Master is clearly under professional and economic pressures that left him 'disappointed' with the ability of well developed countries to enforce the requirements of an international environmental convention such as MARPOL.

From the above, one could argue that the seafarers' trust in the abstract international legal system for governing marine pollution is further compromised by such face-work interactions with inadequate or total lack of PRFs in many ports and oil loading terminals in the world. What my analysis does point out is the important role of the resultant distrust in certain countries on the general framing of the contemporary campaigns to save the environment and reduce carbon emissions from shipping activities. By repeatedly encountering such 'disappointing' face-work interactions, respondents are becoming more sceptical about the validity of the 'global' environmental protection public campaigns especially by western developed nations. The input of this language of globality in dealing with the marine pollution problem and how seafarers link this to their daily faceless and face-work interactions with statutory compliance and enforcement issues is discussed in more detail in the next chapter.

6.5 Concluding Remarks

The MARPOL convention mandates compliance requirements on countries (i.e. flag states – coastal states – port states), ship owners, and seafarers. The seafarers' ability to comply with this convention cannot be detached from the countries' and shipping companies' commitment to their roles as seen from the data discussed in this chapter. In this context, and on the face-work level, seafarers construct two main types of characterisation frames. The first types are the frames based on extreme outcomes (e.g. witnessing dumping activities, prosecutions for pollution charges etc.). The second type are the characterisation frames based on expected value (e.g. young officers assuming adherence with environmental compliance requirements when joining reputable companies). In both cases, the data suggests that the development of

144

these frames was important in determining the resultant trust or distrust in expert systems such as science and technology and essentially in persons perceived to be representing these systems (e.g. auditors and inspectors – senior ranks on-board). The characterisations and their effects on framing the marine pollution problem by seafarers could be classified as follows:

6.5.1 Characterising 'Experts'

On the ship-board level, the framing of perceived 'experts' is largely affected by prejudices and socio-cultural factors (e.g. national culture or national environmental regulations) as previously discussed. However, from the data and discussion presented in this chapter one could argue that actual 'face-work' experiences provide another important factor in characterising 'others' (systems and/or persons) as trustworthy or not. This becomes more influential on the individual's environmental practice if the 'other' is initially trusted as an 'expert' in a certain aspect of professional practice due to their high ranking in the hierarchal structure on board a ship or due to being perceived as more knowledgeable and trained in a certain domain. In this context, the contrasting accounts from seafarers working in the same company and area of trade about exemplary environmental practices of higher ranks suggests that each particular ship - sometimes each shipping company - has developed its own 'environmental culture' that is quite dynamic and highly dependent on trust in the decision making ranks on board.

Along very similar lines, Giddens contends that if and when reflexive individuals invest their trust in abstract systems, they expect that agents of such systems to be trustworthy through monitoring their credentials, adherence to professional codes of practice, and performance (Giddens 1990, p: 87). Clearly, seafarers are not only reflexive individuals but also competent professionals who have the opportunity to examine the legitimacy of the abstract system through face-work interactions with experts representing that system (unlike Giddens' assumptions of lay-expert encounters). Being professional and competent in relation to shipboard matters resulted in a more informed 'face-work' scrutiny of experts' performance especially in relation to environmental issues. However, as the data clearly suggests such professional-expert encounters at access points - in Giddens' terms - were not contributing, in most cases, to maintaining trust in abstract systems as presented in this chapter. On the contrary, the inconsistent and unprofessional performance of out-group experts (e.g. auditors) and in-group senior ranked staff on board (who may be perceived as experts by junior ranks) often resulted in further compromising trust in the abstract legal system.

6.5.2 Characterising Policies

Characterisation frames - at the macro level - of the complex aspects of the marine pollution and compliance problems seem to be more consistent with Beck's approach to reflexivity and risk. Seafarers in this study are clearly engaged in a critical re-appraisal of their risk positions in relation to marine pollution issues even without sufficiently grasping the tools of scientific knowledge about environmental issues (Beck 1992; Beck et al. 1994). In a truly globalised shipping industry the re-framing of the environmental impacts of marine pollution was as dynamic as the 'face-work' encounters with the consequences of a new amendment to an existing marine environmental convention, or as the switching over between companies, ships and even individual senior crew members. In other words, seafarers are linking technical risks to economic, health, and political risks to their own countries, families, and communities. This can be seen from the antagonistic accounts of seafarers comparing the 'cleanliness' of the sea water in their own country's ports and coastal waters with other developed nations that they perceive as practicing exemplary environmental policies.

Drawing on this analysis, and as a result of the compromised trust in the abstract legal system governing marine pollution, seafarers are reflexively framing pollution mitigation technology solutions (e.g. OWSs and ODMEs) as a risk to their job security and to the integrity of the marine environment as well. As seen from the data presented, these framings result in persistent personal attempts to override or by-pass such equipment when and if possible, especially by respondents who, due to economic and organisational difficulties within their shipping companies, may have no other choices. However, this clearly creates a conflict situation with what reflexive seafarers frame as wider 'citizenship' environmental protection responsibilities and the professional roles they strive to fulfil on a daily basis (e.g. accounts of seafarers who try to satisfy 'everybody'). To put it another way, it could be argued that seafarers are finding it increasingly difficult to reach a state of 'ontological security' regarding the protection of the marine environment when faced with such conflicting goals.

6.5.3 Characterising Shipping Companies

In continuation of the reflexive re-framing of pollution risks respondents are engaged in evaluating their company's environmental strategies coupled with a process of characterising good or bad companies depending on the face-work experiences with the practical outcomes of such strategies. In this way, the resultant characterisation frames presented by respondents acknowledge that factors such as organisational culture, economic structure, and availability of resources are important determinants of trust in the management of shipping companies. However, in many cases the lack of proper communication may skew or alter the seafarers' framing of the intentions of their managers ashore. Seafarers characterise a company as being a 'good' company when it employs sound environmental management strategies and communicate its policy to seagoing staff in a transparent manner. Conversely, companies paying attractive salaries but demanding environmental compromises are characterised as 'bad' companies even when the seafarer continues working for them to earn a living in a competitive and globalised labour market. In other words, a 'reflexive' seafarer often characterises his own company as 'bad' when not satisfied with the environmental performance of the company and its seagoing staff. This is done amidst an ongoing process of risk evaluation of the damage to human health, economy, and biological resources caused by pollution from shipping activities.

Following this theme, at the 'in-group' company level, many framing processes emerged as a result of the face-work encounters between off-signing and on-signing crew members during the traditional hand over procedure. For example, in category one ships, some seafarers established a perception that the company management shares with them a 'common goal' of protecting the marine environment in parallel to economic revenue considerations providing a clear model of effective corporate communication strategies (Cornelissen et al. 2007; Donaldson and Fafaliou 2003). However, in some category two and most category three ships respondents' 'hand over' briefings and feedback provided a base for building up a communication barrier with an assumption - which is usually handed over - that this company's sole concern is financial profit. The data attests that category three distrustful seafarers are even trying to maintain a positive face by avoiding the demand of any costly resources from the company (e.g. spare parts for faulty monitoring equipment or the use of shore reception facilities) anticipating that their requests will be rejected.

6.5.4 Characterising Expert Systems

One of the most frequent encounters with 'expert systems' that seafarers deal with on the face-work level are the technology solutions for waste management mandated by MARPOL. In this context, a prominent observation of this study is the reflexive risk frames generated among seafarers regarding technology solutions in general and overboard discharge monitoring equipment in particular. Having suffered from the inefficiency of technical devices installed on board their ships for a long time the replacement of older generations of equipment with new operable 'state of the art' techno-fixes did not seem to dilute the distrust in technology among most seafarers. At times, the fixes even created new sets of problems regarding the lack of training on such newly introduced sophisticated devices. In this context, it is reasonable to argue that when a professional group start accounting the use of technology-based solutions as a 'risk' in its own sense, the resultant dependent environmental practice will not be in favour of sound compliance to the mandatory statutory instruments such as MARPOL.

It is clear from the above accounts that seafarers end up by constructing negative characterisation frames of 'other' people and countries when these 'others' do not contribute to preventing marine environment pollution. They are accounted as 'out-group' and not belonging to their social or national group (not contributing to the public good cause of saving the environment as an abstract notion). The stereotyping of regulators is not 'individualised' but always referred to as 'they' or as a whole 'out-group' block, which seems to contribute to the deepening and salience of the generated characterisation frames (Mullen and Hu 1989).

The above data and discussion highlights a sort of a socio-technical model that has neglected an adequate form of organisational democracy (i.e. decentralised decision making based on competence) and coined a more authoritarian approach on its socio/ professional side. Simultaneously, on the technical side the same model has not allowed seafarers to achieve a balance between an optimum level of environmental performance and practicing sound compliance using 'fail safe' technical devices (Heller 1997). In fact, it is clear that some seafarers and shipping companies started considering the technology as a risk and stopped using it all together. This is detected clearly in the data when seafarers are trying to escape from feelings of helplessness and attempt to perform an active role to protect the marine environment from further pollution but get caught in a situation where neither the rules nor the company is supportive of their attempts.

Finally, the identification of reflexive frames in this chapter helped in assessing the trust and distrust dynamics affecting the environmental performance originated by a particular professional group known as seafarers. However, the data analysis also points out the connections between different reflexive frames deployed by seafarers and the qualitative aspect of the groups' environmental performance especially when being subjected to a global environmental frame (GEF). The identification and analysis of the impact of globality on the reflexive framing processes of respondents regarding protection of the marine environment from pollution is discussed in the next chapter. This is crucial to the further establishment of the relationship between frames, events, grievances, pollution risk perceptions, and environmental practice.

CHAPTER SEVEN - The Global Environmental Frame: Impacts on Seafarers

7.1 Introduction

This chapter demonstrates the relevance of 'reflexive framing' for seafarers working on a range of different ships in terms of the ways they locate their ship borne practices and experiences with the marine environment within a global environmental frame. To achieve this overall aim, this chapter is organised into three major sections. The first section addresses the resources of reflexive framing available to seafarers on board different ships and company types. It also shows how such intended 'informatics' or 'training' resources are viewed in a situated context by seafarers, how they are read reflexively and re-interpreted to form a range of other meanings and impacts. It is clear that such reflexive resources have contributed to creating an enhanced sense of responsibility and commitment towards saving the marine environment from pollution by the majority of respondents in this study. The impacts of the reflexive framing processes on the perceived legitimacy and practicality of the legal and compliance procedures in relation to the marine environment is explored. The discussion extends to define the role of the global environmental frame in dealing with the economic determinism of shipping companies and the persistent focus of policy makers on providing technology solutions to environmental problems.

Section two describes how the contemporary reflexive resources influence the ways in which seafarers re-frame their perceptions of their respective shipping companies especially when employing the language of globality. Seafarers in this study use several key 'measurement points' in order to establish their 'framing' of their own or other shipping companies. Conducting an evaluation using these 'evaluation points', the most prominent 'measurement points' utilised by seafarers for re-framing their companies was the consistency between the company's published policy and actual observed practice by their peers on board. This evaluation was usually influenced by the language of globality utilised by most shipping companies and flag states when describing their overall goals regarding environmental protection.

Section three essentially brings the focus of discussion to explore the impact of the global environmental frame (GEF) and the resultant iterative reflexive framing processes discussed in sections one and two on the seafarers' daily experiences, environmental practices, and perceptions of pollution risks on board different ships in a variety of shipping companies trading in various parts of the world. This section also indicates what 'trust' and 'distrust', resulting from daily on-board experiences, shape what could be termed as the ship's 'environmental culture' which - I argue - could be a very localised ship-specific culture and in many cases may even contrast with the established environmental policy of the owning or managing company.

In this chapter I try to present an important argument, relating to how seafarers combine visible pollution risks and socially constructed risks to end up with reflexive frames that leave them in a condition of stress when failing to act appropriately. Arguably, the global environmental frame (GEF) is the frame that dilutes the boundary between material pollution risks and the socially constructed ones among this labour group. In his later work in particular, Beck accepts that risks are not merely defined by our physical environment, but also by social construction. Responding to his critics, Beck contends: it is cultural perception and definition that contribute to ways of understanding risk (Beck 2009). However, his scepticism about a purely constructivist stance is still prominent as his analysis of the new global risks in his latest publication contend that material dangers have objectively taken a new form. In this study, we can clearly detect that seafarers are varying between physical and constructed notions of risk even when talking about material pollution observations in various parts of the world. This is why I try, in this chapter, to examine whether a relationship exists between the seafarers' beliefs, social constructions, and behaviours regarding marine pollution.

In this chapter, I also seek to examine how the focus on the material transformations of environmental dangers lead seafarers to build up a collective frame so that their own actions - or inactions - result in landmark improvement or destruction of marine and coastal environments thus building more pressure and commitment on themselves. In this context, seafarers are clearly integrating the visible marine pollution with the anticipation of a deteriorating situation as advocated by various media and IT resources that are becoming increasingly available to them. What makes it more difficult for them is that they perceive that their daily 'individualised' practices are going to have a 'global' impact. In an age of reflexivity this is gradually changing the seafarers' focus from localised risks to a wider concept of collective 'global' risks. Clearly, these perceptions are proven to lead to stressful experiences and on the practice side as illustrated below.

7.2   Resources of Reflexive Framing

7.2.1 Focused Maritime Informatics

Many shipping companies, in order to be compliant with the requirements of the STCW95/10 convention and in order to raise the competence level of their staff and crew, provide their fleets with various forms of multi-media 'informatics' and on-board interactive media and video training resources. This trend has grown in the last decade, especially with the implementation of the ISM code on board tankers and the detected disparities between training levels in various Maritime Education and Training institutions (METs) around the world (Anderson 2003; Zhao and Amante 2005). These multi-media resources are in the form of interactive courses, DVDs/ videos, interactive computer based training (CBT) material, VCDs, and printed workbooks. Several companies also supply solutions in the form of web-deliverable training, competency management systems, assessment requirements and e-learning. However, the most widely used forms on-board ships are videos and DVDs that can be either purchased or rented on a rotary basis and are available from ship chandlers and from distribution agents in all major ports worldwide.

In 2008, one of the established UK-based companies in this field designed a CBT called the 'Environmental Officer Training Course' (code no. 864) envisaging the imminent need for such a position on board ships (no explicit mandatory requirement yet) among rising contemporary environmental concerns, a growing trend that inevitably reflects on the shipping industry (Videotel 2008b). This course consolidated many of the previously produced videos and CBTs designed by the same company over the last decade regarding oil spill responses and effects, and MARPOL compliance, bearing in mind the newly introduced areas of air, sewage, and ballast water-borne pollution issues (Videotel 2008a). The graphic representations depicted in this and other media resources available for today's seafarers constitute the devastating effects of ship-based pollution on marine biology, beaches, marine biota, fauna and flora, and fish stocks utilising the graphic images obtained during and in the aftermath of significant oil

152

spills. Moreover, and in line with the recent global focus on the issues of GHGs and global warming, these resources highlight how shipping exhausts and carbon prints contribute to the 'global' environmental problems such as climate change and global warming. This can clearly be seen from the published course outcomes stated on this company's website which reads as follows:

As a result of undertaking this course, the candidate will:
- Be aware of the environmental problems *facing the world* and understand how global warming and climate change threatens our very survival;
- Be familiar with how shipping contributes to *world pollution*, how that can be minimised and the role individual SFs can play in creating a *cleaner planet*.
(Videotel website – my emphasis)

Another popular video that is utilised on board ships, especially tankers, is the "Fighting Pollution" video. This resource comprises a video and supporting booklet and looks at the impact of ship-generated waste on the marine and coastal environments (Videotel 2008a). It also shows how easily oil can pollute the sea and outlines the dangers in discarding MARPOL's banned substances such as plastics that may, at first sight, appear as posing no harm to marine life.

Since there currently an absence of explicit statutory requirements that training seafarers on environmental protection issues could be done utilising such media packages the largest publisher of these packages claims that the above mentioned CBT courses support the requirements of the STCW95 mandatory 'code A' specifying the requirements stipulated at table A-II/1 and table A-III/1 and table A-V/1. Tables A-II/1 and AIII/1 of the STCW code relate to more general versions of knowledge and competence of deck officers and engineers respectively, while table A-V/1 lists the minimum requirements for training and qualification of Masters, officers, and ratings working on-board tankers. This section requires shipping companies and MET institutions to provide a course(s) which clearly explains the effect of oil spill hazards on the marine environment covering 'the effect on human and marine life from the release of oil, chemicals and gases' (STCW code A-V/1).

7.2.2 'Saving the World' Frame

Analyses of the data set reveals that respondents are exposed to an increasing range of reflexive resources such as TV documentaries, TV reception out on the high seas (i.e. using satellite receivers) and - at times - various 'printed' forms of maritime press (magazines, reports, periodicals) that are distributed around the world fleet on a regular basis. The impact of such TV documentaries can be clearly seen in the following account where this rather sceptical respondent expressed how he re-framed the environmental demands mandated to him as a seafarer in the light of wider global environmental pressures. For example, this respondent is clearly reframing his own environmental commitments after being influenced by mass media graphic representations of an imminent 'global catastrophe' such as that which is advocated by the documentary film "An Inconvenient Truth"[1] by Al Gore (referred to in this account).

> 'I think we could really attain the objective of protecting the earth, in whole, I've just seen this film from Mr. Al Gore just a few days ago about the global warming and it is really very scary, so when I look here on the matter of seamen based on that report by Mr. Gore, I don't know if it is true or not? But it is the US itself that used to be the polluter of the world, of the environment, based on these facts that he has acquired in the last 20 years regarding environmental issues. There is one big question, is it just a program that they impose only on seamen?'
> (Respondent E140/C2, Filipino Chief Engineer)

The above account spans several risk perception and distrust concepts that could demonstrate the status of reflexive seafarers in this era of advocating what could be termed 'global risks'. First, the respondent clearly has access to live TV and/or several other media resources on board his ship. Second, as a result of the devastating consequences of pollution depicted by the video, he has clearly started questioning the relevance of the global environmental cry regarding his daily compliance tasks and wondering about his role as a seafarer amidst all these tensions. Third, he shows signs of distrust in institutional compliance on the international level

---

[1] It might be worth noting that the IMO secretariat displayed this particular documentary for the delegates attending the plenary sessions of the MEPC 56 meeting in London while heated debated were underway relating to the types of heavy fuels used in ships and how this effects the GHGs and global warming issues (field observation June 2007 –London).

as he witnesses the refusal of what he perceives as major polluting country to contribute in the collective effort (referring to US rejection to ratify the Kyoto protocol) of saving the environment.

Regarding the availability of TV reception on board ships at high sea, the last decade witnessed the ability to install satellite gyroscopic TV antennas (able to continue to detect broadcasting satellites when the vessel alters course) on many ships worldwide. This enhanced the likelihood of decent TV reception on board ships with a wider variety of viewing options in most geographical areas. Hence, in lieu of the usual classic isolation of the seafarer from the outside world once his ship is out at sea, he is now akin to a normal individual living onshore who is connected and influenced by daily global media resources. The previous limitation of watching local reception only when approaching the shore lines of a country is virtually obsolete nowadays on board many ships. This has permitted a type of 'live' connection between seafarers and daily world news. Moreover, they now have the freedom to select channels and topics they prefer which is an added resource for the reflexive framing process described earlier.

In addition, the global institutions governing maritime issues such as the International Maritime Organisation (IMO) are employing slogans that contribute to this 'global' framing of pollution risks by seafarers. For example, the theme chosen by the IMO for World Maritime Day 2007 was: "IMO's response to current environmental challenges" and the slogan for the year 2009 as shown on the IMO's website and printed on top of all this year's IMO publications is: "*Climate Change: a Challenge for IMO too!*". Such themes and slogans will appear on most IMO publications, circular letters, and media resources that are circulated to ships worldwide to highlight the message and to announce the priority agenda for this global policy making organisation. The argument is that this emphasis on globalising risk issues for this professional group radically altered the framing of professional obligations especially when seafarers are engaged in daily decisive actions that impacts directly on the marine environment.

It is important to note that the above mentioned 'reflexive framing' resources are inevitably confronted and challenged by daily occurrences, day-to-day environmental practices and personal experiences of seafarers on board their ships in different shipping company settings as discussed in the following sections.

7.2.3 The Global Apocalyptic Frame

The global environmental frame (GEF) discussed earlier takes different forms within the set of mediated resources that the contemporary seafarer is subjected to on daily basis. One of these forms is the 'end of the world' theme that is advocated not only by general media resources, but also employed by some specialised maritime press and training resources. The apocalyptic tone in dealing with many 'global' environmental problems (e.g. climate change) is reflected in seafarers' accounts when talking about the urgency of taking action to mitigate what they frame as the long standing problem of marine pollution. They equate the future effects of marine pollution with the catastrophic consequences of global warming that is propagated in the daily news (Giddens 2009). However, in the case of seafarers, some element of empirical observation of pollution exists as they occasionally witness spillages of oil at sea by ships which, arguably, heighten the feeling of obligation and commitment to act on the individual level. However, fulfilment is difficult due to the large disparities in the working conditions of different seafarers in various shipping companies as seen from the accounts of seafarers in this study.

Many global media accounts attempt to create implicit messages of an apocalyptic vision (Mol 2000). According to the data, such messages are framed by seafarers in two distinctive ways. First, when some media resources identify human action(s) as the only means of avoiding the futuristic likelihood of an apocalypse, seafarers relate this to the new wave of environmental regulations in the maritime domain and thus the urgency of their own actions become highly prioritised. Second, as a result of such global frames, an evaluation process of their own shipping companies and countries is triggered - as discussed below - leading to establishing the categorisation of certain companies and countries as 'polluters' which was discussed in previous chapters. However, with the added element of globality, the need for action becomes more associated with the seafarers' individual and professional deficiencies especially when broader institutional compliance is remote (e.g. the case of category three shipping companies - see the following two sub-sections). Put simply, they feel it is important for them to contribute to global calls for environmental protection, however some do not find practical compliance achievable.

These desperate desires to perform well are very clear among seafarers working for category three companies (Respondents D20O/C3 – D23C/C3 – D28O/C3). The global apocalyptic frame type only adds to their frustration and despair. In this context, for the wider public, the latest publications of Beck and Giddens highlight how such a tone may only encourage feelings of despair and contribute to discrediting climate scientists as mere alarmists (Beck 2009; Giddens 2009). In relation to global warming, for example, they contend that such an apocalyptic frame threatens to hinder progress in forming a political will to change the carbon based economy and thus mitigate the consequences of global warming. Looking at seafarers when talking about 'global warming' issues, we find they are confused between the classic problem of the 'ozone hole' and the more contemporary issue of GHG emissions due to a lack of adequate knowledge about such topics. However, as reflexive individuals, the need to act can always be detected in their accounts. In many of these, the detection of the element of 'uncertainty' is prominent especially when talking about their fears about what the future may bring, hence they start 'constructing' what they need to do individually. This uncertainty, or 'non-knowing', as termed by Beck (2009), opens up the window for people to construct wider and more complex 'side effects' of industrial modernity. It is important to highlight that the above mentioned arguments would be largely strengthened by the data analysis and discussion in the following section.

The data analysis of the global environmental frame (GEF) which is inclined to be shaped into an apocalyptic form invites attention to questions concerning how it is possible to handle the growing body of legislation targeting marine - and air - pollution by seafarers. For the public, the repeated announcements of the coming of apocalypse creates despair as people feel they cannot stop such an event, but can only hope that they are among the chosen few to be saved (Mol 2000). In the seafarers' case this frame clearly contributes to the tone of despair sensed in many of their accounts especially among the respondents who work for companies denying their crews access to port reception facilities (PRFs) and refusing to spend money on the maintenance and renewal of overboard oil monitoring and filtering equipment (i.e. maintenance of technology solutions).

7.3 Reflexive Re-Framing of Countries and Companies

Arguably, it is valuable to know which frames might resonate with and seem persuasive to this particular professional group. In this study, it is important to establish how the global environmental frame (GEF) has influenced seafarers' interpretations and resultant actions regarding marine environmental protection across various labour conditions (i.e. in different categories of shipping companies). For this purpose, it is important to highlight that many scholars contend that normative or 'global' goals usually resonate with people (i.e. frame resonance) while frame dissonance occurs when the framer is challenged by practical difficulties (Anderson 2002; Bickerstaff et al. 2008a; Olausson 2009). A clear example of this is the compliance hardships of seafarers with a technically prescriptive marine environmental convention such as MARPOL (e.g. narrated difficulties with ODMEs and OWSs voiced by respondents).

Put in general terms, policy makers frame issues so that target audiences can see how well newly proposed ideas coincide with already accepted ideas and practices. Nowadays, and due to the facilitation of communications across the world, this can be done on a global level (Rantanen 2005; Stamm et al. 2000). In this study, it is clear that maritime policy makers are advocating the ideas regarding pollution prevention from shipping which happen to coincide with more wider frames of 'saving the environment' in general. In other words, they attempt to construct frames that resonate with broader public understandings (Anderson 2002; Olausson 2009). Thus the ideas of frame resonance could potentially explain why the vast majority of seafarers in this study support the wider cause of 'saving the marine environment' but are rather 'uncertain' about the means of achieving this goal on the practical level (e.g. complying to MARPOL) amidst several professional and practical challenges as discussed below.

Analysis of the data set also reveals strong evidence of 'frame dissonance' among respondents between pursuing sound environmental practices and the shipping companies' quest for financial profits in a globalised economic environment (Matten 2004). Most seafarers in this study feel the pressure from such frame dissonance and are re-framing economic revenues of their employers as incompatible with sound compliance with MARPOL. Consequently, seafarers are re-framing two of the main features of contemporary global regulatory tools -

used in the maritime domain - namely the 'technology solutions' and the 'audit culture' (see Chapters seven and eight). These were chosen because the data evidences how contemporary seafarers are increasingly confronted by both these tools with an increasing trend in the last 'few' years. In the following sections, I will explain how the exposure to the above mentioned reflexive resources in the last few years has re-framed the seafarers' views around economic determinism of their companies and around these two main features of contemporary maritime environmental legislations.

On the practical compliance level, with such uncertainty looming over seafarers, exposure to the reflexive framing resources reframed the seafarers' 'trust' in their own countries, companies, and - at times - peers on board. However, the level of pursuance of sound environmental compliance differs between the three categories of respondents in this study as discussed further in this chapter. The argument is that an outwardly sound idea could be forwarded and framed in a plausible manner yet broad compliance could be harder to achieve due to pre-conceptions, established counter frames, and material and practical difficulties encountered by either an optimistic or a desperate target group. In our case, the seafarers' inclusive society on-board ships in different work settings (i.e. different shipping companies) and the diversified origins of crew members encourage the debate around ideal approaches to comply with global marine environmental conventions and who is assigned the blame for failing to do so.

7.3.1 Re-framing Countries

Seafarers frequently refer to the risks their families and children may be subjected to due to marine pollution. They voice their concerns in a set of accounts that could exemplify their prioritisation of the notion of intergenerational equity. Many seafarers also identified the spatial separation between countries producing the pollution risk and the receivers of this risk. According to respondents, whilst developed industrial states are always accused of being the 'producers' of trans-boundary pollution by the global media, seafarers from both sides of the globe (north and south) apply their own judgments regarding each other's countries' contribution to the severity of this growing environmental degradation problem. In this context, Beck (2009) contends that these tensions in the world risk society are due to the 'prevailing lack of knowledge concerning the possibility and reality of unexpected threats'. He adds that

159

scientific debates around environmental issues add to uncertainty which results in 'rumours running wild and hostile stereotypes being revived'.

Stereotyped frames based on the global media categorisations of countries around the world resulted in producing the constructed 'polluter nations' versus 'caring nations' as seen from the following accounts:

> '...a big country like China, they are not sorting their garbage there, and what does for example Sweden do: we divide to glass, paper, what do nine million people do for the environment, we do our best, but we have 1.5 billion people there, so putting it in perspective you can be a little bit angry...'
> (Respondent D9RO/C2, Swedish Chief Officer)

> 'They are more advanced than us in such research, we don't have books, we don't have organisations taking care of such issues, and we don't even have the right legislations to interfere with environmental issues. This is the reason.'
> (Respondent D36O/C1, Saudi Third Officer)

The first Swedish respondent is praising the efforts done by his relatively sparsely populated country in protecting the environment by referring to the national re-cycling scheme implemented and supported by the Swedish people. However, he seems to believe that a densely populated nation like China is not doing its share in 'protecting the environment'. To fully interpret the account, I had to verify to what extent this respondent has been subjected to mediated resources and whether any practical experiences contributed to being distrustful of 'other' countries. This investigation revealed that this Swedish respondent was a keen and regular viewer of nature documentaries (e.g. the discovery channel), his ship mainly traded in the EU region with occasional ocean going voyages and not surprisingly, his experience with PRFs in some ports regarding garbage disposal had contributed to his scepticism about the true intentions of some countries as we can see from this account:

> '...when you compare these garbage facilities, on-board we have to separate garbage from the galley, then we separate plastic, paper, glass, batteries, metal, oily, but when

you throw this, you throw it in one big garbage drum ashore, why we separate here on-board then?!'

(Respondent D9RO/C2, Swedish Chief Officer)

Coining an analytical approach based on established risk and reflexivity theories, the above account, on the one hand, depicts the ambivalence of a reflexive seafarer when perceiving that some environmental policies employed by developed countries may be symbolic rather than genuine (Baker 2007; Bluhdorn 2007) triggering what could be termed as 'ontological insecurity' among reflexive individuals in an age of global risks (Beck 2009). The argument is that such level of 'ontological insecurity' invites seafarers to scrutinise the environmental policies of different nations they visit by closely examining the water quality inside ports and the waste management techniques they employ in each port especially the adequacy of port reception facilities (PRFs). Such ongoing scrutiny and enquiries, as the data set attests, lead to an increasing sense of individual responsibility especially when framing that collective action on the national levels are deficient (e.g. among developing countries). When these observations are complemented by the dominant language of globality, seafarer construct their own frames regarding certain countries seeing them as 'polluters'. What fuels such constructions is the existing distrust in 'experts' (i.e. policy makers) leading to a challenging of the plausibility of scientific claims and a prominent level of expectation of risk(s).

An example supporting this argument is the account of the Saudi respondent who framed his country, or more broadly, oil rich Gulf countries as lagging behind in enacting local legislations to cope with global demands of environmental action. He refers to the lack of adequate legal instruments in his own country to tackle environmental pollution in general. However, it is clear from the accounts of four young Saudi respondents interviewed in this study (D33O-D34O-D35O-D36O). Although they began their careers with high expectations regarding Saudi Arabia's environmental policy, they have since had to re-think and re-evaluate these expectations after witnessing intentional polluting activities in their own territorial waters and elsewhere by fellow crew members and colleagues. This experience has evidently proved stressful for the respondents and clearly contribute to raising questions regarding the validity of the regulatory procedure as seen from the following account:

'The chief officer washed the tanks and discharged the washing oily affluent at sea several times in a special area. Although this was done through the ODME but the idea is not by-passing the device, it is the large amount which was really discharged to the marine environment. *The whole idea is to satisfy the company and cast some good reports.*'
(RespondentD34O/C1)

This group also talked about how their academic courses stressed the global concerns of environmental degradation and that their contributions as a new generation of mariners was vital. What made this worse is that these infringements mainly went without any response or punitive measures from the respective authorities in their country resulting in a growing sense of scepticism and distrust in the genuine willingness of decision makers to pursue the advocated global environmental goals. This group of Saudi respondents reported that when graduating from maritime academies and starting their careers at sea with a renowned multi-national company, they expected much 'better' environmental practice from crew and staff and, more importantly, from their country in order to protect their shore lines, economy, tourism and reputation.

In this context, frame intersections were clearly detected between the characterisation frames discussed in chapter five and the issue of 'trusting' their countries in relation to the rigorous implementation of global marine environmental legal instruments such as MARPOL. Many European and Nordic seafarers defined their countries as 'doing their best' in protecting the environment in general while others from developing countries reflexively framed their own countries as 'not interested' or complacent with regard to enforcing international environmental instruments that they had already ratified. Moreover, SFs from developing countries often framed European countries - whether they visited their ports or not - as more advanced and more willing to protect their marine and coastal environments which in turn reflects positively on the wellbeing and health of their citizens. This enforces my argument that being subjected to the GEF results in reflexive frames among seafarers that transcends their local daily practices and observations and echoes further up the ladder in the form of distrust of the environmental attitudes of their organisations, counties and -at times- global environmental institutions. In the next sub-section, I will take this argument further in order to explore the iterative nature of the resultant reflexive framing resources in today's globalised maritime arenas on this global work force in a more localised setting, namely in different shipping companies.

7.3.2 The Re-framing of Shipping Companies

My measurement point for examining the impact of the language of globality in the more localised setting of different shipping companies was the location of evidence of such 'global' language within the environmental policy texts of some major tanker companies. These policy texts were then compared with the feedback of this study's respondents regarding their own company's policies. Environmental policy texts often constitute a significant part of any shipping company's published standards and values. These texts are usually posted in various public areas on-board every ship adjacent to the ISM document of compliance of the ship (DOC). The text mainly stipulates the company's commitment towards the environment and their strive to achieve higher environmental standards in a sort of idealistic sentencing format (i.e. highlighting idealistic environmental goals and commitments) as shown in the following example for one of the largest tanker owning shipping companies in the world (represented in this study by six respondents):

> Environmental accountability is regarded as one of *the most important measures* by which a company is recognized within the industry. We feel that environmental protection is not only our duty as *responsible citizens of the planet*, but it is essential to developing public and regulatory trust.
> (Vela 2008)- My emphasis.

Furthermore, this company also displays the following text in their quality and fleet reliability commitment which is posted on their website:

> Vela operates and charters safe and *environmentally sound vessels that meet or exceed the standards required by international laws* and relevant codes. The company's quality management system requires the inspection and auditing of Vela owned vessels to ensure that they are consistently well maintained and operate in an efficient, safe and *environmentally sound manner*.
> (Vela 2008)- My emphasis.

We can see how the above text representing an example of the published environmental policies of shipping companies is in line with the global environmental frame (GEF) and represents one of the reflexive framing resources discussed earlier (see section 7.1). In the shipping industry, many smaller companies often benchmark, slightly modify, and adopt the policy texts published by major shipping companies declaring their aspirations to achieve similar high environmental standards. However, the problem is that some of these small companies lack the will and/or the resources to fulfil any of the environmental commitments and obligations stipulated in such 'idealistic' policy texts. In this study, most interviews were finalised by asking the respondent for his feedback and feelings about his company's environmental policy text. Naturally, there were significant differences between respondents with regard to this issue as discussed in this section.

In the following analysis, I start by examining the respondents' feedback on their own company's environmental text as this is considered as an important reflexive framing resource. If any sense of scepticism or distrust is detected, I further explore this specific respondent's experiences with techno-fixes, audit regimes, and/or experience with PRFs in an attempt to verify the reason(s) behind such distrust or scepticism. The reason for this enquiry is to verify how global environmental frames could escalate the perception of environmental risks for this work force when confronted with daily environmental compliance demands. In this context, it is important to highlight that seafarers facing growing environmental legislations are trying to secure victory on multiple fronts while they continuously ask themselves how ideational appeals could be coupled with material leverage. The aspirations, hardships, and attempts to be better citizens and professionals are examined below.

(*See appendix one for an explanation of the categorisation of shipping companies in this study*).

7.3.2.1 Category one shipping companies

This category of respondents are employed on board ships owned by major state owned shipping corporations (or multi-national corporations) usually encompassing large fleets of various types of relatively modern tanker ships. This group of respondents, while showing little signs of scepticism, were found to have the highest rate of faith and trust in their respective companies which reflects in a high level of acceptance - but not total consent - that pursuing economic revenue is inevitable in today's market oriented atmosphere and can equally be balanced with environmental protection. According to the data, shipping companies in this category are advocating that sound environmental practices are not only good for protecting the marine environment, but also bring profit to the company helping it in expanding and/or maintaining the current workforce. While the 'global' environmental goal is expressed explicitly in policy texts, economic revenue goals are usually implied according to many respondents' accounts. In this context, some category one respondents provided the following accounts when asked about their feedback regarding the 'idealistic' text utilised by their company to spell out their environmental policy.

'They really mean it, to improve the standard of the company by applying the rules and regulations, they are trying to gain green awards, and that would reflect on more charterers coming, BP coming, the ship being a standard ship so it is more available for trading in the market...'
(Respondent E21O/C1)

'Frankly, it is not difficult to achieve but on what basis was this text built on? Do they have all the right high standard personnel? This zero pollution depends on one thing only; that all your staff on board is highly professional and high standard.'
(Respondent D24R/C1)

The first respondent (E21O) clearly believes that pursuing 'green awards' for individual vessels in his company's fleet would enhance the business opportunities for his company by bringing in more high quality charterers (e.g. BP shipping) to hire their fleet. However, it is clear that this respondent, likewise others in this category, are convinced that their company pursues a good environmental record not only for scoring economic revenues but for protecting the environment as well. Moreover, they understand that their job security is dependent on keeping the company profitable which, arguably, provides a good incentive for crew members to employ good environmental practices and comply fully with relevant regulations.

The 'green award' is granted to a ship after passing a specific voluntary inspection that might be demanded at some EU ports. The inspection focuses on the vessel's environmental records and standards and grant a 'green award' when no deficiencies are detected which may allow the ship to enjoy deductions in port dues in certain EU ports and terminals. Not surprisingly, campaigns advocating this scheme by certain European ports rely heavily on the role of shipping in controlling global GHG emissions and reducing marine pollution worldwide (Oberthür 2003; Pisani 2002). It is reasonable to argue that this is an example of a company's success in convincing its seagoing staff that better environmental practices can run parallel to pursuing economic revenue which have significant reflections on their daily compliance practices to marine environmental regulations in place.

The second respondent (D24R) is slightly sceptical about his company's environmental policy text. While agreeing that the standards stipulated in the text are achievable, he contends that this would need 'high standard personnel'. Exploring the source of such scepticism within this respondent's interview account revealed that he was subjected to hierarchal and management pressures in his previous company from his superiors on board and was subjected to pressures from the office ashore to dump pollutants at sea. Consequently, this experience contributed to his re-framing of the problem to be a 'human element' one rather than other potential cause which consequently resulted in his prioritization that the ambitious goals written in the policy text could only be achieved by 'high standard' personnel. Hence, the identified risk here relates, as this respondent perceives, to be dependent on individualised attitudes of senior staff on board ships contending that there is a need that crew members are better qualified and willing to improve environmental practices on board their ships. However, this view (i.e. highly qualified and trained personnel are key to improvement) was not shared by respondents working on-board category two and three shipping companies as highlighted below.

7.3.2.2   Category Two Shipping Companies

Respondents in this category start showing signs of disbelief in the authenticity of policy texts either by revoking the need for such idealistic types of text or by simply rejecting them. Some examples of these signs can be seen from the following accounts:

> 'I can tell you, I don't need it, because I have the feeling inside from myself. They do what they have to do according to regulations and if they don't do it then we have a point in the vetting and the ISM is not accepted and so on...'
> (Respondent D1R)

'There are few things here, but at first instance you feel that the company is behaving like most companies because now it is time to have a policy like that. That's one side of the coin and the other side is that this company is also interested in keeping up the environment that is why we have a text like that written down, it is important to them...'

(Respondent D4RO)

The first respondent (D1R/German Master) believes that such policies displayed in various parts of his ship are to fulfil the mandatory requirements of the ISM code and to avoid getting negative remarks or deficiencies in any vetting inspection (inspection done by major oil companies to ensure that chartered tankers are meeting the appropriate standards) or audit that his ship is subjected to. However, he reports that such audit schemes are not needed by him nor by any seafarer who is personally committed to protecting the marine environment. An investigation of the reasons behind this respondent's scepticism was conducted by examining his feedback regarding other elements of global regulatory tools such as technology solutions and audit schemes on-board. Concerning technology, this respondent provided negative feedback about oil detector monitoring equipment (ODMEs) and complained about a certain type which malfunctioned frequently causing numerous difficulties for his staff. This was despite acknowledging that his company usually approves his requests for sending a shore technician to repair this defective device whenever needed. This respondent's bad experience with techno-fixes reflected a higher level of scepticism regarding multiple auditing and inspection regimes attesting that this multiplicity is not needed (e.g. wondering about the rationale behind the repetitiveness and multiplicity of audits while technical devices are predominantly of a poor quality).

The second respondent (D4RO, Swedish Master) clearly believes that his company is simply benchmarking major shipping companies in advocating these policy texts. However, the important point pressed here is that he is convinced that 'it is time' for this initiative to be taken more seriously given the present atmosphere of rising global environmental concerns. This respondent also believes that his company may be keen to save the environment and that such an idealistic text could actually reflect the company's true interests. Not surprisingly in his extended account, this respondent reported a recent improvement in the quality of such devices and that 'user friendly' new versions would reflect positively on the SFs' environmental practices on board. It is also worth noting that this particular respondent reported that his company grants him autonomy in using port reception facilities (PRFs) whenever needed - a practice which is probably quite rare among this category of shipping companies.

With these points in mind, I argue that this cumulative process of positive experiences with employer- company attitudes and practices concerning environmental aspects integrated with a global environmental frame (as discussed above) resulted in reflexively framing the regulatory instruments as legitimate. This frame is seen to elicit the need that individual seafarers should work in collaboration with their companies to achieve what is described by seafarers as 'better environmental practices'. This trend of consent with the company's environmental policies was detected among many seafarers working on this category of medium sized companies which strive to retain their crew members within the company for as long as possible.

7.3.2.3   Category Three Shipping Companies

Almost all respondents in this category reported distrust in their companies' environmental policy texts contending that they significantly contradict their daily experiences in relation to compliance measures to marine environmental conventions. However, experiencing such difficulties led this group of respondents to focus more on the consequences rather than causes of such contradictions. Examples of such accounts follow:

> 'Well, just smile, (sarcastic tone) you look to these texts and laugh. Just posters displayed everywhere, these ISM and policy posters, what about drug and alcohol policy in all companies? Do you think that seafarers don't drink or take drugs? There are many types of policies in every company but is it implemented? The poster is no problem, the implementation is the problem.'
> (Respondent D23C, Egyptian Third Officer).

> 'My feeling is a comic feeling really, the company is advocating some slogans, but the truth is different from all these mottos and slogans. All shipping companies are writing such policies but is there any company willing to write that they throw

pollutants overboard? No, everybody will say no pollution, but the truth is not like this.'

(Respondent D30C, Egyptian Master).

The account of the first respondent (D23C) is an example of strong distrust in the company's environmental policy and intentions behind such policy. This officer interpreted the problem as a lack of genuine will to materialise or implement what is written in such policies which lead him to an extended distrust in a set of other failing policies such as the 'drug and alcohol policy' implemented by his employer. Exploring the source of such distrust in this respondent's interview data revealed that he witnessed his superiors and senior ranks on board ships in his company while fitting by-pass lines (i.e. 'magic pipes'- to by-pass MARPOL's overboard monitoring equipment) for oil discharge monitoring equipment (ODMEs). These magic pipes are installed for the purpose of dumping oily effluents overboard without being detected by the sensors inside these devices which record each overboard discharge time and oil content in the effluent. He also witnessed fraudulent behaviours and actions in relation to the issue of recording the use of port reception facilities (PRFs) for the discharge of the quantities of oily effluents accumulated on-board. For instance, his company was contracted with a de-slopping barge which provides the ship with several stamped copies of slop reception certificates with blank spaces to fill any quantity whenever and wherever needed, attesting that the oily waste has been delivered whilst, in fact, it was dumped overboard.

These infringements to existing conventions and polluting activities were identified by this respondent as persistent attempts by the company to 'save money'. Observing the level of anxiety and stress among respondents in this category regarding such significant MARPOL infringements, I can reasonably argue that these actions were read reflexively by seafarers and clearly had a negative impact on their framing of the whole regulatory process. If we agree that 'frames defines actions' then it is clear from this study that the repetition of such experiences over time in this category of shipping companies resulted in the creation of a sense of despair among seagoing staff who are more likely to be dragged out to such activities thus creating an established negative 'environmental culture' on board a ship or a group of ships in a specific company.

Moreover, if such a 'dumping culture' is established, it very likely to be 'handed over' to newly appointed crew members (e.g. newly graduated officers) and regarded as a norm on board certain ships or companies as evidenced by the interview data. The argument is that witnessing and being forced to dump pollutants is a very stressful experience for contemporary seafarers as it contradicts their strong aspirations to be conscientious citizens and better professionals in an age of reflexivity. Moreover, the state of despair that some seafarers end up with at times could lead – in some cases – to retributive actions in the form of total ignorance to any environmental legislation and more cover-up and dumping activities could take place as seen in the following account of the same desperate third officer:

> 'As a seafarer what I want from the equipment is to print out the right record to show to the port state control, the environment goes to hell after this. Is it covering me in front of any inspector? That is what I need…'
> (Respondent D23C)

Clearly, sound compliance practices are not to be expected from a seafarer reaching this stage of despair and distrust in his company. The above account exemplifies the high level of despair by a crew member who ended up - after many attempts with his company - thinking about forging oily effluents discharge records just for the sake of fulfilling statutory inspection purposes. If we assume that this respondent, likewise his peers, is influenced by the global environmental frame this would only increase the stress and feelings of guilt and despair especially when being unable to act. However, the impacts of these reflexive frames could be translated into a more deviant set of actions that could differ among different work settings and among individual respondents as discussed in the next section.

The second respondent (D30C) is a Master who has worked for the same company for the last 15 years. Similar to the previous respondent, he is deeply sceptical about the environmental policy text and the slogans posted in his ship perceiving that all shipping companies are obliged to publish these policies as a statutory requirement or just as routine practice while what actually happens - on the environmental compliance side - contradicts with such advocated and written policies. Scanning his whole interview data, this respondent also reports a history of hardship with his company management staff persistently refusing to allow him to use port reception facilities (PRFs) and advising him to 'handle the situation' in his own way as an implicit order to dump the pollutants. Moreover, he also reported being sent fraudulent certificates by the company attesting that he discharged his slops in slop barges or PRFs in what seems to be normal practice within this particular shipping company.

Not surprisingly, this respondent perceived statutory audits and inspections as targeting his job security and reported being continuously worried and fearful of his ship being detained at a port as he expects the company would hold him responsible for this detention and terminate his contract. Clearly, such daily experiences by seafarers reflect on their framing of their company as a 'bad' company that is focused only on saving cost. It is clear that such tense working atmospheres in this company is counter-productive to any attempts by sea-going staff towards sound environmental and/or compliance practices. This respondent reported his awareness of the 'global' calls to save the environment in general and mentioned that he was enrolled on an 'anti-pollution training course' recently (as a requirement to re-validate his certificate of competency) where the lecturer stressed the adverse effects of marine pollution. Consequently, this respondent felt very stressed when he found himself, on many occasions, having no other choice but to dump accumulated oily waste overboard.

What adds to the stressful experiences of respondents in this group is that many category three shipping companies prefer to operate their fleets within a geographic region that is confined to the territorial waters of some countries (i.e. coastal trade) famous for lacking the political will to enforce marine environmental conventions. The above two respondents (D23C and D30C), for example, exemplify how such shipping companies resort to operating their fleets in these regions (Gulf and Red Sea) thus minimising the cost and enjoying the protectionist policies that some Gulf nations grant their nationals.

These lenient enforcement standards are reflexively framed by category three respondents as a licence to dump pollutants in the waters of some countries especially when employing policies that do not prioritise environmental protection issues and fail to monitor and prosecute polluters in their areas of jurisdiction. However, the actual observations were not always the sole cause of respondents' frames as explained earlier. These frames were complimented by established constructions regarding the demarcation between an affluent western nation capable and willing to protect its shores and coastal waters and a less affluent nation that is not willing or incapable of doing so. However, in this study, it is clear that this is not a plausible approach as many oil rich gulf nations were seen as environmental pariahs by seafarers due to their negligence in prosecuting pollution violations in their coastal waters (accounts of D23C and D30C). However, looking at the benefits of the reflexive framing process discussed above, we can see that the same professional group who were ignorant about environmental matters until quite recently are now vigilantly observing, analysing, and categorising pollution risks as they roam different ports of affluent and non-affluent countries.

The kind of data displayed above shows how the iterative process of reflexive framing of global regulatory cultures are transcending from top down (i.e. the 'Global Environmental Frame' impact on daily practices of seafarers) and bottom up (personal localised experiences impact on framing regulatory tools). However, the daily practices and environmental compliance tasks on board the ship are also influenced by the reflexive framing processes in different forms; in my concluding remarks section I try verify the commonalities and contrasts in environmental practice between different categories of respondents in this study in an attempt to depict a clearer picture of this iterative process.

7.4   Concluding Remarks

It is evident from the data analysis and discussion above (in this chapter and also bearing in mind what has been discussed in chapters five and six) that strict demarcation between legal obligations (e.g. compliance to MARPOL) and personal responsibility is diluted to a large extent among 'reflexive' seafarers. What is new is that in this mobile professional setting, where everyday action counts, the desired environmental practice will largely depend not only on the individual but also on the institutional support (e.g. support of specific countries, shipping companies...etc.) which varies largely in relation to available resources, commitment, and the existence of political will. The argument is that with such individualised sense of responsibility, seafarers who are excluded from the environmental decision making process (e.g. not supported by their company or trading in areas that lacks enforcement of environmental conventions) are more liable to indulge in despair and - at times - retributive actions that are observed and - at times - benchmarked by their juniors thus forming a 'pollution culture' within the enclosed 'ship' or 'company fleet' social setting. This led many respondents in this study to frame pollution mitigation tools and strategies as 'risks' (e.g. technology solutions – multiplicity and non-harmonisation of audit standards) - an issue that will be elaborated upon in the next chapter.

Not only this, but in response to the demands dictated by the global environmental frame (GEF) (Essary 2007) , respondents employed several practical 'on-board' mediation strategies - at times manipulative - to deal with the growing global environmental concerns that are circumvented on them in the form of daily statutory compliance requirements (e.g. MARPOL and other environmental conventions). Such mandatory compliance requirements were complemented by the growing sense of self commitment and responsibility to protect the marine environment from pollution. Certainly, there are distinctions in terms of daily environmental practices between different categories of respondents in this study as previously discussed. In the next chapter I will draw on such distinctions in order to strengthen my argument that being subjected to the GEF may influence the micro-situational practice of this occupational group in several ways that differ between their countries, companies and areas of trade. To achieve this aim, I try to look at each respondent's framing of daily environmental practice on-board preferably at 'points of intersection' (i.e. at audits- when PRFs are needed-when using techno-fixes). This is to draw a more holistic view of the specific experiences and practices of seafarers that lead to the reflexive framing of marine pollution mitigation practices among seafarers.

Looking at this issue in a holistic way (building on data and discussions presented in chapters five, six, and seven), it is clear that the global environmental frame (GEF) propagated (to seafarers) a spectrum of 'risks' that are dominated by three interrelated characteristics: complexity, uncertainty, and the importance of changing geographical place. For seafarers, complexity lies in the form of a growing number of players (international, regional, and local): organisations involved in the construction of the GEF tailored specifically for the maritime industry. The uncertainty in this context is exemplified by the ambivalence of seafarers regarding who to believe when the media propagates, for example, the apocalyptic views of marine pollution and environmental degradation in the aftermath of pollution accidents (i.e. environmental scientists or maritime policy makers). Throughout the last two chapters we evidenced how this trust relationship was compromised on the faceless and face-work levels, and in this chapter we examined how such trust and distrust relationships were either diluted or deepened as the result of the influential global environmental frame. The input of the continuous changing geographical place also played a crucial role in framing the needs and choices of seafarers especially when - at times - there are no boundaries between the so called developing and developed countries regarding environmental decisions and priorities (i.e. the Global governing body - the IMO - adopts marine environmental legislations that are implemented on all flag states homogeneously – see chapter one).

The data analysis presented also shows that contemporary seafarers as an occupational group cannot easily opt out of the influences of today's wave of environmentalism (used by policy makers in legal texts and by shipping companies in idealistic 'environmental policy' texts). This is a global discourse which employs several strategies to elicit compliance by the public and coins the language of globality as its primary tool (Beck 2009). This trend is clearly represented in this study by various reflexive framing resources even when the subjects are sailing on the high seas. The multi-channel effects of the reflexive framing resources currently available to seafarers contribute to a non-stoppable process re-framing - reflexively - of various countries, companies, and to a lesser extent, their peers on board the ship. The GEF provoked many seafarers - in this study - to look for evidence that confirms rather than rejects an assumption that some countries are better than others and some people have better environmental behaviours than others (i.e. observing their peers environmental compliance practices – see chapters five and six).

Finally it could be argued that the GEF had both positive and negative effects on a labour group such as seafarers. On the one hand, if embraced, it helps to better understand the tensions of the evolving 'risk' environment in the maritime domain (similar to other shore based industries) and make new practices thinkable and possible. On the other hand, however, it leads to a more difficult and stressful relationship with various stakeholders such as policy makers, countries and shipping companies especially when the age of reflexivity clearly leads to higher politicisation of environmental issues and practices (for seafarers this is translated into their attempts to comply). In the next chapter I will explore how seafarers link the reflexive resources and practices discussed above to the wider notion of 'risk' and what the 'conflict management' strategies they propose for mediating such 'risk'.

CHAPTER EIGHT - Conflict Management Frames: Visions for Better Practice

8.1 Introduction

This chapter deals with seafarers' preferences for how marine pollution and compliance problems should be managed or dealt with. Throughout this chapter I attempt to trace the evolution of conflict management frames (CM frames) among respondent groups, evaluate how the frames shape the way they think about resolving or managing the marine pollution problem, and study / discuss / examine the influence of these frames on their general daily compliance practices. Through the process of building up the conflict management (CM) frames I attempt to detect how seafarers reflect critically upon their own positions and assumptions regarding the marine pollution conflict. In this chapter, it will be possible to trace how interviewees re-examine their past experiences in what they perceive as a 'new era of global environmental risks' which - as they contend - necessitates a set of new and tailored conflict management strategies. It is important to highlight that throughout this chapter the term conflict management frames (CM frames) will be used to examine and display how seafarers employ different strategies in dealing with what they frame as an environmental conflict.

8.1.1 Why is there a perceived 'conflict'?

The literature suggests that a 'conflict' can arise when 'two more people or groups perceive their needs, values, views, interests and/or goals as being different or incompatible, whether or not they propose action' (Johnson and Johnson 2000; Lewicki et al. 2003; Tillet 1991). The global environmental frame discussed earlier (chapter seven) resulted in a combination of value, interest, balance, and communication conflicts among seafarers. Different criteria or priorities utilised by different seafarers to evaluate environmental actions or behaviours created a conflict. From this perspective I argue, in this chapter, that reflexive framing of the marine pollution conflict dynamics influenced the way seafarers process the available and potential solutions.

The structure of the discussion starts with identifying the frames developed by respondents to deal with implementation and enforcement deficiencies on the personal, professional, and on-board situational levels. This is to depict their interpretation of the problem and their motivations for resolving it. Following this, a review and discussion around the resultant frames is developed highlighting how respondents believe shipping companies should handle conflict, the best strategies for tackling negative patterns of environmental behaviour, and crew cultural diversity. Moving on to governing bodies, seafarers also present and discuss CM frames targeting the IMO, flag states, and port states and how they should handle the conflict. The above analysis is extended to review wider conflict management strategies employed by some maritime states (flag states) and shipping companies - as framed by seafarers - in order to link individual conflict management frames (CM frames) to the wider policies affecting the marine pollution issues on the international and regional levels.

Seafarers see themselves as both providers and beneficiaries of the public good by protecting the marine environment especially when framing that risks from marine pollution directly affect themselves, their families, their countries…etc (see chapters five, six, and seven). This clearly acts as a major incentive in their strong desire to actively participate towards this goal and may also explain their anxiety when being marginalised and excluded from the environmental decision making process. In this context, seafarers focus on conflict management approaches they believe best advances their own personal, professional, or environmental aspirations and concerns. Whilst the priorities differ between different categories of respondents, they tend to try to achieve their perceived tasks in different ways as discussed below. The typology of conflict management frames presented and discussed below is a result of a process of consulting existing CM framing literature as well as an in-depth data coding and analysis aided by qualitative data analysis software (Davis and Lewicki 2005; Gray 2003; Lewicki et al. 2003). The data reveals that most respondents consciously pay attention to as diverse a range of conflict management strategies as possible. The most prominent CM frames presented by seafarers are: 'mobilising a collective action', 'passivity or avoidance', 'authority decides based on expertise', 'joint problem solving', and to a lesser extent 'appeal to political action' (Gray 2003) . These reflexive CM frames are presented and discussed in the following sections.

8.2   The Evolution of CM Frames

In this section, I discuss how seafarers perceive and evaluate their own and their peers' performance in managing the marine pollution problem and how different values and interests contribute to their framing of CM strategies among themselves as a professional and social group. In terms of risk perceptions, my analysis is also concerned with how seafarers socially construct their own version of the conflict and the resultant potential solutions. It is evident from the data that some conflict management strategies are mobilised when risk frames are detected.

On the individual level, the majority of respondents envisaged - in their accounts - that a major factor that could contribute to reducing or even eliminating the marine pollution deliberate actions by seafarers would be to start educating people from childhood at school or at maritime education and training (MET) institutions, describing what could be termed as a combined 'social and professional learning process'. They acknowledged that this could potentially be a lengthy encounter but would eventually achieve the intended goals. The literature identifies this process as a socially-embedded process of knowledge creation undertaken by individuals and groups by observing each other's behaviours and their consequences which might - or might not - result in changes to social structures (i.e. policy mandate, social norms) (Biermann 2003; Ormrod 2004). However, among seafarers, this environmental social learning process takes the form of an on-going adaptive and communicative process of technical and environmental knowledge that differs according to organisational (i.e. shipping companies, flag states), temporal (i.e. progress over time), and spatial dimensions. For instance, the temporal dimension is clear from the account of an Egyptian 3rdOfficer (category 3) when asked about his observations of environmental behaviours recently:

'Yes, it is improving I notice, even myself when I was a cadet, since I was a junior 4th.Officer, 3rd. officer, it differs maybe the progress relates to experience or awareness or god knows but I am different now from me when I was a cadet.'
(Respondent D23/C3)

It is clear that this respondent, as many others, is realising the change in his own behaviour across the time continuum. In his extended interview account, he thinks that his environmental practice may have steadily improved over recent years due to his improved knowledge about environmental pollution in general and the adverse effects of marine pollution in particular. The argument put forward by many other respondents is that, as a CM strategy, it is important to start such knowledge dissemination processes among younger generations of seafarers - especially new entrants to the industry - to mobilise the vehicle of better environmental practices. The implicit message behind this is that, on the personal level, seafarers - in this study - are ready and prepared to wait for the process to take its time and believe it will eventually lead to improved practices among future generations of mariners. However, the problem is that this is proving to be a difficult goal to achieve bearing in mind the diverse origin and training backgrounds of this global professional group as discussed further ahead in this chapter. For example, a Swedish Master (category two) acknowledges the wide spread of this recent trend of 'improvement' when he was asked whether he observed any changes in the MARPOL compliance process in the last 10 years:

'The company, they are more in line with MARPOL, it is more talked about, [...] we all need to keep improving, so I don't think it's only MARPOL, but the general sense of protecting the environment as a whole, in newspapers, at home, in schools, all that helps, kind of going in line with MARPOL now.'
(Respondent D4RO/C2)

Here too, this respondent is talking about his own observations with an explicit reference to the global environmental frame. He referred to the influence of contemporary media resources in strengthening the notion of environmental protection. However, the bridging between this reflexive frame and the MARPOL convention is what I need to emphasise here in regard to the 'need to improve' in the future associated with heightened feelings of vulnerability of the environment which requires timely personal action(s). My argument is that seafarers are also trying to account for the vulnerability of the marine environment when thinking about potential conflict management strategies and actions which contributes to a heightened sense of responsibility among many respondents in this study. Along similar lines, Beck (2009) contends that this growing sociological conception of environmental vulnerability has a pronounced reference to the future, yet it still combines with a 'profound rooted-ness in the past'.

This is why the CM frames discussed ahead in this chapter are not only connected to the conceptions of rooted environmental 'risks' but also with constructed and anticipated futuristic notions of risky encounters. To summarise the factors identified by this study (see chapters five to seven), the seafarers' framing of vulnerability and environmental risks were observed to have emerged due to the following key reasons:

- Practices of unqualified crew members;
- Lack of preparation or unwillingness of governments (i.e. flag states – coastal states) to improve;
- Non-harmonisation (or deficiency) of technical solutions;
- The perceived excessive cost consciousness of ship owners.

Moreover, the resultant seafarers' conflict management frames also take in consideration the personal vulnerabilities, 'side effects', and barriers they are subjected to while attempting to improve their environmental practice. These include;

- Job security pressures from employers;
- Professional pressures from auditors and inspectors;
- Legal systems of some countries (stringent or lenient);
- Preconceptions of port authorities and terminals;
- Anticipated stricter marine environmental legislations.

I argue that with the above points in mind, we can identify in more concrete ways the reasons underpinning the CM frames utilised by seafarers in this study. For them, it is clear that the threatened unit is not only the 'marine environment' but also the security of their jobs, own and families health, their countries' economies and reputation, personal survival among different legal systems resulting - at times - in multiple constructions about ships and seafarers from the policy makers. This is why the overall task is framed to be quite large and complex to individual players (i.e. seafarers) especially when many of them lack the upper hand in taking the needed decisions. It is true that some of the reasons are outside the scope of 'environmental' issues; however, seafarers in their attempts to generate CM strategies could not help but to include all of the above mentioned factors into play as seen from the following sections in this chapter. Pulling down external and internal factors, seafarers are attempting to view and deal with wider regulatory concerns whilst managing their daily compliance practices in different ways making their task more stressful at times. These CM tension will be discussed more clearly in the following sections. Acknowledging this trend, Beck (2009) contends that in today's global risk society people tend to look for links or networks that may generally lie outside of the 'geographical region of the social unit in question' (Beck 2009:178). He also argues that in this process, individuals bring to light connections that tend to be obscured by the social construction of environmental pollution 'side effects'.

8.3   Conflict Management Frames and Strategies

8.3.1 Promotion of the 'Consequential Knowledge Frame'

This CM frame is employed to serve both 'values' and 'interests' of seafarers (Gray 2003; Gray and Putnam 2005). On the 'interests' front, some seafarers see themselves as 'well educated' (see chapters five and six) and characterise 'others' from different training backgrounds, nationalities, and companies as in need of knowledge enhancement especially in the area of the adverse effects of their ongoing dumping activities on the marine environment, fish stocks, beaches, and tourist industry (McConnell 2002). They perceive that promoting such knowledge would serve to rectify many of their environmental practices as well as basically resulting in less on-board non-compliance practices with obvious benefits for the shipping company they work for. A Kuwaiti Second Engineer, explaining how shipping companies could be situated in a better position, brings forward this (emotional) argument:

'If you educate this person very well and tell him about the negative side of pumping waste oil to sea and what is the effect of that and show him the graphic representation of it not just reading notes, [...] we will see improvement in environmental practice.' (Respondent E21O/C1)

It is clear from this account that the respondent is integrating 'values' and 'interests' in an attempt to devise a CM strategy that - according to his personal vision – could be effective. On the 'values' front - in an extended account - he insists that promoting 'environmental values' (e.g. with graphic and video tapes displayed for crew on-board on regular basis – see chapter six) among uncertified seafarers (i.e. ratings) coming from major seafaring labour-supplying countries is a potential boost to better environmental behaviours in general. On the 'interests' front, he is aware that when the company is better situated in relation to statutory compliance with mandatory legislations, it will also be better positioned to help and support its seagoing staff and crew to comply with current environmental legislations.

What seafarers are discussing here could be described as another form of the reflexive conflict management frame utilising possible individualised solutions without resorting to the need of promoting technical or specific professional knowledge. This personal approach was prominent among many other respondents who compared marine pollution and the 'global warming' issue claiming that enhancing generalised environmental knowledge would boost more personal responsible behaviours among seafarers according to what they perceived as success in the greenhouse gases emissions campaigns.

In this context, many respondents were aware that the observed results of promoting such knowledge would take time and they were clearly ready to accept the extended time frame needed to achieve notable success employing this type of conflict management strategy. Some respondents used - metaphorically - the term 'journey' to highlight their understanding that time is needed to achieve the intended goals. However, they also contended that; eventually this would lead to better personal practices by seafarers towards the marine environment. This corresponds to their belief that education regarding protection of the marine environment should start at school-leaving age.

This brings us back to the concept of 'trust' advocated by Giddens (1990, 1991). While the seafarers' trust in maritime policy makers and experts is compromised by faceless and face work interactions (see chapters five and six), we can still see some level of trust in what is claimed by environmental scientists - through mediated resources - regarding the adverse effects of marine pollution (see chapter seven). However, as the interview data attests, seafarers' trust in science solutions is not free from detected ambivalences and misconceptions. Respondents in this study often had mixed and confused understandings of the global warming issue intermingling it with the ozone depletion files and were ambivalent about whether these could have a relationship with ship based pollution. Such confusions and ambivalences were clearly detected in respondents' accounts when talking about the various tools and strategies needed to manage the conflict. Whether such ambivalences are due to their misunderstanding

181

of scientific data or due to omissions in supplied information cannot be ascertained from this study. However, in this context Wildavsky (1997) pointed out (drawing on empirical studies) that knowledge of the side effects of natural devastations and health risks involves a large amount of non-knowing, wilful omissions, mistakes, exaggerations, and errors (Wildavsky 1997). My argument regarding this is that the seafarers' conflict management frames resulting from such inaccurate or incomplete scientific data constructions could lead to more detachment rather than engagement with the conflict dynamics. This is explained more clearly in the following sections.

8.3.2 The avoidance/ passivity frame

Due to the longevity of the marine pollution problem, and the repeated witnessing and experience of dumping activities whilst on-board, some seafarers have reached a sense of despair resulting in a set of 'passive' CM frames. This despair is more prominent among many category three respondents (see appendix one) who tend to employ a 'passive' frame in relation to the marine pollution conflict preferring to keep themselves distant from more tensions. The data evidences that these interactions dictated distancing themselves from the conflict dynamics and – especially among category three respondents – forced them to adapt with the current situation in order to keep their job. However, feelings of guilt, despair, and resentment were prominent among respondents who reached a state of being helpless in the face of practical or economic pressures exerted on them by their employers. An Egyptian Master (category three) trading in the Gulf area emotionally criticises himself, throughout his interview account, for the state of 'passivity' he reached in the face of his company's persistent refusal to send him a sludge barge (an alternative to land based port reception facilities - PRFs) to discharge the accumulated oily wastes on board his ship:

> 'So I am forced to throw away (dump at sea) and listen to the company's instructions; 'do what you can captain', ok, I think this discussion should be directed to ship owners. We can only obey instructions, what we want never happens…. […]…..I feel this needs to change but I am helpless…..'
> (Respondent D30C/C3)

This respondent, despite being forced to dump, is clearly willing to change the 'dumping at sea' culture dominant in his company but ended up, after many attempts, being disempowered enough to employ his final CM choice which is to 'obey' the company's instructions. This is also the case for most of category three respondents who contend - in various accounts - that they have 'no choice' but to dump pollutants over board (under economic and/or operational pressures). However, some respondents report the lack of port reception facilities (PRFs) and their companies' rejection to pay the relevant expenses without seeking other 'legitimate' waste disposal alternatives (e.g. incineration at sea or decanting through the MARPOL filtration devices). Seafarers reporting these integrated difficulties with feelings of guilt, whilst highlighting their discomfort and refusal of this situation, are attempting to explain the reasons behind such passivity by narrating the difficulties they are subjected to. This is clear from the account of the same Egyptian Master who worked for the same bunker barge operating company for two decades and trading only inside the Arabian Gulf area:

'What should you do if the only port that you deal with has no facility to receive these oily effluents from you, so you will discharge these things to sea, there is no other choice, unless they send us occasionally a barge that takes our bilge.'
(Respondent D30C/C3)

The quote underlines the importance of the corporate role in shaping a passive CM frame among senior seagoing staff. However, it is clear from the data set that seafarers facing such difficulties are becoming more conscious about the nature and anatomy of the problem. They can distinguish between non-compliance due to corporate practices by ship owners, practical difficulties by port authorities, and enforcement difficulties by coastal states. Hence, it is reasonable to argue that, on the bright side, contemporary seafarers are more aware of the problem which is the first step towards framing their own CM strategies in their specific work settings (i.e. different shipping companies, trading areas, etc.). The willingness to act was reported by most respondents from different categories despite the differences in their actual abilities to mobilise such aspirations as we can see from the following account from a Filipino second engineer (category three):

'They do it night time, I wanted to tell the authorities but I didn't, I've been employed in this company for the second time, so let's just keep quiet, but it needs to be addressed, or it must be stopped.'

This respondent clearly preferred to report the dumping practices he detected to the port authorities but failed to do so because of fear of losing his job. Being re-employed on a second contract in his current company, he preferred to be passive and not raise the alarm. However, another form of passivity could be the refusal to dump pollutants only due to the fear of being criminalised if detected by authorities. This fear of criminalisation is clear in the explicit account of an Egyptian Third officer (category 3):

'I refuse to do such actions, I personally know some people who have been caught dumping in European waters, but the company didn't support them. Will they pay millions for him? No he's gone [...] I am not ready to go to prison while the management staff are sitting in the air conditioned offices watching.'
(Respondent D23C/C3).

Clearly the refusal in this case was due to fear of being arrested and criminalised. After weighing his choices this respondent preferred not to dump at sea and is recalling a similar prosecution case for one of his colleagues caught dumping at sea in a European port. The argument brought forward by respondents in this category is to highlight to their peers that keeping their jobs will not work if they are arrested and prosecuted thus losing their certificates and potentially their freedom. Hence, the apparent CM frame presented here could be seen as being defiant against their employer's pressures to dump. Nevertheless, I still argue that such practices fall on the passive side of environmental actions as seafarers in this category, by refraining from dumping sporadically and on an individual basis, still stop short of taking practical steps towards mitigating the problem especially in other geographical areas where marine pollution surveillance was deemed non-existent.

8.3.3 Towards a More Active Role

Other respondents working in better employment conditions (i.e. categories 1 and 2) were clearly more defiant against the act of dumping. Most respondents in category 1 and 2 ruled out any dumping possibilities by themselves and their peers on-board. Not only this, they were more actively engaged in attempting to stop such infringements by other crew members as we can sense from the account of this German Master remembering one on-board confrontation with his Captain when he was a Chief Mate:

'I remember on a chemical Tanker, I got once an order to throw tank washings overboard in the sea of Oland (north Baltic) I said no, the Captain said: I will do it. I said if you do it I will report you, then the story was over, nothing wrong happened.'

The reason behind the defiance is not clear from the quote, however, reviewing his interview it is clear that his dominant CM frame is to deal with the problem on a personal basis, or in other words he committed himself to 'act personally'. He is referring to marine pollution as a 'global' risk that could be mitigated by individual actions. Clearly, employing this personal frame he was able to challenge and stop potential dumping activities that were authorised by the ship's Master without any reference to fear of retributive actions by the Master or by the company. In terms of risk perception, this respondent also reported a high level of familiarity with the risks involved with dumping practices both for the environment and the company in case of being detected. In other words, he is not only well aware of the adverse biological effects of dumping oil at sea but is also cautioning about the legal consequences of such dumping on the company position if detected. Doing this, the references to intergenerational equity and visions for a sustainable future are prominent in his extended interview account. Here we can see an example of personal or individualised CM frames that is embedded in professional roles; a trend that is detected in the accounts of many respondents working for category 1 and 2 shipping companies.

On similar lines, Beck (2009) contends that in the contemporary global risk society the individual could become his own 'moral entrepreneur'. The result is that the person starts to act as if the fate of the world depends on his individual action(s) even when he/she is excluded - at times - from decision contexts which relieves him/her from self-condemnation (Beck 2009). However, among seafarers, this individualisation process triggered different individual CM frames among various categories of respondents in this professional group. My argument is, however, that such frames - triggered by self-reflection - often de-prioritise and sometimes eliminate many plausible options of managing the conflict due to perceptions of economic revenue prevalence of companies, technology failures, or simply due to the dominant distrust in policy makers. These individualised CM frames are discussed more clearly in the following sections.

8.4 Reforming Shipping Companies

8.4.1 The 'Company' Level: Demands for Economic Rationalism

The 'company' is identified by the majority of respondents as a key player in solving the marine pollution and MARPOL compliance problems. They contend that the issue of marine pollution is already sufficiently regulated and the focus should be on enforcing compliance upon the increasingly cost-conscious shipping companies. Employing this CM frame, respondents attributed blame to shipping companies choosing to re-flag their fleets to FOC countries to escape stringent standards and exercise more authority and freedom to choose what to comply with in the current maritime legal sphere (Barton 1999; DeSombre 2000; Van de Voorde 2005). Moreover, respondents presented different, and at times, contrasting views about the means to ensure compliance by shipping companies - mainly framed to be focusing only on economic revenue - with MARPOL and other marine environmental conventions as discussed below.

To exemplify this, the account of a young newly graduated Saudi Third officer (category one) presents a company-focused CM strategy based on his limited experience. He suggests that a slight extension in the duration of stay in port for tanker ships would provide a significant reduction in the amount of oily waste that eventually ends up at sea (i.e. legally or illegally through the decanting process). Doing this, he argues, would be a factor allowing officers to perform tank stripping in a more relaxed atmosphere thus reducing the amount of oily effluents accumulating on board (i.e. needing to be cleaned from cargo tanks resulting in large amounts of oily effluents) later on during the ballast voyage:

> 'Give the seafarer some more comfort on board and this could be done by staying in port five to six hours more, no problem. You have an ocean going passage of 37 days; would it really differ to stay for these few hours more?'
> (Respondent D33O/C1)

This relatively inexperienced respondent, who is still in the observation and learning stage of his career, did not take much time to identify the pressures that his company exerts on the senior ranks on board regarding the cost of extending the duration of stay on-board. He clearly associated such pressures with the corporate profit agenda which eventually leads to the accumulation of more oily effluents on board. Understanding the risks that these wastes pose to the marine environment if dumped, he demands that shipping companies should consider these difficult practicalities and grant more autonomy to senior ranks on board. The rationale behind this proposed CM strategy was to allow more effective stripping of the ship's cargo tanks thus reducing the accumulation of waste oil on board where he observed the chief mate to be struggling to achieve this goal ending up by dumping oily effluents at sea. Looking at this respondent's extended account, and despite him being on his first few trips at sea, he realises the economic constrains that the ships' crews have to deal with on a daily basis and framed his own potential solution, one of which is that the way forward starts with reducing such time limitations on staff members. In other words, he is asking ship owners to deal with the cost issue in a more rational way in the light of the practical difficulties faced by crew members to meet discharge deadlines thus resulting in more oil remaining on board (ROB).

In terms of risk to the marine environment, it is clear that this respondent is concerned about the large quantities of oily effluents that are discharged overboard even in a legal manner (i.e. according to MARPOL's discharge criteria). His view was to possibly reduce the total amount of pollutants that eventually end up in the ocean. This brings us back to the discussion around reflexive framing of pollution risks in contemporary society and how individuals are becoming their own 'moral entrepreneurs'. My argument is that this reflexive route is proving to be a stressful one for seafarers as they try to fulfil demanding self-expectations coupled with professional compliance commitments.

In the same context, category one staff also presented other alternative solutions that companies could explore in order to reconsider their options in dealing with the long standing problem of the inadequacy of port reception facilities (PRFs) in ports and terminals worldwide in an attempt to reduce the outflow of pollutants to sea. Understanding the inherent risks posed by dumping, some respondents suggested either retaining as much as possible from the oily effluents on board or to transfer them to dedicated residual oil tanks (if these exist) or even incinerating it in the open sea (although this may contradict with MARPOL annex six emission standards in some areas). The main objective of these CM strategies was to encourage shipping companies to avoid or reduce the discharge at sea by any means available. However, some of these CM strategies were not practical for seafarers working on board coasters or feeder tanker ships (i.e. limited tonnage tankers trading in coastal areas only) especially when they lack adequate on-board storage capacity.

In the process, many respondents also demanded that shipping companies should de-prioritise 'cost effective' policies when the issue relates to protecting the environment. The conception that companies are only 'profit seekers' dominates most respondents' accounts in this study but is more prominent among category two and three respondents as previously mentioned. A British Chief Officer (category two) explains the attitude of his company towards the accumulated oily wastes (i.e. slops – wash water mixed with latest cargo residues) resulting from cargo tank washings:

> 'They ask you how much have you got on-board? And that depends on the cargo nomination. If they are really struggling to lift the full cargo, they're more likely to say ok we'll pay this time. Why people are risking their jobs to do it? So they need to sit down and say what's causing it, I think that is the key, if it costs money, so what! At the end of the day it is going to save the environment.'

This respondent's company weighs the justified discharge of oily waste with economic revenue (i.e. loss or gain in cargo related freight). Hence the company will allow staff on board to use the port reception facility (PRF) only when they need to displace more cargo to fulfil future cargo contractual obligations and, naturally, avoid losing fright money. These are the types of practices that contribute to establishing frames among seafarers that the ship owner's only concern is profit. As a result, the message this respondent is bringing forward to shipping companies is to be more 'rational' in dealing with issues that relate to the environment and to ultimately recognise the public good in doing so. He also downgrades the priority of the 'cost' issue when the overarching aim is an important one - as he contends - such as 'saving the environment'.

Ironically, we can detect from the above accounts that there is a clear demarcation between what the literature terms 'preferred' and 'enacted' CM frames (Gray and Putnam 2005; Hanke et al. 2003). On the one hand, the 'preferred' CM frames are the frames that respondents used when asked how they think the marine pollution problem could be best resolved. On the other hand, the 'enacted' CM frames are what could be practically exercised by seafarers to reduce the output of pollutants to the marine environment or in some cases - as seen from the above accounts – to dispose of the accumulated waste overboard. Clearly, mobilisation of the practical CM frames is highly dependent on the work setting of each respondent (i.e. category of shipping company, geographical trade area, coastal or ocean going…etc.). However, the seafarers' CM frames were sometimes answered and translated into material actions by some shipping companies as we can see from the following sub-section.

8.4.2 The Ship Owners' Role CM Frames

Seafarers in this study are closely observing and monitoring their shipping companies' CM strategies mainly in response to the global environmental frame (GEF). Naturally, my focus is not the perceived role(s) of shipping companies but rather how seafarers frame this as a viable CM strategy or not. In this context, a novel form of CM strategy utilised by a major shipping company in the face of the lack of 'adequate' PRFs worldwide was detected in the account of an experienced Russian Master (category one –EU region) who 'proudly' talks about his company's newly built tankers . He reports that newly built ships in his large company are purposely designed to have much larger slop and sludge tanks. He contends that this is a new policy employed by his company to overcome the longstanding worldwide problem of inadequate PRFs. This new company oriented CM strategy is clear from his account:

'We have in our company a new design of vessels […]. We have three tank facilities, two slop tanks and a residual oil tank and that means: if in any port there is no PRF we can store the oily residues and keep to another port where we can discharge.' (Respondent D17O/C1)

From this account it is clear that major shipping companies, being aware of the global PRFs problem, and with a vision for a localised solution (i.e. within the company's capability and resources) have chosen to apply major changes in the construction of its new ship buildings in order to overcome this global deficiency and, naturally, to avoid being accused of any sort of marine pollution. Needless to say, such actions contribute to significantly improving the trust relationship between seagoing staff and company management as the Russian Master very proudly affirmed. Both seafarers interviewed in this company felt that their company was supportive of them as staff members and to the overall aim of saving the environment as well. It is worth noting that this particular respondent was very proud of his company's environmental policy and vision, advising other companies to follow suite and insisting on showing me a copy of the 'green award' that his ship had just been awarded by a major EU port.

Nevertheless, the accounts above still depict a sense of despair among seafarers and shipping companies from the longevity of the problem of the global inadequacy of PRFs which lead some ship owners to ask for a design amendment in their newly built tanker vessels to overcome/avoid such problems. Clearly, this may be considered as a practical CM strategy by well-established shipping companies in the face of regulatory implementation difficulties. However, the question still remains; are all shipping companies able (i.e. possess the needed resources) or willing to follow the same route? This study suggests that even on larger tankers where there is extra waste storage capacity, shipping companies may be hesitant to keep them full when approaching the cargo loading phase of the voyage in order to be able to lift larger cargo parcels. Faced with such practical difficulties seafarers usually resort to a demand for 'joint problem solving frames' thus integrating individual and institutional CM frames as discussed below.

8.5 Appeal to political actions

Several respondents recommended handling the marine pollution problem through taking action on the policy level such as enacting new conventions or abolishing existing ones, applying incentives or more sanctions, and/or employing more non-formalised on-board training strategies (video and interactive software or realistic spill drills), or by the mandatory inclusion of more formalised environmental protection training in the syllabi of MET institutions. Clearly, implementing any of these initiatives - or a tailored group of them - require a harmonised effort between policy makers, flag states, port states, different industry stake holders, and maritime education and training (MET) institutions worldwide. However, the current status of liaison between many of these groups is still lacking as respondents contend.

On the maritime policy making level, the majority of respondents perceive the IMO as the overarching international authority in charge of marine pollution issues without recognising that the actual mandate of this intergovernmental organisation (see chapter one) does not grant it prominent enforcement powers. In this context, many seafarers expressed their disappointment in the performance of the IMO by explicitly saying that they expected much more of this international organisation (see chapters five and six). They framed the lack of enforcement of IMO instruments by flag states as a drawback that should be considered urgently by policy makers, an element that emerges from the literature as well (Alderton and Winchester 2002a; Brookman 2002). Very few respondents were aware of the fact that implementation and enforcement fall outside the mandate of the IMO and lie solely with flag states as explained earlier. However, similarly, expressing preferences to flag states (or port states) authority - where it scarcely existed - was also voiced with little expectation that any progress could be achieved in the near future.

Despite these reservations, a few respondents still retained some hope that the IMO still acquires the scientific and technical expertise to handle the marine pollution problem. However, they were sceptical about the means to do this without the power to force member states to fully comply with adopted environmental instruments. The appeals for possessing enforcement powers and demands for an institutional learning and consultation process for policy makers, flag, and port states are presented below.

8.5.1 The Need for Proper Enforcement

Some respondents reported their despair at having to comply with new environmental conventions without even confirming that the previously adopted instruments were being complied with. In the process, they demand that the IMO should have a greater role in ensuring compliance by shipping companies (wrongly perceiving that the IMO possess coercive powers over shipping companies and/or flag states). As an example, the following account depicts a Filipino Second Engineer demanding the active implementation of conventions to help seafarers comply with older pieces of legislations such as MARPOL annex one before thinking about adopting additional legal instruments:

'We have new rules that we have to implement, but they (i.e. flag states) didn't implement the previous one properly. Why don't you enforce the previous rules properly? Make sure it is working, if the first one fails, you don't need a new one.' (Respondent E10RO/C2)

This respondent is referring to the long standing problems of implementation and enforcement of MARPOL annex one (oil). He realises that the lack of enforcement tools are contributing to the longevity of the problem and wonders about the complacency - as he argues - of policy makers in finding solutions to this problem. This led him to be sceptical about the implementation of newly introduced environmental instruments (e.g. MARPOL's air pollution annex) contending that what is needed first is proper enforcement of existing regulations. This 'proper enforcement' reflexive frame was presented by many respondents in this study as a way forward to retain seafarers' trust in policy makers and flag states arguing that without this pre-requisite new regulations will, most probably, have the same fate. Around this point, I argue that reflexive seafarers not only need to see environmental issues regulated properly but they also seek material visible results for regulatory tools (e.g. cleaner water in coastal areas and ports). My argument is that these CM frames eventually lead seafarers to be more sceptical about the true intent behind the forthcoming agendas in environmental policy making in the maritime sphere.

8.5.2 The Need for Consultation/ Participation

Experiencing such implementation difficulties, seafarers suggest that enhancing communication between policy makers and seafarers would contribute to producing more 'realistic' environmental conventions that are not isolated from the actual abilities of seafarers and shipping companies to comply. Put simply, seafarers need to participate or have their say in the enacting of new international legislative instruments to air their thoughts and positions before being confronted with - as they argue - non-achievable goals. However, they are clearly ambivalent about the right approach to pursue this 'preferred' course of action to be able to legitimately voice their concerns.

Based on several observations from the data and on field observation notes taken at the IMO, the lack of active representation of seafarers in policy making arenas (e.g. the IMO) could be identified as potential reasons for such ambivalence (field observation, MEPC meetings 54, 55, and 56 - IMO London). Most trade unions enjoying a consultative status in the IMO and dealing with seafarers' issues (e.g. ITF, IFSMA) are focused on agendas regarding better wages, safe manning levels, fatigue, and/or improving seafarers' living and working conditions (ITF 2005; Lillie 2004; Talley 2007; Wadsworth et al. 2006). Such unions were not detected to be engaged in raising any prominent agendas which voice their members' hardships and concerns in relation to the growing trend of demanding environmental legislations in the maritime industry. In the following sub-section, seafarers explain some of the practical and constructed barriers that prevent them from proper compliance with the current set of marine environmental legislations.

8.5.3 Calls for Better Treatment

Accounts of mistreatment and feelings of indignity were detected in the seafarers' interview data as early as the pilot study of this research. Many respondents reported that port officials treated them as potential polluters until proven otherwise. Some respondents were explicit about the stress such treatment represents to them at a time when they need to concentrate on their jobs and not be distracted by such continuous threats (i.e. the sensitive loading and discharging operation in tanker ships while at ports or terminals). The CM frames among respondents regarding this issue were articulated around the need that port authorities should improve their treatment of ships' crews and stop having such prejudices. However, at the same time, many respondents thought that instead of such collective mistreatment of seafarers, countries should make more effort to monitor pollution activities, not only inside ports but also in the waters falling under their jurisdiction. This is clear from the account of this stressed Greek Chief Officer:

'Coastal state authorities think that all tankers, they think we like to pollute... [...]... you can see this from their treatment?! I don't know why this thinking is still the same in various ports? May be that is why if you go outside at sea you see all ships are throwing the garbage outside in the sea, one can see them throw, I don't know why?' (Respondent D19O/C2)

The quote underlines the feelings of stigma that this respondent experiences due to being repeatedly mistreated by port officials. Still ambivalent about the reason(s) behind this treatment, he suggests that this could be because of the dumping activities conducted by many ships outside port areas either before or after port entry, leading port officials to treat every visiting ship as a polluter. On this point, other respondents warned that such mistreatment could result in retributive actions by some seafarers in the forms of intentional dumping close to the coastal areas of these countries. The CM frame presented regarding this issue was the call for abolishing such preconceptions and prejudices and focus on monitoring and pollution surveillance activities to target and verify the actual polluters and prosecute them.

8.5.4 The Need for Exemplary Leadership

Another prominent CM frame was the need for exemplary leadership on-board ships. This frame was detected when seafarers talk about how it is important for them to follow the examples set by senior ranks on-board. In the seafaring profession, the classic frame of the master and senior ranks as role models exemplifying decent behaviour still exists among many junior ranked respondents. It is clear that when this frame is contradicted by demanding or authorising dumping practices, or even turning a blind eye to them, seafarers become more stressed on the personal and professional levels. An Egyptian Master who experienced some pressures to dump from higher ranks in his previous company contends:

'All these mistakes comes from the leaders, if the leader is good everybody will follow him, no way he will tell you one day: can you throw these oily effluents to the sea? You have to build and educate leaders; if you don't fix the head everything will be ruined...' (Respondent D24R/C1)

This respondent's framing of the exemplary leadership issue led him to conclude that most of noncompliance practices with MARPOL were due to a personal decision taken by a senior staff member to save money for the company or to reduce his workload. He talked about Masters who turned a blind eye to dumping practices conducted by their own senior staff and Chief mates who resort to dumping to reduce their interaction with technical devices thus reducing their working hours. Naturally, this was seen to create a bad example for junior ranked officers and ratings, encouraging them to follow the same undesired practices. Consequently, the CM

194

frame employed by this respondent was that shipping companies should be ensuring higher levels of training and professional integrity before recruiting senior ranked positions in their fleets. The hope is that such highly trained senior staff would not conduct or tolerate any dumping activities by their crew members thus setting a good example for all.

To sum up the above CM strategies so far, respondents who framed their companies as having relatively sound environmental policies tend to focus on promoting themselves, their peers, and ratings on board regarding personal environmental practices. Alternatively, respondents who frame their companies as 'profit seekers only' tend to focus on CM strategies that either appeals for a higher authority to coerce compliance (e.g. senior ranks, company management) or to a hegemonic political action either by flag states, port states, or a global governing body. However, it is clear that the majority of respondents in this study are resorting to more personalised CM frames focusing on the improvement of individual environmental practices among themselves as a professional group. This brings us back to Beck's argument regarding the individualisation of risk in contemporary global risk society in which he contends that people, even when disempowered, feel that the fate of the planet lies in their hands and depends on their perusal actions and that their personal actions are the ones that will count (Beck 2009). Hence, for seafarers who are generally distrustful of senior ranks, experts, and policy makers (see chapter six and seven) the dominance of individualised types of CM frames clearly results in a heightened sense of self-responsibility provoking stressful grievances among most respondents in this study.

8.5.5 Carrots and/or Sticks

This classic CM frame was frequently employed by seafarers from all three categories of shipping companies. The data analysis reveals that when respondents suggest rewards and sanctions, this was largely dependent upon their framing of people, countries, and policy makers (see chapter six). For example, respondents characterising their own countries as environmental pariahs are highlighting the necessity to employ some global disciplinary systems to rectify long standing problems such as the lack of PRFs (sometimes suggesting that the IMO should take action). These potential new systems are envisaged to be used as tools to stop offenders from further polluting the marine environment by incorporating clear sanctioning elements. For example, the appeal for sanctioning port facilities for not complying

195

with MARPOL mandatory requirements could be detected clearly from the following account of a frustrated Russian Master:

> 'Every 'good' port should provide adequate PRFs, who don't do that should be black listed in the worldwide port guides.'
> (Respondent D17O/C1)

This experienced respondent, after voicing his concern regarding the lack of PRFs, suggests that a 'naming and shaming' policy should be implemented for ports and loading terminals, likewise similar polices which identify and publicise the names of poorly performing ships and their respective flags by port state control. He believes that doing this will force / encourage port authorities to improve their facilities and services fearing the impact of bad publicity on their trade levels and reputation. This also adds to the argument discussed earlier that the majority of seafarers in this study are more inclined towards the utilisations of, what they frame as, smarter tools rather than adopting formal legal instruments that end up, as some previous regulations, to be - as they claim - merely a 'paper practice'.

In terms of incentives, few respondents described how the process of financial rewards can enhance both individual and company capacities to deliver 'better' environmental performance. In this context, EU ports are currently offering a significant reduction in port dues for 'greener' ships subject to a comprehensive inspection process (Field study observation FSI 16 meeting at the IMO – June 2007 - interview data). However, on the individual level the seafarers' economic incentives CM frame takes a more simple form by suggesting a bonus pay for seafarers to encourage improved environmental performance as this Egyptian Third officer (category three- Gulf area) suggests:

> 'For example if a system comes out saying that in every environmentally friendly ship each one of the crew will have 100 $ bonus, you will see that no one will throw even a cigarette in the sea.'
> (Respondent D23C/C3)

Clearly this respondent prefers adopting a rewarding policy contending that shipping companies are capable of funding such initiatives. He believes that bonus financial incentives given to each crew member on board a compliant ship would be a fail-proof policy that ensures levels of compliance that exceeds the mandatory requirements by MARPOL. My argument is, while compliance with MARPOL is frequently mentioned, the focus of seafarers' CM frames is clearly shifted to disciplining the individual's environmental practice first and then expecting that statutory compliance would easily follow as a consequence. This is problematic as, with international crews, judging others with one's own standards could only lead to more stress and marginalisation of seafarers from certain groups, nationalities, and training backgrounds. For example, this was clear from the characterisation frames employed by some Nordic seafarers regarding crew members from Asia, or seafarers who were previously employed by certain smaller companies flying flags of open registers...etc. (see chapters five and six).

8.5.6 The need to Benchmark 'Better' Practices

Some respondents, especially category three seafarers, due to their framing of certain countries as successful in implementing environmental policies, suggest that such polices should be benchmarked by what they frame as 'non-performing' countries. In many instances they strongly demand the right to copy or benchmark the environmental policies and practices employed by certain western developed countries and adopt these policies in developing nations. Whilst such frames could either be based, as previously discussed, on social constructions of risk or on material observations encountered during their voyages to different parts of the world, the resultant CM strategies are clearly very demanding and prominently strong. This is clear from the account of this Iraqi Chief Engineer:

'The ports must force the ships to deliver garbage, this practice of issuing documents
of reception of garbage and oily waste without this happening should be sanctioned
by the Port State Control.'
(Respondent E28O/C3)

This respondent refers to some EU ports where he experienced a genuine and thorough check of the ship's waste disposal records. He contends that his experience proves that in some countries the port inspectors and auditors are not keen on checking the authenticity of the relevant documents thus opening the window for fraudulent practices (e.g. forging waste reception receipts). Framing proper enforcement and genuine monitoring as plausible CM strategies he demands wider global implementation of such practices to ensure compliance by ships.

Realising the difficulty of achieving this on the practical level, several respondents contend that a potential solution to the marine pollution problem is to scrap 'old ships' as in the case of many developed countries. They argue that such a strategy was successful when employed by several developed nations especially when observing that their fleets are composed only of recently built ships with less technical problems. They contend that older ships should be withdrawn from service and scrapped accusing such ships of being a major source of pollution. Not only this, they also suggested that restraining political actions by port states such as banning older generation of ships from trading in their waters or entering their ports (an extreme measure already taken by some EU countries after the Erika and Prestige accidents in the Bay of Biscay). I argue that such diversely observed CM frames are not only based on dumping observations of older ships but also on a rather heightened sense of pollution risk which clearly led many seafarers to suggest practically difficult solutions rather than focusing on the more realistic strategies in hand. These rather extreme CM frames (i.e. banning and scrapping of old ships) were, in part, due to the dominant distrust that technology solutions could deliver significant improvements when installed on these tanker ships. However, regarding problematic technology solutions, some respondents still ask for harmonisation of strategies and technical solutions as discussed below.

8.5.7 The collective Technical Solution: Standardisation

No significant differences existed in the way each category of respondents viewed the potential for improving technical solutions to mitigate marine pollution. All respondents agreed that consensus must be attained between all stake holders involved in the process of enacting new harmonised technical standards or reviewing and amending existing ones. However, the differences detected between groups were the ultimate aims and objectives of this demand of 'standardisation' of technical overboard discharge monitoring equipment (i.e. oily water separators (OWSs) and oil detector monitoring equipment ODMEs). Respondents working on newer generations of tankers (mostly category 1 and and some cat. 2) and not experiencing severe difficulties with existing technical equipment on board saw the further improvement and standardisation of this equipment as an ultimate gain for the marine environment. On the other hand, respondents working on-board older ships (category 3) saw the standardisation as a potential relief from their daily hardships in dealing with such equipment leading to less fatigue and a reduction to long working hours spent in dealing with older filtration devices (i.e. 'value' frames Vs 'interest' frames).

Moreover, the data also suggests that differences in framing technical solutions could be the result of cumulative experiences held by different respondents in dealing with technology solutions. Clearly, bad experiences with certain types and specific brands of equipment served to strengthen these negative CM frames. In this context, seafarers who are suffering from the stresses of dealing with older existing equipment (on-board relatively older generations of tankers) have reached what the literature identifies as a 'frame lock'. This is a situation in which one holds steadfastly to a particular frame (e.g. 'technology solutions' do not work) rather than considering the validity of other solutions to the problem (Gardener and Burgess 2003). Hence the CM frames held by these respondents usually deviate away from standardisation or harmonisation of technology solutions dismissing the usefulness of this route and focusing on other alternatives (i.e. personal and/or institutional). I argue that a major contributor to this 'frame lock' is the time factor (i.e. the longevity of the conspicuous problem of marine pollution as observed by seafarers in various parts of the world's oceans, seas and ports) integrated with the widely spread operational difficulties of many older brands of filtration devices. The endurance and persistence of problems with technical equipment over an extended period of time also resulted in re-enforcing this 'lock' and lead to frustrated seafarers who perceive no end in sight despite slightly improved conditions (e.g. acknowledgement by a few number of respondents that newer generations of equipment are better). Nevertheless, many respondents are still willing to give technology solutions a chance on the condition that it is to be standardised to facilitate training and for ease of operation.

8.6 Concluding Remarks

The key individualised CM frames employed by seafarers are:
- The need for enhancing seafarers' environmental awareness collectively;
- The need for better treatment to seafarers in ports worldwide;
- The need for exemplary leadership on-board each ship.

The key three institutionalised CM frames presented by seafarers are:

- Proper enforcement by coastal states;
- Standardisation of technology solutions in the industry;
- Economic rationalism among shipping companies.

Most respondents employing either one or more of the above CM frames demand a termination to what they term as the 'destructive' pollution activities affecting the marine environment. It is important to acknowledge, however, that most respondents employing such frames are well aware of the current tensions in the shipping sector in relation to the division between flag states, companies, and training backgrounds of seafarers. Whether these demanding CM frames are fulfilled by individualised actions, coercive regulatory instruments, or by ensuring enforcement by port or flag states remain a divisive issue among respondents. What is clear is that the CM frames presented are highly dependent not only on their actual experiences as assumed earlier in the study, but also on other preferences such as their category of shipping company, and more importantly the spatial aspect (i.e. geographic area of trade). For example, respondents are clearly aware that CM strategies applied in the EU waters may not fit with ships trading in the Red Sea and Gulf area, and what applies for trading in territorial and coastal waters may differ from what works inside certain ports and countries. To sum up, based on this study's data, I argue that the CM frames presented by seafarers are clearly influenced by triangulated structural factors that could be summarised as follows:

- Unequal implementation and enforcement capabilities by flag states, port states, and coastal states and the inability of the governing bodies to ensure compliance.
- Negative patterns of behaviours observed by seafarers on the personal, company, and flag levels aided by the highly mobile and roaming nature of their profession.
- Cultural and geographical stratification and variance in perceived compliance requirements (e.g. coastal, territorial waters, inside ports, high seas, European waters, African shores....etc.).

One advantage of the generation and employment of CM frames is that respondents are clearly evaluating the resources of the parties involved, the global institutions available for helping in the conflict management process (mainly focusing on the IMO), and the localised organisational conditions (e.g. within shipping companies). Not only this, they also realise that solutions need support from seagoing staff especially senior ranks, hence their focus on the effect on-board hierarchical tensions and exemplary leadership styles or strategies. In other words, they take into account categorically the three levels discussed earlier namely the global, company, and individual conditions of the conflict.

On the company level the established frames about economic determinism and the need for profit constructed by respondents represent a significant barrier between seafarers and managers ashore when voicing their hardships and concerns, creating a more stressful atmosphere where many seafarers fell oppressed by their management. On the individualised level, the sheer existence of cultural differences between various seafarers represents a challenge to materialise most collective CM frames. Notably, value systems among a group on board a ship often clash and this is intensified by feelings of helplessness - at times - in certain companies, flags, or when trading in certain parts of world.

Seafarers, in their attempts to mobilise their CM frames (i.e. take practical steps towards potential solutions), identified several factors that may inhibit the formation of productive and mutually trusting relationships among themselves, between them and port officials, auditors, inspectors and port state control officers (i.e. perceived experts – see chapter five). Among these factors are lack of proper communications between busy staff on board (especially during extensive loading and discharging operations in tankers) and auditors boarding the ship in ports and terminals, as well as lack of proper feedback following such audits and inspections (see chapters five and six). Another factor detected in the data and which could fuel the distrust in policy makers and monitoring groups are the subordinate feelings by many seafarers in relation to mistreatment in ports (especially for open register crews) by some port officials and port state control officers, which contributes to misperceiving the issue of cooperation for protecting the marine environment with its implications on mutual goal setting and power sharing (Gold 2005; Morris 2002). Naturally, what seafarers detect as barriers turn later to demands to remove such barriers which contribute to building up CM frames by most respondents.

Seafarers' individual CM frames are seen to reflect institutional ones. In the process of building CM frames, seafarers are detected to be influenced by some international and regional strategies implemented by IMO and some EU countries in recent years. For example, several

European countries decided to ban the passage of single hulled tankers carrying heavy and persistent oils passing or entering their territorial waters and exclusive economic zones (EEZs) in the aftermath of large oil spill disasters (e.g. Erika 1999, prestige 2002) in what is considered as unilateral action by the IMO (Kim 2003) . Responding to pressures from European member states, the IMO had to speed up the phasing out scheme of single hull tankers in 2002 to avoid further unilateral action by individual states or regional groups (IMO 2002). However, the issue of the efficacy of the double hull as protection from oil spills in cases of high energy collisions and the economic aspect of building and converting ships to double hulls is still an issue for debate among IMO delegates (Brown and Savage 1996; Hung and Chen 2007; Zheng et al. 2007). I may argue that actions advocated on the international and regional levels - in this specific case - is reflected on the seafarers' CM frames resulting in perceptions of solutions in harmony with what is advocated in the policy making arenas. This results in seafarers from developing nations accusing their countries of being lenient or complacent in enforcing firm environmental laws and demanding mitigation measures that could be difficult to implement on the ground.

To sum up, and focusing more closely on the personal experiences of seafarers when visiting ports for loading and discharging purposes, the main CM barriers identified by respondents revolve around the variations of MARPOL implementation measures among countries, companies, and on-board ships as discussed in this chapter. Naturally, seafarers demanded more transparency, harmonisation of implementation measures, better feedback (coining the no blame culture), and occasionally the use of either financial incentives and/or sanctions.

On reflection of the data and discussion presented in this chapter, there is no doubt that some of the CM strategies presented by seafarers are not only dependant on practical experiences and observations, but represent a blend of reflexive frames resulting from their charged experiences and constructed values and interests. These frames clearly describe the relationship of the marine pollution problem to the particular regime designed for its abatement. They also highlight how seafarers as a 'global' professional group distinguish, intentionally or non-intentionally, between political, institutional, and environmental success of not only an established maritime convention such as MARPOL but also the marine environmental governance as a whole.

CHAPTER NINE – Conclusion

9.1 Introduction

In this chapter, the presentation and discussion of my findings and conclusions will be carried out at three main levels. The first level is concerned with the reflexive framing of marine environmental legislations and their relevance to the seafaring profession. The second level relates to the seafarers' framing of shipping companies' environmental policies and practices, while the third level relates to the seafarers' framing of their peers and of daily compliance practices on board. On the sociological side, this thesis examined the link between the 'frames' and 'actions' or 'inactions' of this professional group. This endeavour has been pursued by applying reflexive modernisation theory to this particular work force and by analysing the relationship between global concerns, personal experience, and workplace tensions and barriers to sound environmental practice. Moreover, the study has explored - based on qualitative data - different perceptions of a range of environmental compliance practices in the context of a global regulation such as MARPOL.

Seafarers - contributing to this study - developed salient reflexive frames on these three levels. However, the consequences of employing such frames - with regard to compliance practice - differs at each level and these are influenced by various social, geographical, and professional factors. At the first level, seafarers' commitment to complying with international environmental instruments such as MARPOL was hindered - in many cases - by national implementation difficulties (e.g. lack of reception facilities) and interpretation difficulties (e.g. difficulties in MARPOL technical text comprehension), and further difficulties (e.g. fear of criminalisation or self-incrimination) especially in the light of numerous criminalisation cases against seafarers in the aftermath of pollution accidents or incidents. At the second level, seafarers were striving to balance their personal aspirations to protect the marine environment against corporate and managerial demands in a quest to reach a state of - using Giddens' term - 'ontological security' (i.e. a sense of order and continuity in regard to an individual's experiences). This led them to reframe marine environmental compliance issues and to the generation of new on board practices among seafarers to be able to keep their jobs while avoiding being criminalised at the same time in what could be considered as an example of pursuance of incompatible goals. This level was observed among respondents working on various categories of shipping companies by examining the ways in which they employed or modified their compliance practices to MARPOL as a result of such reflexive frames.

Reflexive frames of the complex aspects of the marine pollution and compliance problems have contributed to multiple trade-offs and led to reframing of environmental issues among seafarers. In a globalised shipping industry the re-framing of environmental tensions was as dynamic as the introduction of new amendments to an existing marine environmental convention, or the switching over of companies, ships and even the replacement of individual senior crew members. Despite the dramatic change in environmental practices due to such variations, respondents working in stressful conditions seem to hold on to their 'value' frames concerning marine environmental protection.

While reflexive frames - at the company level - presented by respondents acknowledge that factors such as organisational culture, economic structure, and availability of resources are important determinants of trust in the management of shipping companies, the lack of proper communication and practical implementation strategies may skew or alter the seafarers' framing of the intentions of their managers ashore. Seafarers characterise a company as being 'good' when it employs sound environmental management strategies and communicates its policy to the seagoing staff in a transparent manner. Conversely, companies paying attractive salaries but demanding environmental compromises are characterised as 'bad' companies even if the seafarer has worked for these companies for a considerable number of years. On the - on board - third level, seafarers constructed their own frames regarding certain peer groups from different nationalities and training backgrounds based on their environmental compliance practices. Such characterisations have led seafarers to create a set of reflexive frames that have contributed to their aspirations of better environmental practice which proved, in many cases, stressful and unachievable. The journey towards building up of the seafarers' reflexive framing journey is outlined below.

9.2   The Seafarers' Reflexive Framing Journey

One of the sociological aims of this thesis was to examine perceptions and reactions of a 'reflexive' seafarer using the vehicle of the 'reflexive modernization' theory of modern societies. The study applied this theory to a global workforce and revealed how problematic coping with the demands of modernity could be to seafarers as a nomadic group. Doing this, the study analysed the relationship between global concerns, personal experiences of seafarers and workplace perceptions of a range of compliance - and non-compliance - practices relating to the MARPOL convention as a particular global expert system.

Being subjected to increasing global reflexive resources (e.g. the GEF), the seafarers in this study continued their reflexive, evaluative, and critical journey towards reframing their own countries, other countries, and other regions worldwide, either by relying partly on their daily observations and experiences or on what was communicated through various media and interactive educational resources. In this study, the 'intersection' or 'measurement' points for seafarers to trust their own or other countries were twofold: one relating to the availability of port reception facilities in a particular port and the quality of water parameters in the ports, coastal areas, and territorial waters which was considered by respondents as a sign for the effective implementation and enforcement of marine environmental conventions. The second measurement point relates to pre-occupations and established constructions regarding certain countries which were underpinned, in most cases, by the influences of the global environmental frame (GEF).

That is why, on the one hand, seafarers trading in MARPOL special areas lying within the EU waters - where states are expected to comply strictly with MARPOL - find themselves confused when not finding or when denied access to port reception facilities (PRFs) in what they frame as developed western countries (Mattson 2006; Sahatjian 1998). The updates of daily media resources (available to all seafarers trading in these geographical areas) constantly attest and advocate that such 'developed' countries do care about reducing or even eliminating pollution to the environment (Anderson 2002) giving an idealistic view as perceived by seafarers in this study. On the other hand, seafarers trading in the Gulf and Red sea areas (i.e. trading within the waters of less developed countries perceived to be lenient in implementing MARPOL) and experiencing similar problems aspire that these countries follow the 'exemplary' path of European countries even when, for some of them, their whole seafaring career was confined within the Gulf area. Hence, it is reasonable to argue that this is yet another example of reflexive frames that are built by being subjected to a combination of the global environmental frame (i.e. in this case, that all EU countries perform better on the environmental side) complimented by empirical observations available from the roaming nature of the seafaring profession. The result in this case was an autonomous licence granting seafarers the liberty to evaluate geographical locations (sometimes the coastal waters of certain countries) where dumping pollutants would not constitute the risk of being detected or prosecuted, while in other areas it is 'risky' to commit such infringements. However, most respondents expected that the near future carries the prospect of more stringent environmental regulations in the maritime regulatory sphere which will contribute to mitigating the dumping culture among seafarers worldwide.

Linking the above findings to the main risk perception theories, we can see how seafarers who feel incapable of fulfilling their environmental protection obligations show a higher sense of anticipation of futuristic risks. In this context, risk theorists contend that risk by definition is situated in the future; therefore risks exist in a permanent state of being a potential and are actualised only through anticipation (Van Loon 2000). In this study, the accounts of many seafarers show fear and anticipation of the adverse effects of marine pollution on their own families, country and - at times - their economic revenues. Following this, for Beck, what emerges when facing risk is a social awareness of the catastrophic impacts of risks; from this emerges a specific kind of critical reflection as a form of self-critique and self-transformation in the face of what is perceived as disastrous (Beck 2009; Beck et al. 1994). According to the interview data, we can see how category three seafarers (i.e. the most oppressed group – see appendix one) are blaming themselves for not being able to comply with MARPOL and prevent further pollution activities by their peers on board. However, despite having no choice but to continue working for such companies, the grievances voiced in their interview accounts depict prominent feelings of what Giddens' labels as lack of 'ontological security'. The consequences of such feelings and their reflections on compliance practices with MARPOL was varied as highlighted below.

In a slightly different theoretical approach, based on Beck's recent arguments, seafarers in this study could be observed as becoming their own 'moral entrepreneurs' (Beck 2009). In other words, some respondents, after being subjected to the global environmental frame (GEF), feel that the fate of the marine environment depends on their current and future personal practices on board ships. With such a 'reflexive' heightened sense of responsibility, and while witnessing multiple signs of institutional non-compliance (as discussed in chapters five and six), the anticipation of success or failure of future marine environmental legislations and the need for more personalised actions became very prominent in their accounts (i.e. the ruling out of institutional actions and the prioritisation of personal actions). However, to translate such aspirations into practice, this ability to act was primarily dependant on the specific work setting of each respondent (i.e. category of shipping company where each respondent is employed).

As outlined earlier, seafarers working for large shipping corporations (e.g. category one – in this study) were found to be in a better consensual relationship with their employers as they ended up reflexively framing their company as a 'good' company with an expectation that this company will continue performing well on the environmental compliance side. The data strongly suggests that such consensual feelings and working towards a common goal (i.e. seafarers agree to comply with MARPOL as does their company) remain intact and broken only if the person comes across an empirical experience which is accounted as a breach of norms or an infringement to international, regional, or legal requirements. This consensual relationship allows the seafarer to focus more on ensuring better environmental practices rather than trying to achieve incompatible goals (e.g. dumping pollutants to satisfy corporate masters – avoid being criminalised). However, in the case of seafarers working in smaller corporations (e.g. category two), they are trying to cope with the usual cost consciousness of their employers by attempting to balance between saving cost and sound performance on the environmental practice side. As this proves extremely difficult, at times, especially when trading in a MARPOL special area where the discharge of oily effluents is not permitted, it is clear that most respondents in this category are striving to find alternatives other than dumping for their daily waste disposal problems.

Clearly, seafarers working on board ships owned by other companies (i.e. category three companies) are caught between their personal aspirations to save the marine environment and the predominant 'dumping' culture on board ships belonging to this category. Moreover, trading in coastal waters of particular geographic areas that are framed to be lacking in marine pollution surveillance and monitoring, or within the jurisdictions of countries which are framed to be environmental pariahs, encourages the dumping culture that eventually becomes a stressful norm among seafarers working for these companies. Seafarers working for these companies expressed their inability to comply with MARPOL as ship owners exploit the lenient conditions in coastal areas of these states (i.e. no policing or environmental surveillance) which becomes a permeant source of stress for seafarers forced to evade the regulations on a daily basis.

On the sociological front, the implications of the global environmental frame on seafarers as an occupational group could be summarised in three main points; first, seafarers of all categories 'constructed' a sense of necessary involvement to protect or save the marine environment. However, we can see that seafarers reflexively frame the way ahead differently, some will advocate individual ameliorative action and others will delegate / assign such responsibility to governmental and industrial entities (e.g. specific countries or shipping companies). But on the practice side, the ability to comply remains different and - for some seafarers – difficult, as seen from the data analysis and discussion presented in previous chapters. Second, such 'constructed' potential pollution 'risks' became an inevitable result of the dominant 'distrust' in the legitimacy of the whole regulatory system especially with the contribution of faceless and face-work interactions (see chapters five and six).

Consequently, marine pollution is reflexively framed by seafarers as a long-term hazard that reflects not only on their life, health and wellbeing, but also the security of their jobs. However, we could verify how such framings of 'risk' and 'risky' encounters affected some seafarers more than others depending on the nature of their employers, the geographic span of their voyages, and their ability to access modern mediated resources. Similarly, the reliance on technology and expert systems as mitigation strategies for the potential pollution risk is clearly undermined by the very nature of these strategies and the economic and cost factors that are taking primacy for ship owners in the maritime sector (see discussions about viability and effectiveness of technology solutions in chapter eight).

On the conflict management (CM) side, the seafarers' CM frames were seen to be highly dependent either on 'interests' or 'values' or, occasionally, on both. For example, the group showing a high environmental orientation is more inclined to suggest effective political actions from policy makers to rectify the compliance and implementation difficulties. In contrast, the group which suffers most from procedural and technical difficulties (i.e. interests) are more inclined to demand administrative and managerial reforms from their companies to reduce their daily working tensions and avoid being criminalised (e.g. category three). However, both groups end up by acknowledging that neither of these measures would work without mobilising what they term as 'the personal initiative' (i.e. the seafarers should act on an individual basis to protect the marine environment).

Put simply, it is clear that seafarers, while presenting their CM strategies, take either the position of activists, passive spectators, or victims depending on their social, cultural, spatial, or professional status. However, all respondents in this study took the opportunity at interviews to have their say in how the conflict could or would be solved and/or managed. Doing this, they are attempting to satisfy their professional needs and the needs dictated by the established global environmental frame (GEF) simultaneously (see chapters five to seven). In other words they are trying to satisfy the value side of their needs (i.e. protecting the marine environment) and their interest side (keeping their job - fulfilling corporate demands....etc.). My argument is that while the GEF successfully mobilised seafarers on the basis that they are global actors, it also significantly contributed to increasing their feelings of stress and helplessness when faced with institutional and technical difficulties beyond their control.

The economic consciousness of shipping companies emerged as a major theme in this study. Costs and benefits seem to have influenced the implementation processes of MARPOL including the seafarers' ability to comply with practical daily requirements. In all cases where the respondents' assumptions about their companies were skewed towards 'lack of resources' in relation to sound implementation requirements, this matched a low degree of output in environmental performance. This, I argue, sends the wrong message to seafarers in general regarding future and potential environmental legislations that may be met with scepticism even before they are adopted and signs of these in the interview data are emerging.

While economic determinism in the shipping industry represents one of the most significant barriers to sound environmental practice, it can be detected that when economic scarcity diminishes (e.g. in category 1 and 2 ships) other factors - such as environmental values -shape seafarers' compliance practices to an increasing degree. This coincides with the view of Inglehart's comprehensive 26 year study which concluded that the subjective wellbeing of individuals and their support to environmental protection is directly linked to sound socio-economic conditions (Inglehart 1995). Nevertheless, some seafarers working for affluent well renowned shipping companies start losing trust in management when they witness or observe any explicit breach of environmental conventions. The point I make here is that the influence of the experiential factor on established beliefs of seafarers lead to the formation of reflexive frames that defined a set of needed actions among this group, which proved difficult to achieve in many occupational settings.

In this economic (shipping companies') profit seeking context previous research suggested that MARPOL represented very concentrated costs while, at the same time, scattering distributed benefits for ship owners (Mattson 2006; Sahatjian 1998). This research suggested that there was no vision that MARPOL would result in implementation problems. With passing time, low implementation and enforcement scores by some target groups (e.g. especially Flag of Convenience states - FOCs - compliance and implementation rates) became a natural consequence. Based on this, it is reasonable to argue that the significance of these aspects is also likely to increase in the near future with attempts to widen the scope of implementation of the new requirements for air pollution from shipping and the intended fast-tracked shift to distillate fuels being currently discussed in the IMO (field observation IMO MEPC 57 March 08- London - 'Impacts of Climate change on the Maritime Industry' Conference Malmo - Sweden 2nd. to 4th. June 08).

Seafarers in this study argued that institutional changes are required within the IMO to expand its mandate to be able to actively provide adequate aid and resources to incapable flag states and then to question, and monitor the performance through a credible and transparent scheme. Some fairly recent studies suggest that the efforts of the IMO's technical cooperation committee in this respect in recent years were not successful as it always focused on funding the acquisition of new technical capabilities to some developing member states giving less priority to institutional change in these countries' maritime administrations (Zhu 2006). With the recent changes in converting the IMO member state voluntary audit scheme to a mandatory system some positive changes are hoped for (IMO, 2013). However, one of the limitations of this study is the inability to further explore seafarers' expectations regarding the ideal approaches - in their views - to assist flag states to comply with growing compliance measures under MARPOL.

However, the story is rather different on the practical on-board level (i.e. daily compliance practices). Many framing processes emerged as a result of the influence of the unique 'hand over' culture where off signing staff and crew using word of mouth describe to their on signing peers the strategies and practices they employ to either comply or evade the mandatory compliance requirements on a particular vessel. In category one shipping companies, seafarers established a frame that the company management share with them a 'common goal' of protecting the marine environment and this picture is handed over to newcomers. However, in some category two and all of category three respondents' accounts, the 'hand over' word of mouth briefings and feedback provided a base for building up a communication barrier especially when it strengthens the assumption that the company's sole concern is financial profit. The data also attests that category three seafarers are even trying to maintain a positive face by avoiding the demand of any costly resources from the company (e.g. spare parts for faulty monitoring equipment or demanding the use of shore reception facilities) claiming that such requests are expected to be rejected by the company managers (see chapter seven and eight).

The global reflexive frames discussed above are focused on strategies and actions (e.g. procedures and compliance tasks, auditing and monitoring…etc.) rather than goals (e.g. pollution reduction or elimination). This is an indication that the seafarers group is experiencing what previous studies refer to as 'qualitative difficulty' and are striving to enhance their performance in relation to environmental practice in general (Futoran et al. 1989). As a result of such global reflexive frames, seafarers are detected to be consuming a considerable amount of time engaged with in-group conflict and rivalry discourses over environmental practices rather than focusing on task content (i.e. the technical problem solving or the ability to read / comprehend equipment operation and maintenance manuals). When framing technology solutions, respondents worry most about how risky decisions are made by regulators and shipping company managers, whose interests are served, and who have assumed authority in the situation and, in many cases, start framing technology solutions as a 'risk' that is to be avoided (see chapter six). In what follows, I will sum up the main arguments relating to stake holders (in the hierarchical order suggested by respondents) identified by respondents in this study as the most influential regarding the issue of compliance to current and future marine environmental regulations.

9.2.1 Framing Shipping Companies

In the shipping sector, it may be relatively easy for a shipping company to paint a portrait of environmental ethics and corporate citizenship, but it is still rather difficult for affected residents, port and coastal states to believe them and reasons for doubt are plentiful (Kimerling 2001). These doubts are deepened with the anonymity of most pollution incidents attributed to the shipping sector and the non-availability of advanced detection and surveillance technologies in many parts of the world. According to the limited literature dealing with corporate environmental behaviours of shipping companies, neither ship owners nor regulations alone can face or impose the high price of environmental quality in such a 'cost conscious' industry (Fafaliou et al. 2006). Arguably, this environmental quality is scarcely demanded by the users of the shipping service, the manufacturers, traders, freight forwarders, or the final consumers (Haralambides 1998). However, for seafarers, as inside concerned observers, shipping companies play an important role in the environmental compliance chain. The study clearly evidences (see chapter seven) that this work force is continuously monitoring and evaluating the effects of unfair environmental practices on the sea water and port area quality in the geographic areas they trade in. This is generated by the reflexive frames developed that necessitate actions - if they are able to - otherwise triggering either stress due to perceived personal in-capacitance or detected unwillingness of shipping companies (see chapters five to seven).

Shipping companies are seen as having distinctive characters that contribute to how seafarers should operate especially on the environmental practice side. In this study, these characters (or corporate identities) emerged from practical environmental policies - not policy texts - of such companies and their willingness to bear the high costs of being compliant with statutory instruments such as MARPOL. From this perspective, an organisational identity is constructed among seafarers through the development of 'in-group' and 'out-group' narratives, rhetoric, and stories, compelling different types and levels of trust, scepticism, and distrust in shipping companies. Most of these are either strengthened or weekend by actual observations of seafarers throughout their tours of duty on a specific company's fleet, hence maintain or compromising trust in their employers. This was detected also to propagate upwards towards the coastal states and their rigor in enforcing the maritime conventions they ratified to protect their own marine and coastal environments (i.e. trust and distrust in regulatory bodies – see chapters five and six).

The data analysis points out that trust and distrust in shipping companies served to firstly, differentiate the seafarers' reflexive framing of various shipping companies with implications on the perceived environmental practices of such companies. Second, legitimising deviant environmental practices (i.e. preparing seafarers to accept a state of 'inevitable' dumping activities when working for 'bad' companies) by what is framed as 'bad' companies thus finding excuses for non-compliance to MARPOL and other regional and local environmental regulations further encouraging collective distrust in such companies. In contrast, the data clearly evidences that these frames contributed to eliciting initial high expectations regarding environmental practice from what are perceived by respondents to be 'good' companies. Third, such frames also served to encourage complacency and the spreading of rhetoric rather than accurate factual information about certain companies, especially in relation to their flags, nationalities and training backgrounds of employed crew members (i.e. employment policy), ownership origins, or even the training background of their crew members.

9.2.2 Framing Regulatory Institutions

This study identified three main components of vested trust (or distrust) in regulatory institutions among seafarers. First, perceived competence of the specific risk management entity (e.g. regulatory agency, coastal state) which represents the degree of technical expertise of the regulating body and has extended to cover this body's agents and/or representatives (i.e. experts). Second, faith in the intended goals of regulatory instruments coupled with or without absence of bias in the regulating body (e.g. the IMO). Third, the consistency and relative harmony between different regulatory bodies observed to pursue similar goals and objectives (e.g. auditing compliance with MARPOL by international, regional and local governing bodies). The study therefore suggests these are the ways in which regulatory institutions are reflexively framed by seafarers which determine the type and/or level of trust vested. This is in conformity with recent studies suggesting that this trust clearly relates to an institution's historical record of competence, whether there is enough familiarity (or adequate understanding) of statutory instruments produced by this institution, and how this then feeds through apperception of mutuality of values (Poortinga and Pidgeon 2006). The IMO occupied the highest share of trust and distrust in the respondents' account as explained below. This mostly results from an inherent misunderstanding of the IMO's mandate which is essentially an intergovernmental organisation and not a supra-national one, which leaves the onus of implementation and enforcement on member states rather than the IMO body.

Respondents in this study - after observing local and institutional compliance difficulties - identified the IMO as the main regulatory body responsible for adopting maritime safety and environmental protection. However, seafarers, due to the above discussed reasons - offered sharply contrasting views of the institutional effectiveness of the IMO. While some seafarers generally acknowledge its political effects and the general environmental awareness it entailed, others claim that there is no evidence of significant improvement among the actors (at least with whom they interact). This classic model of distrust in policy makers contributed to more scepticism about newly introduced marine environmental legislations especially in the absence of any sanctioning mechanisms to enforce the current ones by the relevant coastal states. It is important to note here that most aspirations of seafarers regarding the ineffectiveness of the IMO wrongly assume that this intergovernmental organisation possess any enforcement powers.

9.2.3 Framing Different Countries

Framing of different coastal states was frequently integrated with perceptions of pollution risks among respondents. For example, category three respondents initially perceived that many developing countries (even if they are oil wealthy states) were pursuing an agenda that favoured economic development over environmental protection activities. Conversely, they possessed established frames that a European quality of life relied on characteristics like clean air, water, and aesthetic beauty that underpins the environmental practices of their citizens wherever they go. Category one and some category two respondents saw developed EU countries, European owned companies and flag states as pursuing compatible objectives related to protection of the marine environment and movement of trade, largely because of their economic viability.

Framing of pollution risk as discussed in this thesis may also be seen as a systematic way employed by seafarers to deal with pollution hazards and insecurities to human health introduced primarily by the global environmental frame (GEF) in lieu of 'modernisation' advocated by Beck in his discussion of the risk society (Beck 1992; Lidskog and Sundqvist 2004; Matten 2004). In this context, the risk literature warns of the "naturalisation" of humans in the increasing environmental risk discourses. In this study, seafarers seem to focus more on 'manufactured risks' (i.e. ones constituting human agents) rather than 'external' or natural risks (Giddens 1999). This focus on manufactured risks may constitute a strategy to try to get involved in the mitigation of pollution which human agency is perceived to be a major contributor towards a terminal outcome or in the way of doing so. The attempts of 'getting involved' in environmental decision making processes by seafarers was clear in their numerous attempts to establish their role in the mitigation of marine pollution in different professional settings (see chapter eight) even when such roles were limited to criticising / resisting infringements and the persistent calls for better practices due to the limitations of shipping companies. One clear example of this was the acceptance of most respondents of various environmental audit schemes despite their reservations regarding the inconsistency, lack of harmonisation, and the occasional non-professional conduct of such audits in some coastal states.

In this context, the qualitative data collected in relation to environmental audit schemes in the maritime sector waves a cautionary flag; that persistent attempts to integrate the agendas of multiple stake holders (i.e. major oil companies, port states, flag states, and coastal states….etc.) proves to be problematic to integrate. The legitimacy of different audits schemes presented in this thesis draw a clear line between three types of successes claimed by different stake holders. Policy makers in their pursuit to follow-up global environmental calls generate audit procedures focused on what could be termed 'political success', seeking to fulfil what they prioritise as general policy agendas. At the same time, shipping companies and ship owners are seeking a form of 'institutional success' trying to either create a more appealing working atmosphere for their staff (e.g. category one) or creating a good reputation and public image (especially large oil Multinational Corporations - MNCs - owning their own tanker fleets) . Finally, seafarers are predominantly seeking perceived 'environmental successes' through their attempts to arrive at a state of 'ontological security' which can be clearly detected from their persistent attempts to enhance the potential benefits to the marine environment if countries', companies', and personal environmental practices are properly implemented and enforced.

9.3 Contribution of This Research

Having discussed some of the conceptual / theoretical innovations developed by this study, this section will present the sociological and empirical contributions of the thesis in a more explicit form utilising the substantive elements of the study.

9.3.1 Sociological Contributions

One of the innovative contributions of the thesis was the careful application of Reflexive Modernisation (RM) theory and its embedded concepts of risk, trust, the precautionary principle and technology solutions to a global working group. The application of this approach allowed an in-depth analysis of the relationship between seafarers' global concerns, personal experiences and perceptions of a range of choices and practices regarding the protection of the environment based on a rich qualitative dataset. The task was done by utilising MARPOL as a particular global 'expert system' enjoying ratification by the vast majority of maritime states.

A further original contribution was the application of this conceptual framework to a nomadic workforce (i.e. Methodologically more able to observe differences). This method contributed to producing a qualitative study that depicts a clearer understanding of the ways in which global environmental concerns are perceived in different work settings and how these contribute to developing different workplace cultures and practices. The study located clearly the heightened sense of risk mainly triggered by various reflexive framings of seafarers engaging with expert systems at faceless or face to face levels. This was achieved by a carefully structured approach combining the notions of reflexivity, risk and trust to arrive at a developed reflexive framing approach that underpinned the coding and analysis of the qualitative data.

The thesis contributes as well to the scarce literature discussing the reflections and practices of regulatees regarding some of the main concepts presented by the reflexive modernisation literature namely the precautionary principal, technology solutions and the audit culture in the context of risk and trust. This is evidenced in this study by the different forms of risk perception identified and by the various levels of trust emerging from the qualitative inquiry. Moreover, the analysis provided by this study highlighted the relationships between the application of the RM tools and workplace cultures and clarified the different resultant workplace cultures and practices especially when 'global' environmental concerns are playing the central role. This study also analysed the emergence and generation of social conflict management frames and strategies by respondents who deliberate compelling solutions to their daily environmental compliance practice based on the integration between global concerns and local available/allowable practices in specific work settings (i.e. different shipping companies trading in different geographic location and trade patterns).

The thesis also contributes to the body of literature attempting to better understanding of the ways in which professional groups in late modern society perceive global institutions governing environmental pollution. In this context, it adds to our knowledge of how global regulatory tools are received, perceived, and acted upon differently in different work settings and different geographic locations by a diverse and global professional group.

9.3.2 Empirical Contributions

The empirical contribution based on the findings of this research study is three-fold. It can be presented in the form of three explicit messages to maritime policy makers, corporate entities in the shipping sector, and the wider population of seafarers respectively.

First, the study contributes to policy reform by sending a clear message to maritime policy makers (i.e. initiators/generators of expert systems) who need to seriously re-consider the diverse nature of targeted regulatees especially in the maritime and shipping sectors. The assumption that a global regulatory tool will enjoy uniform compliance was not borne out by the empirical findings of this study. This study highlighted that even in the same global work force there may be many differences in the interpretation of legal scripts and in the application of technology solutions depending on types of work settings and cultures. This assumption by policy makers also led to a variant perception of pollution risk(s) among the targeted group of the regulatory tool. The study evidences that with a heightened sense of risk, regulatees raise the ceiling of expectations from policy makers and apply more critical strategy to ensure the ultimate goal of the regulation is achieved. Facing difficulties (e.g. technical or statutory compliance difficulties by peers or flag states) results in compromising trust in the overarching legal system opening the door to potential infringements. With the persistent calls - by policy makers - regarding the need to harmonise the compliance with global legal tools, a careful reconsideration needs to in place in drafting, implementing, and enforcing such pieces of international law prior to adopting the legal text. A review of the various conflict management strategies generated by this study's respondents could well be a viable starting point.

Secondly, the findings of this study contribute to organisation and regulatory compliance studies literature by waiving a cautionary flag to corporate entities in the maritime and shipping industries emphasising the need to maintain the trust relation between the corporate entity and the employees especially regarding environmental policies. In this context, the study highlights clearly the consequences of compromised trust relations and how this could result in building up of negative perceptions among employers leading - potentially - to environmental compliance problems. Naturally, achieving sound compliance to environmental regulation is a major concern for shipping companies as it depicts a benign corporate image of the corporate entity in the public domain, an element of vital importance to the recruitment of cargoes and a sustainable economic revenue. The study contributes by highlighting the inherent difficulties to end of pipe technology solutions in the shipping sector and sheds more light on the impacts of the trade pattern and geographic area of trade on the sound daily compliance of seafarers as the end link of the compliance chain, areas very scarcely addressed by environmental compliance studies in the maritime and shipping sectors. Put simply, this study evidences that for a shipping company to be classified as 'good' by its own employees, there needs to exist a genuine attempt towards investing all available resources to ensure full and sound compliance to environmental regulations.

Thirdly, this study contributed to an in-depth understanding of the potential tensions in a global workplace and within a global work force regarding environmental practice. In the context of perceiving environmental risk and compliance demands, it became clear from the careful analysis of the qualitative data set that seafarers frame their peers on board based on a multiplicity of factors. The study not only detected the different perceptions regarding different nationalities and/or training backgrounds among peers on board but also detected - more importantly - the different characterisations of 'others' based on observing and evaluating their environmental practice. The study strongly suggests that an acceptable 'professional' identity was clearly bestowed to crew members - by their leaders/peers on board - who succeed in employing sound daily compliance practices whilst negative characterisations about a fellow crew member was mainly linked to his/her inability to perform in an environmentally considerate manner. Naturally the measurement point was statutory compliance practices mandated by the dominant 'expert system' (i.e. MARPOL) as explained earlier.

In relation to the specific nature of the seafaring profession, this study contributes to a realisation of the continuous evaluation process to the integrity and cleanliness of the marine and coastal environments employed by seafarers in their nomadic profession being influenced by a global environmental protection frame. Being at the receiving end of global environmental regulations they were found to be engaged in a continuous assessment process in an attempt to verify whether the increasing body of marine environmental legislations are yielding positive outcomes or not. The study highlights their perceptions about marine pollution based not only on visible observations but also on established frames about various countries and regions in the world. I argue that this realisation is vital to policy makers upon drafting new marine environmental legislations or amending the current ones.

9.4   Limitations and Further Research

9.4.1 Limitations

One of the main limitations of this study was the inability to pursue a more longitudinal form of study for the development of the seafarer's reflexive frames over a long period of time. It is evident that marine environmental legislations are dynamic in the recent decade and the evolution of such regulations necessitate further research to take this temporal element into account by tracing the development of reflexive frames among this professional group and identify the resultant actions and practices over time. The comparison between classic environmental practices - by seafarers - and the current compliance conditions clearly results in change of frames among seafarers especially when linked to personal and professional aspirations. Further work would be needed to trace such salient reflexive frames among this work force especially after introducing new legal instruments that tackle - for example - ballast water, an element carried on ships for decades without previously being accounted as a pollutant.

Other limitations of the study were the inability to include other stakeholders within the qualitative inquiry (shipping companies and policy makers) due to time, funding and research management limitations. Hence, the decision taken after reviewing the initial results of the pilot study was to focus on seafarers and the reflexive framing approach providing a good theoretical vehicle to examine their perceptions and reactions to MARPOL throughout the study. Once the Global Environmental Frame (GEF) was located within the qualitative data set, it was difficult to verify clearly whether these frames and the discussions of the globality of environmental problems which emerged are only due to maritime resources and informatics (discussed in chapter seven) or due to an integrated digest from being subjected to global calls to saving the environment at sea and whilst spending their leave time ashore. Whilst I consider this study to be limited at this level, further research could explore the actual sources and effects of each motivating factor on the global environmental frame in a more longitudinal study as alluded to earlier.

In terms of methods, the categorisation of shipping companies into three main categories is another limitation. Arguably, types of shipping companies could be classified into many more categories in relation to their ownership, fleet size, and geographical scopes of trade, overall tonnage, and much more. However, for the purpose of this study's enquiry it was limited to three categories only to facilitate the analytical process. Whilst all my qualitative data were collected either at British ports or at a regional maritime training institution, it was difficult to choose and/or balance between these three categories prior to selection of respondents.

9.4.2 Further Research

Seafarers in this study voiced their concerns regarding the drafting, implementation, and daily compliance practices of MARPOL as a global regulatory tool. Whilst this study examined the reasons behind the seafarers' framing of regulatory bodies, shipping companies, and peers on-board, further in-depth research needs to examine the main regulatory body's priorities and the power relations driving environmental agendas and how these are considerate - or not - to the disparities and differences of regulatees in the maritime industry. Further research can also select specific shipping companies representing various records of environmental compliance - using port state control data for example – and attempt to examine how each company allocates different resources (human – training – financial) to environmental compliance in such an evolutionary regulatory area.

From the discussion above we can see that further research needs to explore the reasons behind the IMO's hard choices between "effectiveness oriented" and "compliance oriented" information before thinking about adopting new environmental legal instruments. The former is to assess whether regime members (i.e. state parties) are achieving regime goals, while the latter is to assess whether particular actors are fulfilling regime commitments. A research task needs to be directed to the identification of the IMO stance on this issue in an attempt to verify the level of transparency in the dissemination of "compliance" or "effectiveness" information and the means of using such a resource in improving the state of compliance with marine environmental conventions. This task will also attempt to reveal the link between collected information in the past two decades about MARPOL compliance and the introduction of new amendments to this convention. This research may contribute to explaining the high dynamic status of MARPOL and other maritime conventions.

9.5   Closing Statement

It is clear from this study that cultural understandings of pollution risks cannot be generalised and will be divisive rather than homogeneous. For seafarers, when a set of reflexive frames become dominant (e.g. the global environmental frame – GEF - highlighting pollution risks to the environment), they tend to see themselves, their peers, their company, and regulators from a single perspective in significantly different forms. Doing this, they often fail to notice several positive aspects, but rather take a personalised view leading to classifying these different stake holders along a single axis (i.e. environmental practice and sound compliance) often ignoring some commonalities and overlapping ties. Clearly, face-work and faceless interactions contribute to the building up of such frames leading to a set of stratified environmental practices as evidenced by this study. Nevertheless, I recommend that one way to take this forward is by building a bridge between such situated professionals and expert systems by allowing them to be more fully represented in the IMO (i.e. to have their say) when new rules, conventions, amendments, and protocols, are drafted in order to arrive to an instrument scrutinised by seafarers as well as politicians.

Further research in the area of the potential forms of engagement of seafarers' in future marine environmental legislations is recommended by this study to provide a platform for this global workforce to have their say in future regulatory tools on the environmental side. This research may also open a dialogue between seafarer representatives and regulatory bodies around the evolution of scientific and technology solutions and how these can be moderated to be fit for purpose on board ships worldwide.

Last, this empirical study added to the political debate that is being set in motion by the perception of a global ecological crisis by a nomadic workforce group transcending the limitations of space and place. If we can acknowledge that a reflexive citizen now realises such limitations in a second face of modernity rather than merely acknowledging it, seafarers did that as well in their own ways. Reflexive seafarers, in their quest to arrive at a state of 'ontological security', strengthened the argument that the environment can no longer be perceived solely as an outside that can be adopted to their employers – or regulators – purposes, but increasingly as an inherent part of society. This opened the door to many future research questions; what do we need to facilitate environmental compliance for seafarers worldwide in such a dynamic regulatory environment? Do we need more scientific research to locate a feasible technology, or more specialised roles and tasks on board that can result in more allocated training for future seafarers, or to draft regulatory tools that prove to be more persuasive to seafarers with such diverse training backgrounds?

Finally, however, on the positive side, it is reasonable to argue that seafarers as a professional group have developed new capacities, dispositions, ambitions, and new forms of understanding across the time continuum. They are engaged in a continuous process of self-evaluation and face a struggle to fulfil what they frame as environmental obligations to arrive at an ontological state of rest with ever changing regulatory and physical environments.

BIBLIOGRAPHY

Abbott, D., Quilgars, D. and Jones, A. (2006) *The Impact of Social and Cultural Difference in Relation to Job Loss and Financial Planning: Reflections on the Risk Society.* Available at: <URL: http://www.qualitative-research.net/index.php/fqs/article/view/52> [Accessed: 25 July 2008]

Abou-Elkawam, M. (2008) Seafarers and Port Reception Facilities: The Usual Warm Welcome! In: Wittig, W. and Prieser, C. (eds.) *The Human Element at the Ship/Port Interface.* Bremen: Buchwerft-verlag.de, pp. 17-27.

Acejo, I. (2012) Seafarers and transnationalism: ways of belongingness ashore and aboard, *Journal of Intercultural Studies*, 33(1):69-84.

Adam, B., Beck, U. and Van Loon, J. (2000) *The Risk Society and Beyond: Critical issues for Social Theory.* London: Sage.

Adam, B. and Van Loon, J. (2000) Repositioning Risk: The Challenge for Social Theory. In: Adam, B., Beck, U. and Van Loon, J. (eds.) *The Risk Society and Beyond: Critical issues for Social Theory.* London: Sage.

Akamangwa, N. (2013) 'Global Environmental Regulation and Workers in the Shipping Industry', PhD Thesis, Cardiff University.

Alderton, T. and Winchester, N. (2002a) Flag States and Safety: 1997-1999. *Maritime Policy and Management*, 29(2):151-162.

Alderton, T. and Winchester, N. (2002b) Globalisation and Deregulation in the Maritime Industry. *Marine Policy*, 26:35-43.

Alvesson, M. and Willmott, H. (2002) Identity Regulation as Organizational Control: Producing the Appropriate Individual. *Journal of Management Studies*, 39(5):619-644.

Andersen, M. S. and Massa, I. (2000) Ecological modernisation: origins, dilemmas and future directions. *Journal of Environmental Policy and Planning*, 2:337-345.

Anderson, A. G. (2002) The Media Politics of Oil Spills. *Spill Science and Technology Bulletin*, 7(1-2):7-15.

Anderson, H. (1997) Nationality of Ships and Flags of Convenience: Economics, Politics, and Alternatives. *Tulane Maritime Law Journal*, 21:139-150.

Anderson, P. (2003) *Cracking the Code: The relevance of the ISM code and its impact on shipping practices.* London: The Nautical Institute.

Anthony, O. G. (2006) Criminalization of seafarers for accidental discharge of oil: Is there justification in international law for criminal sanction for negligent or accidental pollution of the sea? *Journal of Maritime Law and Commerce*, 37(2):219-243.

Bahree, B., Vitzhumm, C. and Mitchener, B. (2002) Oil Spill Strikes Spanish Coast. In: Tanker Disaster. *Wall Street Journal*. Nov 20, 2002. p. A.2.

Bailey, N., Ellis, N. and Sampson, H. (2012) 'Exploring differences in perceptions of risk, and its management, amongst personnel directly associated with the operation of ships', SIRC Publication, April, ISBN 1-900174-42-1.

Baker, S. (2007) Sustainable development as symbolic commitment: Declaratory politics and the seductive appeal of ecological modernisation in the European Union. *Environmental Politics*, 16(2):297-317.

Ball, I. (1999) Port waste reception facilities in UK ports. *Marine Policy*, 23(4-5):307-327.

Barness, B. (1995) *The Elements of Social Theory*. London: UCL press.

Barrieu, P. and Sinclair-Desgagne, B. (2006) On precautionary policies. *Management Science*, 52(8):1145-1154.

Barton, J. R. (1999) 'Flags of Convenience': Geo-economics and Regulatory Minimisation. *Tijdschrift voor Economische en Sociale Geografie,* 90(2):142-155.

Beck, U. (1992) *Risk society: towards a new modernity.* London: Sage.

Beck, U. (1995) *Ecological Politics in an Age of Risk.* Cambridge: Polity Press.

Beck, U. (1996) World Risk Society as Cosmopolitan Society?: Ecological Questions in a Framework of Manufactured Uncertainties. *Theory Culture Society,* 13(4):1-32.

Beck, U. (2000) Risk Society Revisited: Theory, Politics and Research Programmes. In: Adam, B., Beck, U. and Van Loon, J. (eds.) *The Risk Society and Beyond: Critical Issues for Social Theory.* London: Sage.

Beck, U. (2009) *World at Risk.* Cambridge: Polity Press.

Beck, U., BOnss, W. and Lau, C. (2003) The Theory of Reflexive Modernization: Problematic, Hypotheses and Research Programme. *Theory, Culture and Society,* 20(2):1-33.

Beck, U., Giddens, A. and Lash, S. (1994) *Reflexive Modernization: Politics, Tradition and Aesthetics in the Modern Social Order.* Cambridge: Polity Press

Beck-Gernsheim, E. (2000) Health and Responsibility: From Social Change to Technological Change and Vice Versa. In: Adam, B., Beck, U. and Van Loon, J. (eds.) *The Risk Society and Beyond: Critical Issues for Social Theory.* London: Sage.

Bell, A. (1994) Climate of Opinion: Public and Media Discourse on the Global Environment. *Discourse Society,* 5(1):33-64.

Bell, D. (1993) Port state control v flag state control: UK government position. *Marine Policy,* 17(5):367-370.

Benford, R. D. and Snow, D. A. (2000) Framing Processes and Social Movements: An Overview and Assessment. *Annual Review of Sociology,* 26:611-639.

Benton, T. (1994) Biology and social theory in the environmental debate. In: Redclift, M. and Benton, T. (eds.) *Social theory and the global environment.* London: Routledge, pp. 28-50.

Bhattacharya, S. (2007) Seafarers' Participation in Safety Management on Board Cargo Ships. *SIRC Symposium 2007.* Cardiff, UK: SIRC, pp. 157-176.

Bickerstaff, K., Lorenzoni, I., Pidgeon, N. F., Poortinga, W. and Simmons, P. (2008a) Reframing nuclear power in the UK energy debate: nuclear power, climate change mitigation and radioactive waste. *Public Understanding of Science,* 17(2):145-169.

Bickerstaff, K., Simmons, P. and Pidgeon, N. F. (2008b) Constructing responsibilities for risk: Negotiating citizen - State relationships. *Environment and Planning A,* 40(6):1312-1330.

Bickerstaff, K. and Walker, G. (2003) The place(s) of matter: Matter out of place - Public understandings of air pollution. *Progress in Human Geography,* 27(1):45-68.

Biermann, F. (2003) Global environmental change and the Nation State: The scope of the challenge. *PIK Report,* (80):1-9.

Bloor, M., Datta, R., Gilinskiy, Y. and Horlick-Jones, T. (2006) Unicorn among the cedars: On the possibility of effective 'smart regulation' of the globalized shipping industry. *Social and Legal Studies,* 15(4):534-551.

Bloor, M., Baker, S., Sampson, H. and Dahlgren, K. (2013) 'Issues in the Enforcement of Future International Regulations on Ships' Carbon Emissions', Cardiff University, 45-6, online at www.sirc.cf.ac.uk.

Bloor, M., Sampson, H., Baker, S., Walters, D., Dahlgren, K., Wadsworth, E. and James, P. (2013) Room for Manoeuvre? Regulatory Compliance in the Global Shipping Industry, *Social and Legal Studies,* 22(2):171-189.

Bloor, M., Sampson, H., Gekara, V. (2013) 'Global governance of training standards in an outsourced labor force: The training double bind in seafarer license and certification assessments'. *Regulation and Governance*. DOI: 10.1111/rego.12042.

Bluhdorn, I. (2007) Sustaining the unsustainable: Symbolic politics and the politics of simulation. *Environmental Politics*, 16(2):251-275.

Boden, D. (2000) Worlds in Action: Information, Instantaneity and Global Furures Trading. In: Adam, B., Beck, U. and Van Loon, J. (eds.) *The Risk Society and Beyond: Critical Issues for Social Theory*. London: Sage.

Boehmer-Christiansen, S. (1994) The Precautionary Principle in Germany - Enabling Government. In: O'Riodan, J.C. (ed.) *Interpreting the Precautionary Principle*. London: Earth Scan, pp. 31-60.

Boyle, A. E. (2005) Globalising Environmental Liability: The Interplay of National and International Law. *J Environmental Law*, 17(1):3-26.

BPS (2004) *Code of Conduct, Ethical Principles and Guidelines* Available at: <URL: http://www.bps.org.uk/downloadfile.cfm?file_uuid=6D0645CC-7E96-C67F-D75E2648E5580115&ext=pdf> [Accessed: 10th March 2006]

Brewer, P. R. and Gross, K. (2005) Values, Framing, and Citizens' Thoughts about Policy Issues: Effects on Content and Quantity. *Political Psychology*, 26(6):929-948.

Brookman, C. S. (2002) IMO environmental regulations - Is there a case for change to the standard entry-into-force requirements? *Marine Technology*, 39(4):232-238.

Brown, R. S. and Savage, I. (1996) The economics of double-hulled tankers. *Maritime Policy and Management*, 23(2):167-175.

Bryan, T. and Wondolleck, J. M. (2003) When Irresolvable Becomes Resolvable: The Quincy Library Group Conflict. In: Lewicki, R., Gray, B. and Elliott, M. (eds.) *Making Sense of Intractable Environmental Conflicts*. London: Island Press, pp. 63-90.

Burningham, K. and Cooper, G. (2001) Being Constructive: Social Constructionism and the Environment. *Sociology,* 33(2):296-316.

Cariou, P., Mejia Jr., M. Q. and Wolff, F-C. (2007) An econometric analysis of deficiencies noted in port state control inspections. *Maritime Policy and Management,* 34(3):243-258.

Carpenter, A. and Macgill, S. M. (2000) The new EU directive on port reception facilities for ship-generated waste and cargo residues: An evaluation. *Water Studies,* 9:173-183.

Celik, M. (2008) Designing of integrated quality and safety management system (IQSMS) for shipping operations. *Safety Science.*

Charmaz, K. (2000) Grounded Theory: Objectivist and Constructivist Methods. In: Denzin, N. and Lincoln, Y. (eds.) *Handbook of Qualitaive Research*. Thousand Oaks, CA: Sage, pp. 509-536.

Chen, L. (2000) Legal and practical consequences of not complying with ISM code. *Maritime Policy and Management,* 27(3):219-230.

Chesters, G. and Welsh, I. (2002) *Reflexive Framing and Ecology of Action: Engaging with the Movement 'For Humanity Against Neoliberalism'*. Available at: <URL: http://www.shiftingground.freeuk.com/isapaper.htm> [Accessed: 10th April 2006]

Chesters, G. and Welsh, I. (2005) Complexity and Social Movement(s): Process and Emergence in Planetary Action Systems. *Theory Culture Society,* 22(5):187-211.

Chesters, G. and Welsh, I. (2006) *Complexity and Social Movements: Multitudes at the Edge of Chaos*. Abington: Routledge.

Chiasson, N. et al. (1996) In-Group-Out-Group Similar Information as a Determinant of Attraction toward Members of Minority Groups. *Journal of Social Psychology,* 136(2):233-241.

Chircop, A. (2002) Ships in distress, Environmental Threats to Coastal States, and Places of Refuge: New Directions for an Ancient regime? *Ocean Development and International Law,* 33(2):207-226.

Collins, H. and Yearley, S. (1992) Epistemological Chicken. In: Pickering, A. (ed.) *Science as practice and culture.* Chicago: University of Chicago Press, pp. 301-326.

Cormack, D. and Fowler, D. (1986) Operational oil discharges from ships: Impact on the North Sea. *Oil and Chemical Pollution,* 3(4):307-325.

Cornelissen, J. P., Haslam, S. A. and Balmer, J. M. T. (2007) Social Identity, Organizational Identity and Corporate Identity: Towards an Integrated Understanding of Processes, Patternings and Products. *British Journal of Management,* 18(s1):S1-S16.

Cvetkovich, G., Siegrist, M., Murray, R. and Tragesser, S. (2002) New information and social trust: Asymmetry and perseverance of attributions about hazard managers. *Risk Analysis,* 22(2):359-367.

Davis, C. B. and Lewicki, R. J. (2005) Environmental Conflict Resolution: Framing and Intractability. An Introduction. *Environmental Practice,* 5(3):200-206.

De Young, R. (2000) New Ways to Promote Pro-environmental Behavior: Expanding and Evaluating Motives for Environmentally Responsible Behavior. *Journal of Social Issues,* 56(3):509-526.

Delamont, S. (1992) *Fieldwork in Educational Settings: Methods, Pitfalls and Perspectives.* London: Falmer.

Demeritt, D. (2001) The Construction of Global Warming and the Politics of Science. *Annals of the Association of American Geographers,* 91(2):307-337.

Denzin, N. and Keller, C. (1981) Frame Analysis Reconsidered. *Contemporary Sociology,* 10(1):52-60.

DeSombre, E. (2000) Flags of Convenience and the Enforcement of Environmental, Safety, and Labor Regulations at Sea. *International Politics,* 37:213-232.

Dickens, P. (1996) *Reconstructing nature: alienation, emancipation and the division of labour.* London: Routledge.

Donaldson, J. and Fafaliou, I. (2003) Business Ethics, Corporate Social Responsibility and Corporate Governance: A Review and Summary Critique. *European Research Studies,* 6(1-2):97-117.

Eden, S. (1998) Environmental issues: knowledge, uncertainty and the environment. *Progress in Human Geography,* 22(3):415-432.

Edley, N. (2001) Unravelling Social Constructionism. *Theory Psychology,* 11(3):433-441.

EEA (1999) State and Pressures of the Marine and Coastal Mediterranean Environment. Environmental Assessment Series No. 5.Copenhagen: European Environment Agency.

Ekberg, M. (2007) The Parameters of the Risk Society: A Review and Exploration. *Current Sociology,* 55(3):343-366.

Elliott, M. (2005) Risk Perception Frames in Environmental Decision Making. *Environmental Practice,* 5(3):214-222.

Entman, R. (1993) Framing: Toward clarification of a fractured paradigm. *Journal of Communication,* 43(4):51-58.

Equasis (2007) *Equasis Data Base*. Available at: <URL: http://www.equasis.org/EquasisWeb/public/About?fs=HomePage> [Accessed: 5th February 2008]

Essary, E. H. (2007) Speaking of Globalization: Frame Analysis and the World Society. *International Journal of Comparative Sociology*, 46(6):509-526.

Fafaliou, I., Lekakou, M. and Theotokas, I. (2006) Is the European shipping industry aware of corporate social responsibility? The case of the Greek-owned short sea shipping companies. *Marine Policy*, 30(4):412-419.

Fineman, S. and Sturdy, A. (1999) The Emotions of Control: A Qualitative Exploration of Environmental Regulation. *Human Relations*, 52(5):631-663.

Fingas, M. and E. Brown, C. (2007) Oil spill remote sensing: A forensic approach Oil Spill Environmental Forensics. Burlington: Academic Press.

Fisher, K. (1997) *Locating Frames in the Discursive Universe*. Available at: <URL: http://www.socresonline.org.uk/socresonline/2/3/4.html> [Accessed: 10th November 2006]

Fletcher, C. (1990) The Relationships Between Candidate Personality, Self-Presentation Strategies, and Interviewer Assessments in Selection Interviews: An Empirical Study. *Human Relations*, 43(8):739-749.

Frame, B. and Brown, J. (2008) Developing post-normal technologies for sustainability. *Ecological Economics*, 65(2):225-241.

Futoran, G. C., Kelly, J. R. and McGrath, J. E. (1989) TEMPO: A Time-based System for Analysis of Group Interaction Process. *Basic and Applied Social Psychology*, 10(3):211-232.

Gallagher, J. J. (2002) The Application of Strict Criminal Liabilities to Spillage of Oil: The Practical Impact on Effective Spill Response. *Spill Science and Technology Bulletin*, 7(1-2):39-44.

Gamson, W. (1975) Frame Analysis: Book Review. *Contemporary Sociology*, 4(6):603-607.

Gamson, W. (1992) *Talking politics*. Cambridge, New York: Cambridge University Press.

Gamson, W. (1995) Constructing Social Protest. In: Johnston, H. and Klandermans, B. (eds.) *Social Movements and Culture*. London: UCL Press.

Gardener, R. and Burgess, G. (2003) Analysis of Colorado Growth Conflict Frames. In: Lewicki, R., Gray, B. and Elliott, M. (eds.) *Making Sense of Intractable Environmental Conflicts*. London: Island Press, pp. 387-405.

GESAMP (2006) Updated memorandum of 1994 on the joint group of experts on the scientific aspects of marine environmental protection. Available at: <URL: http://gesamp.imo.org/gesamp.htm> [Accessed: 15th July 2006]

Giddens, A. (1984) *The constitution of society: outline of the theory of structuration*. Cambridge: Polity Press.

Giddens, A. (1990) *The Consequences of Modernity*. Cambridge: Polity Press.

Giddens, A. (1991) *Modernity and Self-identity: Self and Society in the late Modern Age*. Stanford, California: Stanford University Press.

Giddens, A. (1994a) *Beyond Left and Right: The Future of Radical Politics*. Stanford: Polity Press.

Giddens, A. (1994b) Living in a Post-Traditional Society. In: Beck, U. (ed.) *Reflexive Modernisation: Politics, Tradition and Aesthetics in the Modern Social Order*. Cambridge: Polity Press, pp. 56-109.

Giddens, A. (1998) *The Third Way: Renewal of Social Democracy*. London: Polity Press.

Giddens, A. (1999) Risk and Responsibility. *Modern Law Review*, 62(1):1-10.

Giddens, A. (2009) *The Politics of Climate Change*. Cambridge: Polity Press.

GISIS (2008) *Port Reception Facilities*. Available at: <URL: http://gisis.imo.org/Public/PRF/SearchAdvanced.aspx> [Accessed: 20th December 2006]

Glaser, B. and Strauss, A. (1967) *The Discovery of Grounded Theory: Strategies for Qualitative Research*. Chicago: Aldine.

Goffman, E. (1974) *Frame Analysis: An Essay on the Organization of Experience*. Cambridge, Massachusetts: Harvard University Press.

Gold, E. 2005. The Fair Treatment of Seafarers. *WMU Journal of Maritime Affairs*, 4:129-130.

Gouldson, A. and Murphy, J. 1997. Ecological modernisation: restructuring industrial economies. In: Jacobs, M. ed. *Greening the Millennium?* Oxford: Blackwell.

Granitz, N. A. and Ward, J. C. 2001. Actual and Perceived Sharing of Ethical Reasoning and Moral Intent Among In-Group and Out-Group Members. *Journal of Business Ethics*, 33(4):299-322.

Gray, B. (2003) Framing of Environmental Disputes. In: Lewicki, R., Gray, B. and Elliott, M. (eds.) *Making Sense of Intractable Environmental Conflicts*. London: Island Press, pp. 11-34.

Gray, B. and Putnam, L. L. (2005) Means to What End? Conflict Management Frames. *Environmental Practice*, 5(3):239-246.

Gray, D. E. (2004) *Doing Research in the Real World*. London: Sage Publications.

Gray, J. R. and Sims, M. D. (1997) Management system audits for ship operators - The auditor's experience. *International Maritime Technology*, 109(3):233-255.

Grosso, J. M. and Waldron, J. K. (eds.) (2005) *Trends in criminal enforcement in the marine industry: More targets and expanding theories of liability*. 2005 International Oil Spill Conference, IOSC 2005.

Grotius, H. (1916) *Freedom of the Seas*. London: Oxford University Press.

Guillemin, M. and Gillam, L. (2004) Ethics, Reflexivity, and "Ethically Important Moments" in Research. *Qualitative Inquiry,* 10(2):261-280.

Gunningham, N. (2007) Designing OSH Standards: process, safety case and best practice. *Policy and Practice in Health and Safety,* 5(2):3-24.

Hacking, I. (2000) *The social construction of what?* Cambridge, Massachusetts: Harvard University Press.

Haines, F. and Sutton, A. (2003) The engineer's dilemma: A sociological perspective on juridificaton and regulation. *Crime, Law and Social Change,* 39(1):1-22.

Hajer, M. A. (1997) *The Politics of Environmental Discourse: Ecological Modernization and the Policy Process*. Oxford: Oxford University Press.

Hammersley, M. (1984) The Researcher Exposed: A Natural History. In: Burgess, R. (ed.) *The Research Process in Educational Settings: Ten Case Studies*. London: Falmer, pp. 39-67.

Hanke, R. Rosenberg, A. Gray, B. (2003) The Story of Drake Chemical; A Burning Issue. In: Lewicki, R., Gray, B. and Elliott, M. (eds.) *Making Sense of Intractable Environmental Conflicts*. London: Island Press, pp. 275-302.

Haralambides, H. (ed.) (1998) *Quality shipping: market mechanisms for safer shipping and cleaner oceans*. Rotterdam: Erasmus Publishing.

Haralambides, H. E. and Yang, J. (2003) A fuzzy set theory approach to flagging out: towards a new Chinese shipping policy. *Marine Policy,* 27(1):13-22.

Hawkins, K. (1984) *Environment and Enforcement: Regulation and the Social Definition of pollution*. Oxford: Oxford University Press.

Hed, B. (2005) *Criminalisation of Seafarers*. Available at: <URL: http://www.swedishclub.com/upload/18/2005-1.pdf> [Accessed: 15th February 2007]

Held, D. (2000) The Changing structure of International Law. In: Held, D. and McGrew, A. (eds.) *The Global Transformations Reader: an introduction to the globalization debate*. Cambridge: Polity Press, pp. 162-176.

Held, D., Goldblatt, D. and Perraton, J. (1999) *Global Transformations: Politics, Economics and Culture*. Cambridge: Polity Press.

Heller, F. (1997) Sociotechnology and the Environment. *Human Relations,* 50(5):605-624.

Hopf, C. (2004) Research Ethics and Qualitative Research. In: Flick, U., von Kardoff, E. and Steinke, I. (eds.) *A Companion to Qualitative Research*. London: Sage Publications, pp. 334-339.

Hopkins, A. and Wilkinson, P. (2005) *Safety Case Regulation for the Mining Industry* Australian National University. Available at: <URL: http://ohs.anu.edu.au/publications/pdf/wp%2037%20-%20Hopkins(2).pdf> [Accessed: 21st December 2008]

Hung, C. F. and Chen, C. P. (2007) The approximate method to predicate the crashworthiness of ship double hull structures. *Journal of Taiwan Society of Naval Architects and Marine Engineers,* 26(3):139-150.

ILO (2004) *The Global Seafarer: Living and Working Conditions in a Globalised Industry*. Geneve: International Labour Office.

ILO (2006) *94th. (Maritime) session of the International Labour Conference*. Available at: <URL: http://www.ilo.org/public/english/dialogue/sector/sectors/mariti.htm> [Accessed: 10th April 2006]

IMO (1990) Petroleum in the Marine Environment. Document MEPC 30/INF. 13 submitted by the United States. London: International Maritime Organization.

IMO (2002) *MARPOL 73/78 : articles, protocols, annexes, unified interpretations of the International Convention for the Prevention of Pollution from Ships, 1973, as modified by the protocol of 1978 relating thereto*. Consolidated ed., London: IMO.

IMO (2006a) March 2006 CAB. *Current Awareness bulletin*, p. 4.

IMO (2006b) *MARPOL 73/78: articles, protocols, annexes, unified interpretations of the International Convention for the Prevention of Pollution from Ships, 1973, as modified by the protocol of 1978 relating thereto*. Consolidated ed., London: IMO.

IMO (2006c) *Sub-Committee on Flag State Implementation (FSI) Agendas*. Available at: <URL: http://www.imo.org/home.asp> [Accessed: 10th April 2006]

Inglehart, R. (1995) Public Support for Environmental Protection: Objective Problems and Subjective Values in 43 Societies. *Political Science and Politics*, 28(1):57-72.

International Oil Spill Conference (1999) *International Oil Spill Conference Proceedings*. Seattle: API.

ITF (2005) Seafarers' Bulletin, No.19/2005. London: International Transport Workers' Federation.

Jeon, Y.-H. (2004) The application of grounded theory and symbolic interactionism. *Scandinavian Journal of Caring Sciences*, 18(3):249-256.

Johnson, D. W. and Johnson, F. P. (2000) *Joining together: group theory and group skills*. 7th. ed. Boston: Allyn and Bacon.

Kaufman, S. (2003) *Frames, Framing and Reframing* Conflict Research Consortium, University of Colorado. Available at: <URL: http://www.beyondintractability.org/essay/framing/> [Accessed: 15th November 2006]

Khee, A. and Tan, J. (2005) *Vessel Source Marine Pollution: The Law and Politics of International Regulation*. Cambridge: Cambridge University Press.

Kim, I. (2007) "Milking" oil tankers: The paradoxical effect of the Oil Pollution Act of 1990. *Natural Resources Journal,* 47(4):849-866.

Kim, I. (2003) A comparison between the international and US regimes regulating oil pollution liability and compensation. *Marine Policy,* 27(3):265-279.

Kimerling, J. (2001) Corporate ethics in the era of globalization: The promise and peril of international environmental standards. *Journal of Agricultural and Environmental Ethics,* 14(4):425-455.

Kimmel, A. (1988) *Ethics and Values in Applied Social Research*. London: Sage publications.

Knapp, S. and Franses, P. H. (2007) A global view on port state control: econometric analysis of the differences across port state control regimes. *Maritime Policy and Management* 34(5):453-482.

Koenig, T. (2006) Compounding mixed-methods problems in frame analysis through comparative research. *Qualitative Research,* 6(1):61-76.

Kohlbacher, F. (2006) The use of qualitative content analysis in case study research. *Forum Qualitative Sozialforschung,* 7(1): Art. 21.

Lane, T. (2000) *The global seafarers' labour market: Problems and solutions* Available at: <URL: http://www.icons.org.au/images/93SIRC.pdf> [Accessed: 10th April 2006]

Lash, S. (1994) Reflexivity and its Doubles: Structure, Aesthetics, Community. In: Beck, U. (ed.) *Reflexive Modernisation*. Cambridge: Polity Press, pp. 110-173.

Lash, S. (2000) Risk Culture. In: Adam, B., Beck, U. and Van Loon, J. (eds.) *The Risk Society and Beyond: Critical Issues for Social Theory*. London: Sage.

Lash, S. and Urry, J. (1994) *Economies of signs and space*. London: Sage.

Leschine, T. M. (2002) Oil Spills and the Social Amplification and Attenuation of Risk. *Spill Science and Technology Bulletin,* 7(1-2):63-73.

Levy, M. Haas, M., and Keohane, R. (1993) Improving the Effectiveness of International Environmental Agreements. In: Haas, P. et al. eds. *Institutions of the Earth: Sources of Effective International Environmental Protection*. Cambridge, Massachusetts: MIT Press.

Lewicki, R., Grey, B. and Elliot, M (eds.) (2003) *Making Sense of Intractable Environmental Conflicts*. London: Island Press.

Li, K. X. and Zheng, H. (2008) Enforcement of Law by the Port State Control (PSC). *Maritime Policy and Management,* 35(1):61-71.

Lidskog, R. and Sundqvist, G. (2004) From consensus to credibility. *Innovation: The European Journal of Social Science Research,* 17(3):205-226.

Lillie, N. (2004) Global Collective Bargaining on Flag of Convenience Shipping. *British Journal of Industrial Relations,* 42(1):47-67.

Lin, B. and Lin, C.-Y. (2006) Compliance with international emission regulations: Reducing the air pollution from merchant vessels. *Marine Policy,* 30(3):220-225.

LLOYD'S LIST (2006a) 'PGM's $1.5m fine for oily water separator violations'. *LLOYD'S LIST*. 3 July 2006. p. 3.

LLOYD'S LIST (2006b) 'US fines Wallenius $6.5m for pollution'. *LLOYD'S LIST*. 24 March 2006. p. 3.

Lomborg, B. (2001) *The skeptical environmentalist : measuring the real state of the world.* Cambridge: Cambridge University Press.

Lumbers, K. (2006) *Marine Pollution Prevention: Reducing the Risk of Port State Control Detentions.* London: Lloyd's Register / UK P&I Club.

Lupton, D. and Tulloch, J. (2002) `Risk is Part of Your Life': Risk Epistemologies Among a Group of Australians. *Sociology,* 36(2):317-334.

Lutzen, K., Cronqvist, A. and Magnusson, A. (2003) Moral stress: Synthesis of a concept. *Nursing Ethics,* 10(3):312-322.

MacPhee, B. (2007) Hitchhikers' guide to the Ballast Water Management Convention: an analysis of legal mechanisms to address the issue of alien invasive species. *Journal of International Wildlife Law and Policy*, 10(1):29-54.

Manning, P. (1977) Frame Analysis. *The American Journal of Sociology,* 82(6):1361-1364.

Matten, D. (2004) The impact of the risk society thesis on environmental politics and management in a globalizing economy - Principles, proficiency, perspectives. *Journal of Risk Research,* 7(4):377-398.

Mattson, G. (2006) MARPOL 73/78 and Annex I: an assessment of its effectiveness. (International Convention for the Prevention of Pollution from Ships). *Journal of International Wildlife Law and Policy,* 9(2):175-194.

May, C., Gaska, L. and Atkinsona, T. (2001) Resisting and promoting new technologies in clinical practice: the case of telepsychiatry. *Social Science and Medicine,* 52(12):1889-1901.

Mayring, P. (2004) Qualitative Content Analysis. In: Flick, U., von Kardoff, E. and Steinke, I. (eds.) *A Companion to Qualitative Research.* London: Sage, pp. 266-269.

McConnell, M. (2002) Capacity building for a sustainable shipping industry: a key ingredient in improving coastal and ocean and management. *Ocean and Coastal Management,* 45(9-10):617-632.

McKechnie, R. and Welsh, I. (2002) When the Global Meets the Local: Critical Reflections on Reflexive Modernisation. In: Dunlap, R., Buttel, F. H., Dickens, P. and Gijswijt, A. (eds.) *Sociological Theory and the Environment.* Oxford: Rowman & Littlefield Publishers.

Meng, Q.-N. (1987) *Land-Base Marine Pollution: International Law Development.* Boston: Martinus Nijhoff Publishers.

Meyer, C. B. (2001) A case in Case Study Methodology. *Field Methods,* 13(4):329-352.

M'Gonigle, R. and Zacher, M. (1979) *Pollution, Politics and International Law: Tankers at Sea.* Los Angeles: University of California Press.

Mills, J., Bonner, A. and Francis, K. (2006) Adopting a constructivist approach to grounded theory: Implications for research design. *International Journal of Nursing Practice,* 12:8-13.

Mitchell, R. (1994a) *Intentional Oil Pollution at Sea: Environmental Policy and Treaty Compliance.* Cambridge, Massachusetts: MIT Press.

Mitchell, R. (1994) Regime Design Matters: Intentional Oil Pollution and Treaty Compliance. *International Organisation,* 48(3):425-458.

Mitchell, R. (1994) Heterogeneities at Two Levels: States, Non-State Actors and Intentional Oil Pollution. *Journal of Theoretical Politics,* 6(4):625-653.

Mitchell, R. (1998) Sources of Transparency: Information Systems in International Regimes. *International Studies Quarterly*, 42(1):109-130.

Mol, A. P. J. (1995) *The Refinement of Production: Ecological Modernisation Theory and the Chemical Industry*. Utrecht: International.

Mol, A. P. J. (1997) Ecological Modernisation: Industrial Transformations and Environmental Reform. In: Readclift, M. and Woodgate, G. (eds.) *The International Handbook of Environmental Sociology*. Cheltenham: Edward Elgar.

Mol, A. P. J. (2000) Globalization and environment: between apocalypse-blindness and ecological modernization. In: Spaargaren, G., Mol, A. P. J. and Buttel, F. H. (eds.) *Environment and Global Modernity*. London: Sage, pp. 121-150.

Mol, A. P. J. (2001) *Globalization and Environmental Reform: The Ecological Modernization of the Global Economy*. Cambridge, Massachusetts: MIT Press.

Morris, H. (2002) *Globalisation affects today's seafarers*. Available at: <URL: http://www.icons.org.au/pdfs/Speech_021001.pdf> [Accessed: 15th February 2007]

Mullen, B. and Hu, L.-T. (1989) Perceptions of Ingroup and Outgroup Variability: A Meta-Analytic Integration. *Basic and Applied Social Psychology*, 10(3):233-252.

Munnichs, G. (2004) Whom to Trust? Public Concerns, Late Modern Risks, and Expert Trustworthiness. *Journal of Agricultural and Environmental Ethics*, 17(2):113.

Obando-Rojas, B., Welsh, I., Bloor, M., Lane, T., Badigannavar, V. and Maguire, M. (2004) The political economy of fraud in a globalised industry: the case of seafarers' certifications. *The Sociological Review*, 52(3):295-313.

Oberthür, S. (2003) Institutional interaction to address greenhouse gas emissions from international transport: ICAO, IMO and the Kyoto Protocol. *Climate Policy*, 3(3):191-205.

OECD (2002) *Regulator Issues in International Maritime Transport*. Available at: <URL: www.oecd.org> [Accessed: 15th March 2006]

Olausson, U. (2009) Global warming--global responsibility? Media frames of collective action and scientific certainty. *Public Understanding of Science*, p. 0963662507081242.

Orlikowski, W. J. and Gash, D. C. (1994) Technological frames: making sense of information technology in organizations. *ACM Transactions on Information Systems*, 12(2):174-207.

Ormrod, J. E. (2004) *Human learning*. 4th ed. New York: Merrill.

Palvakis, P., Tarki, D., Sieber, A. J., Guido, F, and Vincent, G. (2001) On the Monitoring of Illicit Vessel Discharges: A reconnaissance Study in the Mediterranean Sea. Brussels: Directorate of Environmental Quality of natural Resources, European Commission.

Perri 6 (2005) What's in a frame? Social organization, risk perception and the sociology of knowledge. *Journal of Risk Research*, 8(2):91-118.

Pisani, C. (2002) Fair at sea: The design of a future legal instrument on marine bunker fuels emissions within the climate change regime. *Ocean Development and International Law*, 33(1):57-76.

Poortinga, W. and Pidgeon, N. F. (2003) Exploring the dimensionality of trust in risk regulation. *Risk Analysis*, 23(5):961-972.

Poortinga, W. and Pidgeon, N. F. (2005) Trust in Risk Regulation: Cause or Consequence of the Acceptability of GM Food? *Risk Analysis*, 25(1):199-209.

Poortinga, W. and Pidgeon, N. F. (2006) Prior attitudes, salient value similarity, and dimensionality: Toward an integrative model of trust in risk regulation. *Journal of Applied Social Psychology*, 36(7):1674-1700.

Power, M. (1997) *The Audit Society: Rituals of Verification*. New York: Oxford University Press.

Pritchard, S. (1985) *Oil Pollution Control*. London: Croom Helm.

Punch, M. (1986) *Politics and Ethics of Field Work*. London: Sage Publications.

Raftopoulos, E. (2001) "Relational Governance" for marine pollution incidents in the Mediterranean: Transformations, development and prospects. *International Journal of Marine and Coastal Law,* 16(1):41-76.

Rantanen, T. (2005) Giddens and the 'G'-word: An interview with Anthony Giddens. *Global Media and Communication,* 1(1):63-77.

Rapley, T. (2004) Interviews. In: Clive Seale, G.G., Jaber, F. and Gubrium, D. S. (ed.) *Qualitative Research Practice*. London: Sage, pp. 15-34.

Reynolds, K. J., Turner, J. C. and Haslam, S. A. (2000) When Are We Better Than Them and They Worse Than Us? A Closer Look at Social Discrimination. *Journal of Personality and Social Psychology,* 78(1):64-80.

Rice, G. (2006) Pro-environmental behaviour in Egypt: Is there a role for Islamic environmental ethics? *Journal of Business Ethics,* 65(4):373-390.

Richards, J. P., Glegg, G. A. and Cullinane, S. (2000) Environmental regulation: Industry and the marine environment. *Journal of Environmental Management,* 58(2):119-134.

Rose, H. (2000) Risk, Trust and Scepticism in the Age of the New Genetics. In: Adam, B., Beck, U. and Van Loon, J. (eds.) *The Risk Society and Beyond: Critical Issues for Social Theory*. London: Sage.

Sahatjian, L. (ed.) (1998) *International Oil Spill Conference*. APA.

Sampson, H. (2004) Navigating the waves: the usefulness of a pilot in qualitative research. *Qualitative Research,* 4(3):383-402.

Sampson H. and Bloor, M. (2012) 'The effectiveness of Global Regulation in the shipping industry: a critical case study'. *Revista Latino-americana de Estudos do Trabalho (RELET),* 17(28):45-72.

Sampson, H., Ellis, N., Gould. E., Tang, L., Turgo, N. and Zhao, Z. (2012) 'Safety and Shipping 1912-2012', Report commissioned by Allianz which underpins their subsequent publication 'Safety and Shipping 1912-2012: From Titanic to Costa Concordia, an insurer's perspective from Allianz Global Corporate and Specialty' available from Allianz GCS.

Sampson, H., Gekara, V.O. and Bloor, M. (2011) Water-tight or sinking? A consideration of the standards of the contemporary assessment practices underpinning seafarer licence examinations and their implications for employers. *Maritime Policy and Management,* 38(1):81-92.

Sampson, H. (2011) Spilling oil, spilling blood: Cost and corporate decision making concerning safe working practices. *Policy and Practice in Health and Safety,* 9(1):17-32.

Schaeffer, N. and Maynard, D. (2001) Standardization and Interaction in the Survey Interview. In: Gubrium, J. and Holstein, J. (eds.) *Handbook of Interview Research.* Sage Publications, pp. 578-585.

Schwarzwald, J., Koslowsky, M. and Allouf, M. (2005) Group Membership, Status, and Social Power Preference. *Journal of Applied Social Psychology,* 35(3):644-665.

Selkou, E. and Roe, M. (2004) *Globalisation, Policy and Shipping.* Cheltenham: Edward Edgar Publishing.

Silverman, D. (2001) *Interpreting Qualitative Data: Methods for Analysing Talk, Text and Interaction.* London: Sage Publications.

Singhota, G. S. (1995) IMO's role in promoting oil spill preparedness. *Spill Science and Technology Bulletin,* 2(4):207-215.

Smith, H. D. (2002) The role of the social sciences in capacity building in ocean and coastal management. *Ocean and Coastal Management,* 45(9-10):573-582.

Snow, D., Burke Rochford Jr, E., Worden, S. and Benford, R. D. (1986) Frame Alignment Processes, Micromobilisation, and Movement Participation. *American Sociological Review,* 51(4):464-481.

Stamm, K. R., Clark, F. and Reynolds Eblacas, P. (2000) Mass communication and public understanding of environmental problems: The case of global warming. *Public Understanding of Science,* 9(3):219-237.

Steinberg, P. (2001) *The Social Construction of the Sea.* Cambridge: Cambridge University Press.

Stets, J. E. and Biga, C. F. (2003) Bringing Identity Theory into Environmental Sociology. *Sociological Theory,* 21(4):398-423.

Strauss, A. and Corbin, J. (1998) *Basics of Qualitative Research: Techniques and Procedures for Developing Grounded Theory.* 2nd. ed. London: Sage.

Suarez de Vivero, J. L. and Rodriguez Mateos, J. C. (2004) New factors in ocean governance. From economic to security-based boundaries. *Marine Policy,* 28(2):185-188.

Talley, W. K. (2007) Earnings differentials of seafarers. *Journal of Labour Research,* 28(3):515-524.

Tang, L. and Sampson, H. (2012) The interaction between mass media and the Internet in non-democratic states: the case of China. *Media Culture and Society,* 34(4):457-471.

Tang, L. and Sampson, H. (2011) 'Training and Technology: Findings from the Questionnaire Study', SIRC Symposium, Cardiff University, 6-7th July.

Tarui, N. and Polasky, S. (2005) Environmental regulation with technology adoption, learning and strategic behaviour. *Journal of Environmental Economics and Management*, 50(3):447-467.

Tatman, A. K. (2005) Development of a human element assessment tool (HEAT) for the maritime industry. *RINA, Royal Institution of Naval Architects International Conference - Human Factors in Ship Design, Safety and Operation*, pp. 133-141.

Taylor, D. E. (2000) The Rise of the Environmental Justice Paradigm: Injustice Framing and the Social Construction of Environmental Discourses. *American Behavioural Scientist*, 43(4):508-580.

Tesh, S. N. (1999) Citizen experts in environmental risk. *Policy Sciences*, 32(1):39-58.

Tillet, G. (1991) *Resolving conflict: a practical approach*. Sydney: Sydney University Press.

Trbojevic, V. M. (2006) Risk Criteria for the Shipping Industry. *Quality and Reliability Engineering International*, 22(1):31-40.

Turgo, N., Sampson, H., Acejo, I., Ellis, N. and Tang, L. (2013) 'Understanding the Relationships between Ship and Shore Personnel', SIRC Symposium, Cardiff University 3-4th July.

UNCLOS (1983) *U.N. Convention on the Law of the Sea, 1982*. New York: Oceana.

Vallega, A. (2001) Ocean governance in post-modern society--a geographical perspective. *Marine Policy*, 25(6):399-414.

Van de Voorde, E. E. M. (2005) What Future the Maritime Sector?: Some Considerations on Globalisation. In: Adib Kanafani, K.K. (ed.) *Global Competition in Transportation Markets: Analysis and Policy Making*. Volume 13 ed. JAI, pp. 253-277.

Van Dyke, J., Zaelke, D. and Hewison, G. (1993) *Freedom for the Seas in the 21st Century*. Washington D.C.: Island Press.

Van Leeuwen, S. (2004) Auditing international environmental agreements: The role of Supreme Audit Institutions. *Environmentalist,* 24(2):93-99.

Van Loon, J. (2000) Virtual Risks in an Age of Cybernetic Reproduction. In: Adam, B., Beck, U. and Van Loon, J. (eds.) *The Risk Society and Beyond: Critical Issues for Social Theory*. London: Sage.

Vanderzwaag, D. (2002) The precautionary principle and marine environmental protection: Slippery shores, rough seas, and rising normative tides. *Ocean Development and International Law,* 33(2):165-188.

Vela (2008) *Standards and Values*. Available at: <URL: http://www.vela.ae/-Standards-&-Values-Vela10.html> [Accessed: 15th July 2006]

Videotel (2008a) *Marine Training Catalogue*. London: Videotel.

Videotel (2008b) *STCW Computer-based Assessment and Training: ENVIRONMENTAL OFFICER TRAINING COURSE*. Available at: <URL: http://www.videotel.co.uk/catalogue/S09_18.asp> [Accessed: 20th July 2006]

Wadsworth, E. J. K., Howard, A.P., Kirsty, E.J., Wellens, B., McNamara, R. and Smith, P. (2006) Patterns of fatigue among seafarers during a tour of duty. *American Journal of Industrial Medicine,* 49(10):836-844.

Walters, D. (2009) 'Supply chains and best practice in the management of health and safety', SIRC Symposium 2009, Cardiff, 8- 9th July, ISBN 1-900174-37-5.

Walters, D., Bhattacharya, S. and Xue, C. (2011) 'Managing Health and Safety through the Supply Chain: A Case Study of Supply Chain Influence in the Shipping Industry', SIRC Symposium, Cardiff University, 6-7th July, ISBN 1-900174-39-1.

Walters, D., Wadsworth, E.J.K., Sampson, H. and James, P. (2012) 'The Limits of Influence: the role of supply chains in influencing health and safety management in two sectors', report submitted to the IOSH Research Committee, www.iosh.co.uk/research reports.

Walters, D. and Sampson, H. (2013) 'Supply Chain Leverage and Health and Safety Management in Shipping – The Case of the Container Trade' SIRC Symposium, Cardiff University 3-4th July.

Webb, J. (2004) Organizations, self-identities and the new economy. *Sociology,* 38(4):719-738.

Webster, A. (2004) State of the art: Risk, science and policy - Researching the social management of uncertainty. *Policy Studies,* 25(1):5-18.

Weinberg, J. M. and Kleinman, K. P. (2003) Good study design and analysis plans as features of ethical research with humans. *IRB; a review of human subjects research,* 25(5):11-14.

Wells, P. G., Duce, R. A. and Huber, M. E. (2002) Caring for the sea--accomplishments, activities and future of the United Nations GESAMP (the Joint Group of Experts on the Scientific Aspects of Marine Environmental Protection). *Ocean and Coastal Management* 45(1):77-89.

Wells, P. G., Höfer, T. and Nauke, M. (1999) Evaluating the hazards of harmful substances carried by ships: The role of GESAMP and its EHS working group. *The Science of the Total Environment,* 237-238:329-350.

Welsh, I. (2000a) *Mobilising Modernity: The Nuclear Moment.* London: Routledge.

248

Welsh, I. (2000b) Nuclear Risks: Three problematics. In: Adam, B., Beck, U. and Van Loon, J. (eds.) *The Risk Society and Beyond: Critical Issues for Social Theory*. London: Sage.

Welsh, I. and Chesters, G. (2001) *Re-Framing Social Movements: Margins, Meanings and Governance*. Cardiff University. Available at: <URL:http://www.cardiff.ac.uk/schoolsanddivisions/academicschools/socsi/publications/wor kingpaperseries/numeric-11-20.html> [Accessed: 15th October 2007]

Wildavsky, A. (1997) *But is it True?: Citizen's Guide to Environmental Health and Safety Issues*. Cambridge, Massachusetts: Harvard University Press.

Willemyns, M., Gallois, C. and Callan, V. J. (2003) Trust me, I'm your boss: trust and power in supervisor-supervisee communication. *International Journal of Human Resource Management*, 14(1):117-127.

Winchester, N., Lillie, N., Greer, I., Hauptmeier, M. and Anner, M. (2006) Industrial Determinants of Transnational Solidarity: Global Union Politics in Shipping, Autos and Apparel. *European Journal of Industrial Relations*, 12(1):7-27.

Wonham, J. (1998) Agenda 21 and sea-based pollution: Opportunity or apathy? *Marine Policy*, 22(4-5):375-391.

Woodgate, G. and Redclift, M. (1998) From a 'sociology of nature' to environmental sociology: Beyond social construction. *Environmental Values*, 7(1):3-24.

Yearley, S. (1996) *Sociology, Environmentalism, Globalization*. London: Sage.

Yin, R. (2003) *Case Study Research: Design and Methods*. 3rd, Edition ed. California: Sage Publications.

Young, S. C. (2000) The Origins and Evolving Nature of Ecological Modernisation. In: Young, S.C. (ed.) *The Emergence of Ecological Modernisation: Integrating the Environment and the Economy?* London: Routledge, pp. 1-39.

Zhao, M. and Amante, M. S. V. (2005) Chinese and Filipino seafarers: A race to the top or the bottom? *Modern Asian Studies*, 39(3):535-557.

Zheng, Y., Aksu, S., Vassalos, D. and Tuzcu, C. (2007) Study on side structure resistance to ship-ship collisions. *Ships and Offshore Structures,* 2(3):273-293.

Zhu, J. (2006) Asia and IMO technical cooperation. *Ocean and Coastal Management,* 49(9-10):627-636.

APPENDIX ONE

Main Field Respondents and Categorisation of Shipping Companies

I: Seafarers interviewed on board their tanker ships whilst in port (Milford haven and Cardiff).

Resp. No.	Date of Interview	Nationality	Rank	Respondent Code/Category	Flag	Trading Area
1M	12th May 2007	German	Master	D1R/C2	Isle of Man	EU Waters
2M	12th May 2007	Filipino	2nd.Eng.	E2R/C2	Isle of Man	EU Waters
3M	12th May 2007	Filipino	Pump Man	R3R/C2	Isle of Man	EU Waters
4M	14th May 2007	Swedish	Master	D4RO/C2	Sweden	EU Waters and Ocean going
5M	14th May 2007	Filipino	2nd.Off.	D5RO/C2	Sweden	EU Waters and Ocean going
6M	15th May 2007	British	Chief Off.	D6C/C2	Liberia	Coastal EU Waters
7M	15th May 2007	Filipino	Bosun	R7C/C2	Liberia	EU Waters
8M	26th May 2007	Swedish	Chief Eng.	E8RO/C2	Sweden	EU Waters and Ocean going
9M	26th May 2007	Swedish	Chief Off.	D9RO/C2	Sweden	EU Waters and Ocean going
10M	26th May 2007	Filipino	2nd.Eng.	E10RO/C2	Sweden	EU Waters and Ocean going
11M	13th June 2007	Filipino	Chief Off.	D11R/C2	Sweden	EU Waters
12M	13th June 2007	Filipino	2nd Eng.	E12R/C2	Sweden	EU Waters
13M	18th June 2007	Norwegian	Master	D13O/C2	Norway	Ocean going
14M	18th June 2007	Filipino	Chief Eng.	E14O/C2	Norway	Ocean going
15M	18th June 2007	Norwegian	Chief Off.	D15O/C2	Norway	Ocean going
16M	18th June 2007	Russian	2nd Off.	D16O/C1	Liberia	Ocean going
17M	18th June 2007	Russian	Master	D17O/C1	Liberia	Ocean going
18M	19th June 2007	Greek	2nd Off.	D18O/C2	Greece	Ocean going
19M	19th June 2007	Greek	Chief Off.	D19O/C2	Greece	Ocean going

II: Respondents interviewed whilst attending short and professional courses at the AASTMT – Alexandria – Egypt.

Resp. No.	Date of Interview	Nationality	Rank	Respondent Code/Category	Flag	Trading Area
20M	22th July 2007	Nigerian	Chief Off	D20O/C3	FOC	W. Africa and EU Waters
21M	23rd July 2007	Kuwaiti	2nd Eng.	E21O/C1	National only	Ocean Going
22M	24th July 2007	Egyptian	Master	D22R/C1	National only	Mainly Gulf area
23M	24th July 2007	Egyptian	3rd Off.	D23C/C3	FOC	Coastal Gulf area
24M	25th July 2007	Egyptian	Master	D24R/C1	National only	Mainly Gulf area
25M	29th July 2007	Iraqi	Chief Eng.	E25O/C3	National and FOC	Ocean Going
26M	29th July 2007	Egyptian	Chief Off	D26C/C3	FOC	Coastal Gulf area
27M	29th July 2007	Egyptian	Master	D27O/C1	National only	Ocean Going
28M	31st July 2007	Iraqi	Chief Eng.	E28O/C3	FOC	Ocean Going
29M	31st July 2007	Sudanese	Chief Eng.	E29R/C3	FOC	Mainly Gulf area
30M	1st Aug 2007	Egyptian	Master.	D30C/C3	FOC	Coastal Gulf area
31M	5th Aug 2007	Egyptian	3rd Eng.	E31O/C1	National and FOC	Ocean Going
32M	6th Aug 2007	Egyptian	3rd Off.	D32O/C1	National Only	Ocean going
33M	12th Aug 2007	Saudi	3rd Off.	D33O/C1	National and FOC	Ocean going
34M	13th Aug 2007	Saudi	3rd Off.	D34O/C1	National and FOC	Ocean going
35M	14th Aug 2007	Saudi	3rd Off.	D35O/C1	National and FOC	Ocean going
36M	15th Aug 2007	Saudi	3rd Off.	D36O/C1	National and FOC	Ocean going
37M	26th Aug 2007	Egyptian	3rd Off.	D37O/C1	National Only	Ocean going
38M	27th Aug 2007	Kuwaiti	2nd Off	D38O/C1	National Only	Ocean going
39M	28th Aug 2007	Libyan	Chief Off	D39R/C2	FOC	US and Canadian waters
40M	28th Aug 2007	Syrian	Chief Off	D40O/C3	National and FOC	Ocean going

- For analytical purposes shipping companies of respondents were categorised in to three categories according to the following criteria:

1- According to the Ship's 'flag', whether it is a national flag or flagged to an open register country (i.e. FOC).
2- State or private/independent ownership.
3- Ownership origin (i.e. EU owner or developing country owner- state or private).

- Category one is for National Flags or established open registers, state owned, and essentially included in the INTERTANKO top 10 largest state owned Tanker Companies in the world (these are represented in this study with 3 companies and 14 out of 40 respondents – two refused to be recorded and excluded).
- Category two is for either national flags/ 2nd. EU registers/ established FOC when owned by private /independent owner or company registered in an EU country.
- Category three is for ships flying an open register flag (FOC) and owned by a non-EU company or independent owner.

(The rationale behind this grading choice will be highlighted in the methods chapter)

Respondent codes:

-For data presentation and discussion purposes each respondent was given a code indicative of his professional affiliation on board (i.e. Officer or Engineer), geographic scope of trade (i.e. regional , coastal or ocean going), and his ship/company grade explained above.
-Key to respondent codes is as follows: (e.g. D35O/C1 - E32O/C1 - R7C/C2)

D: indicates a deck Officer or Master
E: indicates an Engineer officer or Chief Engineer
R: Rating

- This is followed by the respondent's number and a letter indicative of scope of trading area;
O: indicates ocean going trading area (i.e. cross continents)

R: indicates regional trading area only (i.e. whether confined to the EU region or Gulf and red seas areas).

C: indicates coastal trade or bunkering operations confined to the coastal areas of one or more countries (i.e. whether in European coastal waters or Gulf and red sea areas). Two of the above letters indicates a ship trading in both scopes (e.g. E10RO indicates a respondent working on board a ship trading primarily in a regional zone and occasionally undertakes ocean going long voyages).

Finally the code may be followed by the respondent's company category where needed.

APPENDIX TWO

Participant Information Sheet

Title of Research Project: Seafarers and Growing Environmental Concerns: Risk, Trust, Regulation and Workplace Culture and Practice

Name of Researcher: Mohab Abou-Elkawam
Cardiff University – School of Social Sciences

Researcher Contact details:
Seafarers International Research Centre (SIRC)
Cardiff University, 52 Park Place, Cardiff, CF10 3AT   UK
Personal mobile phone: 07*********

Funding Body: The Nippon Foundation – Japan.

Part a: What is the Research Study About?

- The study is about the perceptions and reactions of shipping companies and seafarers towards marine environmental regulations. The study also seeks to verify the aims and objectives of these regulations and the achievement of compliance levels.

- The study seeks to explore the effect of the introduction of new regulations relating to the marine environment on the compliance levels of concerned shipping companies and seafarers on board ships trading worldwide.

- The study aims to identify problematic areas in the views of companies and seafarers to be able to fully comply with marine environmental regulations.

- The study explores the feedback of shipping companies and seafarers on their views about more practical means of enforcement and monitoring compliance to marine environmental regulations and conventions.

- The study will finally try to explore how the seafarers on various shipping companies think about the issue of protection and preservation of the marine environment in general.

The questions posed during the interview will revolve around the above mentioned issues.
The proposed interview should be around 45 Minutes to one hour.
The major outcomes of this research would be highlighted in the thesis of the researcher and publications in refereed academic journals (without any reference to specific personnel or company names).

Part B: Declaration to the Participants

- Individuals will not be identified in any publication/dissemination of the research findings without their written permission.
- All information collected during conversation/interviews will only be viewed by the researcher / his supervisor (if requested) and remain strictly confidential.

If you take part in the study you have the right to:

- Refuse to answer any particular question, and to withdraw from the study by notifying the researcher at any time and up to August 2008. (the time of submitting the thesis)
- Ask any further questions about the study that occurs to you during your participation. (refer to contact details of the researcher above)
- Request access to a copy transcript of your interview prior to its inclusion in the research data.

The School Ethics Officer (and also the Chair of the School Research Ethics Committee) is:
Professor Søren Holm
Cardiff Law School
Tel: +44 (0)29 208 75447
Fax: +44 (0)29 208 7409
Email: Holms@cf.ac.uk

(A copy to be kept by respondent)

APPENDIX THREE

Informed Consent Form

Title of Research Project: Seafarers and Growing Environmental Concerns: Risk, Trust, Regulation and Workplace Culture and Practice

Name of Researcher: Mohab Abou-Elkawam

Cardiff University – School of Social Sciences

As an informed participant of this research project, I understand that:

1. My participation is voluntary and I may cease to take part in this project at any time, without penalty.
2. I am aware of what my participation involves.
3. This research will be conducted and managed to maintain the anonymity of respondents and confidentiality of data and/or information offered in interview.
4. All my questions about the study have been satisfactorily answered.

I have read and understood the above, and give consent to participate:

Participant's Signature:_____ **Date:**_____

I have explained the above and answered all questions asked by the participant:

Researcher's Signature:_____ **Date:**_____

APPENDIX FOUR

Seafarers' Interview Schedule

Section one: Demographic Questions (All ranks)

1- Could you tell me, how long have you been working at sea in total?

2- How many years of these were with the company you are working with now?

3- What types of ships does your current company own?

4- What was the trading pattern of your last ship?

5- What was your last certificate of competency? (Last training course in case of ratings)?

6- From Which Maritime Education and Training institution did you have your latest training or certification?

7- What is your current rank? How long have you been in this rank?

8- Are you planning to continue working at sea for the rest of your working career? Why? Why not?

Section Two: Core Generalized Questions

In this section the questions will need to cover the social, cultural, technical and legal aspects of the marine pollution problem *(I thought about separating them each in a sub-section....but on second thoughts I decided to ask about these issues together to avoid making the respondent concentrate on talking on one aspect most of the interview...)*

1) Why do you think some seafarers are not complying with marine environmental conventions?

(....trying to unravel reasons for non-compliance from the seafarers' perspectives).

2) What do you feel when you hear criminalization of seafarers in the aftermath of accidents or incidents resulting in pollution to the marine or coastal environments?

(...exploring knowledge about such problem and how it could affect compliance to Marpol and ...potentially other environmental conventions).

3) Could you talk to me about the use of reception facilities by the ships in your company?

(…may open an account about the cost consciousness of the shipping company….with follow up could open a discussion about tensions between management ashore and management on board).

4) New satellite technologies are able now to detect pollution in the high seas…what is your comment about this?

(…whether they believe directly that this is achievable and shift frames…or suspect….unravels seafarers' trust or distrust in technology)

5) What do you think about the current international system of regulating the issue of marine pollution?

(…with some follow up about Marpol…knowledge and competence issues about regulations and how could it be improved from their views….the issue of consulting the regulatees raised before!)

6) Could you talk to me more about your daily duties in relation to compliance to Marpol requirements? <u>For Ratings</u>: how do you get the orders about your daily duties in relation to compliance to Marpol? Are you being supervised while carrying out such duties?

(…To try answering the question of….is the technology the problem or the people using it?).

7) Have you read the Marpol text….what do you think about it? <u>For Staff only.</u>

(…To explore the level of knowledge of statutory requirements….or lack of knowledge….or extent of understanding…which leads to dominant perceptions at the end).

8) Have you ever asked your company for advice regarding any compliance requirements to environmental regulations? What was their response?

(…to explore and identify…if any…tensions between management staff ashore and management staff on board which may reflect on sound compliance and the final framing of the problem by both players).

9) Do you think that the trading area of your latest ship for example have an effect on the issue of compliance to Marpol?

(…to try comparing between the effect of different trading patterns and their effect on the framing of compliance problems…if any).

10) What are the sorts of auditing and monitoring you are subjected to either from your own company or from local authorities in port?

(...to explore the effect of the dominant Audit society on seafarers...and whether they feel that such audits are genuine or not).

11) How do you think we can enhance environmental knowledge or awareness among seafarers?

(...to unravel the dominant frame of inadequacy of MET institutions worldwide in addressing the adverse effects of marine pollution among current and future seafarers....a frame which also emerged from the IMO interviews).

12) In your opinion...do you think that we can promote pro-environmental behaviours among seafarers by means other than regulatory enforcement? How?

(...to explore the simplistic and practical views of seafarers about tackling the problem).

13) Do you discuss the environmental issues in your management meeting on board? What are the dominant themes in such discussions? For senior staff only

(...exploring "problem solving" frames –if any- presented by respondents....and identifying priority issues discussed).

14) Tell me how the Chief Officer (or Second Engineer) deals with the monitoring equipment of discharged effluents (i.e. OWS or ODME)...does he assign any duty to you relating to this? Does he stay with you during the operation...*another form or a revisit of question no.6 above in case the respondent didn't reply to the first one.*

(...Unraveling dominant ...attitudes...and the role of hierarchy in dealing with tech fixes on board ships).

14) In the last ten years of your career at sea did you notice an improvement in the area of compliance to Marpol? Why? Why Not?

(...exploring regulatory successes and failures from the seafarers' perspectives in relation to the ultimate goals of marine environmental regulations)

15) Why do you think we should protect the marine environment from pollution...in general? How could we do that in your view?

(...to reveal whether respondents lean towards anthropocentric oe ecopocentric approaches or in other words self-interests or ecological concerns ....the follow up to this question may explore the collective action frames presented earlier in the pilot study)

16) Do you think the ultimate goal of Marpol is to reduce marine pollution or to eliminate it all together?

(...to open up a discussion that may help...among other issues....to reveal whether seafarers think of environmental regulations as being genuine ...or just symbolic and why).

17) What do you think is the effect of media interpretations in the aftermath of accidents resulting in oil pollution? Do you think this could affect you? Why? Why not?

(...to explore whether external pressures on seafarers could result –or not- in "frame adjustments" or "frame transformations" when talking about marine pollution ....)

18) Some regulators are claiming that the solution of the marine pollution problem is in the hands of seafarers...do you believe so? Why? Why not?

(...need to reveal if they think of themselves as part of the problem or part of the solution and why)

19) What would you do if, in your watch, see a ship discharging oil while in port or at sea? Why/ why not? For senior ranks only

(...to open-up a discussion about one compliance requirement...which might be known or not and also detect frames of fear of self-incrimination and their potential effects –if any)

20) In your opinion, what is the difference between compliance to safety conventions and compliance to environmental conventions? To Staff Only.

(...to open up a potential discussion about "compliance" oriented thinking VS "effectiveness" oriented thinking in the seafarers' views and how they interpret the goals of such conventions)

21) Why do you think that some European countries, for example, seem to be caring more about the marine environment than some developing countries? Did you detect any evidence of that?

(...opening-up accounts about perceived differences in pro-environmental behaviors between the north and south...may also open discussion about effects of governments, NGOs, and public at large in relation to the marine pollution problem).

22) How do describe the living and working conditions on board the ships in your company? Ratings only

(...to trigger a discussion about job satisfaction or not...of seafarers with the current de-regulated shipping industry atmosphere and its effects on environmental attitudes and behaviour).

23) Joining different ships in your company could sense any differences in compliance behaviours to marine environmental regulations to marine environmental regulations? Why is that? How could you sense such differences if any?

(...exploring the sense making of seafarers in relation to marine pollution and may open an account about the effect of group work and on board management in compliance issues.....also could help in establishing more information about dominant behaviours in relation to the marine environment and reasons for them).

24) Your company may have an environmental policy statement or a published annual report...have you read that? What do you feel reading these policies?

(To reveal how seafarers perceive published policy slogans and texts....whether this elicits compliance....promotes loyalty....or result in resistance or rejection....)

Section Three: Daily Compliance General Questions

- *Selected respondents based on their answers in section two.*

1- In your current rank, could you outline to me the duties associated with it which is related to compliance with marine environmental regulations?

2- In your working practice, how do you balance between these compliance duties and doing your other daily duties safelyand efficiently?

3- In your work on board, what sorts of monitoring or auditing procedures (mechanisms) are there (in place) in relation to compliance to marine environmental regulations and conventions?

4- From your experience, how can any shipping company contribute in the promotion of compliance to marine environmental regulations?

5- In your opinion, do you think that compliance to marine environmental regulations is a moral issue ...or just an exercise of power?

6- Why – in your view - did the issue of regulating the marine environment had to be an international issue? What do you think about the international bodies formulating these marine environmental regulations?

7- In your opinion, can Maritime Education and Training institutions contribute in promoting compliance to such marine environmental regulations?

8- In your experience working at sea for ...years, how can nation states promote this issue of compliance to marine environmental regulations among its national fleets – or among foreign ships visiting their ports and terminals?

9- What are the detection and monitoring regimes (mechanisms) of compliance that you know about? In your opinion, are they effective? Why?

10- Do you think, in relation to this compliance issue, that there is a question that I did not ask? What is that? ...do you want to add anything from your own experience about this issue or about regulating the marine environment in general?

APPENDIX FIVE

Examples of NVivo Nodes

NVivo revision 2.0.163   Licensee: Mohab AbouElkawam

Project: Field Analysis Mohab   User: Mohab   Date: 10/17/2007 -
12:28:05 PM
NODE CODING REPORT

    Node: Infringements
    Created: 9/17/2007 - 12:47:04 AM
    Modified: 10/17/2007 - 11:38:06 AM
    Documents in Set: All Documents
    Document 1 of 7 Part1P
    Passage 1 of 4   Section 1.1.12, Para 62, 128 chars.

62: you find that their standards are less than the standards than
the crew is applying….so if they lose oil to the sea….no problem…

    Passage 2 of 4   Section 1.1.27, Para 122, 224 chars.

122: Well, we see cases close to ports….for example we see oil….it
happens a lot…..that people wash their tanks and throw slop water to
sea…..by overriding the ODME and it is obvious …….we can see obvious
strong oil traces at sea

    Passage 3 of 4   Section 1.1.30, Para 134, 114 chars.

134: I absolutely approve……because as long as the regulations
exist….there are short cuts….to override the regulations.

    Passage 4 of 4   Section 1.1.31, Para 138, 279 chars.

138: Well the simplest thing we heard about….many people discharge
through the ODME but they override the oil content meter ……so he
throws the slop water….instead of being compliant….it is not
complying…….so the percentage of oil in the water would be greater
than the allowed content

    Document 2 of 7 Part2P
    Passage 1 of 6   Section 1.34, Para 101, 33 chars.

101: you have many other alternatives

    Passage 2 of 6   Section 1.46, Para 131, 109 chars.

131: sometimes some people who lack the moral initiative …they can
put a fake lock which could be easily removed….

Passage 3 of 6   Section 1.52, Para 144, 122 chars.

144: I heard that some people are making on their ships a pipe…you know…a pipe….he removes the overboard pipe…and put this pipe

Passage 4 of 6   Section 1.92, Para 229, 118 chars.

229: .so humans try thinking how they can carry on with their jobs & get over these obstacles so they handle the situation…

Passage 5 of 6   Section 1.94, Para 233, 96 chars.

233: why doesn't he flush the ODME …the system is easy….but when he finds difficulty in flushing it……

Passage 6 of 6   Section 1.108, Para 262, 108 chars.

262: to avoid difficulties which leads the operator to by-passes and short cuts…which is easier…the second issue

Document 3 of 7 Part3P
Passage 1 of 4   Section 1.24, Para 58, 139 chars.

58: but it was never tested at all……despite recording that it was tested….but nobody was actually testing it……nobody had any idea how it works…

Passage 2 of 4   Section 1.39, Para 88, 58 chars.

88: and I was obliged to flog the record of my own rest hours…

Passage 3 of 4   Section 1.73, Para 157, 191 chars.

157: .but they didn't care about the drip trays…..it was not shifted to slops as it was done simultaneously with the tank cleaning process….so it usually went to sea….and this is a big time saver.

Passage 4 of 4   Section 1.97, Para 209, 231 chars.

209: but what I want to say collectively…..is that ships in the company ….not all of them are complying……well the worldwide trading ships were not complying when they get out of the areas of control…..the Gulf…the Red Sea……Arabian sea……

Document 4 of 7 part4P
Passage 1 of 3   Section 1.22.1, Para 89, 165 chars.

89: for example the Red Sea … everybody throws his oil in it … some ships stop & wash their tanks… there are the some problem in the Persian (18:47) gulf … people throw…

Passage 2 of 3   Section 1.22.1, Para 89, 201 chars.

89: they do not know how to control vessels … one ship going out of (port name in the red sea area) has 15 or 20 meters bilge as recorded … reaches (another port in the red sea) with nothing (no bilge).

Passage 3 of 3   Section 1.36.1, Para 146, 252 chars.

146: they usually take the Master to prison ….. if he does not report any pollution promptly …. he is taken to prison… he is prosecuted …. Criminally convicted and jailed…. The civil side of the case is only valid if the Captian reports about the pollution

Document 5 of 7   Part5P
Passage 1 of 9   Section 1.1.22, Para 99, 155 chars.

99: For example…..some crew members if not supervised properly were throwing the garbage overboard so he can get rid of it without the knowledge of the Captain

Passage 2 of 9   Section 1.1.23, Para 103, 126 chars.

103: ..he just wants to relax…..instead of labour & working….they just take shortcuts….and save time….escaping from responsibility.

Passage 3 of 9   Section 1.1.25, Para 111, 50 chars.

111: they were fatigued so they throw these….overboard.

Passage 4 of 9   Section 1.1.27, Para 119, 127 chars.

119: but I noticed that the people who are complying with the rules in their own countries….they didn't do that when they came here…

Passage 5 of 9   Section 1.1.28, Para 123, 367 chars.

123: Some of the engine room ratings were not Egyptians….if they were in their own country they wouldn't be able to be negligent like this….but because they discovered that there is no inspection from the ports….so they dump oil in the Suez Gulf….while we were underway…..claiming that Egypt never care about that…..if he know that there is punishment he wouldn't do that.

Passage 6 of 9   Section 1.1.36, Para 157, 135 chars.

157: some of these ships….berthed on the terminal….and when they leave sailing to the gulf ….I could see….a slick of oil following the ship.

Passage 7 of 9   Section 1.1.37, Para 161, 57 chars.

161: you can see the oil trace clearly in the wake of the ship

Passage 8 of 9   Section 1.1.40, Para 173, 93 chars.

173: .the engine room rating who dumps oil……is not working in my department but I did care to know

Passage 9 of 9   Section 1.1.48, Para 208, 332 chars.

208: do they have waste or not….some ship go inside ports or terminals and they don't deliver the waste…where did it go?......it must have been thrown to sea…..a voyage of two …three months and arriving to port….defiantly there are lots of garbage and lots of oily waste…..oil waste….by logic….if not handed in port….it was thrown to sea…

Document 6 of 7 Part6P
Passage 1 of 6   Section 1.1.15, Para 70, 118 chars.

70: There are some people aware of this and they don't comply…..and they pump large amounts of oil out at sea in the night

Passage 2 of 6   Section 1.1.20, Para 91, 100 chars.

91: Well…the secure feeling….they are saying…don't worry…..I did it several times before ……no problem…..

Passage 3 of 6   Section 1.1.21, Para 95, 263 chars.

95: This happens in open sea…..many ships are there…..it is very difficult to know who……unless you take a sample…..but this is in the middle of the ocean……it is very difficult to specify who….and this is the point….they think they are safe……and no one can detect him.

Passage 4 of 6   Section 1.1.26, Para 115, 85 chars.

115: .then he stops the ODME & register what he did….then continue to pump out normally………

Passage 5 of 6   Section 1.1.27, Para 119, 28 chars.

119: Yes, pump normally to sea…..

Passage 6 of 6   Section 1.1.28, Para 123, 138 chars.

123: Where……definitely he will not drink it…..if he discharged it in a shore facility he must have documents to prove that…..where did it go…..?

APPENDIX SIX

Publications Based on this Research Study

Abou-Elkawam, M. (2011) 'Seafarers and Growing Environmental Concerns: To Comply or Not to Comply - Choices and Practices', SIRC Symposium, Cardiff University, 6-7 July, ISBN 1-900174-39-1. Available at: http://www.sirc.cf.ac.uk

- **Abou-Elkawam, M**. (2009) GLOBAL ENVIRONMENTAL CONCERNS: LOCAL SHIPBOARD PRACTICE - THE SEAFARERS ORDEAL. 1st SIRC-Nippon Fellow Maritime Conference. January 2009. Cardiff. UK Available at: http://www.sirc.cf.ac.uk/pdf/SIRC-NF%20Conf%2009.pdf

- **Abou-Elkawam, M**. (2008) "Seafarers Quest for 'Better' Auditing Regimes" The Sea (Nov- Dec 08).Mission to Seafarers. London .UK.

- **Abou-Elkawam, M**. (2008) "Seafarers and Port Reception Facilities: The Usual Warm Welcome". Proceedings of the 1st. International Ship-Port Interface Conference - The Human Element, 19 - 21 May 2008, Bremen / Germany.

APPENDIX SEVEN

Scholarly and PDP Activities during Study

Professional and Practical Courses / Conferences / Meetings Attended / Contributed to:

Most recent

April 2014 - Conducting / coordinating a workshop on behalf of the IMO to train PSC officers in the Red sea and Gulf of Aden region on compliance to MARPOL and the Ballast Water Management Convention – Jeddah – Saudi Arabia – PERSGA HQs

December 2013 - Conducting / coordinating a workshop on behalf of the IMO to train PSC officers in the Red sea and Gulf of Aden region on environmental auditing aspects – Jeddah – Saudi Arabia – PERSGA HQs.

June 2013 – Coordinating / Delivering MARPOL workshop for the PERSGA region in Hurghada / Egypt in Collaboration with IMO Technical Cooperation Division (TC). EMARSGA Centre Hurghada.

Conferences / Meetings attended

2011/ Present
Attending / contributing to IMO Council/ Assembly meetings – and various other committees - as the accredited Representative of the League of Arab states to the IMO and as a maritime consultant / member of the League of Arab States Delegation.

2009/2011
Attended IMO's MEPC / STW / FSI Committees and sub-committees representing Egypt.

Attended / Presented paper 1st. International Ship-Port-Interface Conference (ISPIC 2008). Bremen – Germany 19-21 May 2008. (See published paper)

Attended Impacts of Climate Change on the Maritime Industry Conference (ICCMI 2008) World Maritime University (WMU), Malmö, Sweden, 2nd. To 4th. of June 2008.

Attended 'Empowering Professional Women in the Maritime World International Conference' 02 – 04 April 2008. Malmö, Sweden.

Attended / Presented paper at the British Sociological Association Annual Conference 2008 - Social Worlds Natural Worlds. 28th. to 30th. March 2008. Warwick University: Coventry. UK.

Regular Attendance of IMO MEPC Committee meetings 52, 53, 54, 56, 57 and FSI 15. London – UK
(January 2006 – May 2008).

Personal Development Courses - PDCs (Including Managerial and IT skills)

1. Completed Personal Development Program (November2007 – July 2008) Speaking and Presenting, Listening and Awareness, The Art of Negotiation, Problem Solving, Teamwork, Successful Networking, Leadership Styles, and Team Briefings. Upon Completion a Certificate of "Professional Development" is awarded. Cardiff University, Cardiff, UK.
2. Publishing a Journal Article in the Social Sciences (October 2007). Cardiff University, Cardiff, UK.
3. Qualitative Analysis in the Social Sciences (January 2007). Cardiff University.
4. Microsoft Word: Working with Long Documents (November 2006). Cardiff University.
5. Rapid Reading (January 2006). Cardiff University.
6. Researching/Writing a Literature Review in the Social Sciences (October 2005). Cardiff University.
7. Academic Writing in the Social Sciences (November 2005) Cardiff University.

APPENDIX EIGHT

List of Abbreviations (in Alphabetical Order)

- AASTMT: Arab Academy for Science, Technology, and Maritime Transport.
- BATNEEC: Best Available Technologies Not Including Excessive Cost.
- BWM: Ballast Water Management.
- CFCs: Chlorofluorocarbons.
- COC: Certificate of Competency.
- COW: Crude Oil Washing.
- ECAs: Emission Control Areas.
- EEDI: Energy Efficiency Design Index.
- EEZ: Exclusive Economic Zone.
- EM: Ecological Modernisation.
- FOCs: Flags of Convenience.
- FSC: Flag State Control.
- GEF: Global Environmental Frame.
- GESAMP: Joint Group of Experts on the Scientific Aspects of Marine Environmental Protection.
- GHG: Green House Gases.
- IAPP: International Air Pollution Prevention Certificate.
- ILO: International Labour Office.
- IMO: International Maritime Organisation.
- IOPP: International Oil Pollution Prevention Certificate.
- MARPOL: The international convention for the prevention of pollution from ships.
- MEPC: Marine Environment Protection Committee.
- MSC: Maritime Safety Committee.
- NOx: Nitrogen Oxides.
- ODME: Oil Detector Monitoring Equipment.
- OECD: Organisation for Economic Co-operation and Development.
- OWS: Oily Water Separators.
- PM: Particulate Matter.

- PPM: Part Per Million.
- PRFs: Port Reception Facilities.
- PSC: Port State Control.
- SBT: Segregated Ballast Tanks.
- SEEMP: Ship Energy Efficiency Management Plan.
- SOLAS: The Safety of Life at Sea Convention.
- SOPEP: Ship Oil Pollution Emergency Plan.
- SOx: Sulphur Oxides.
- STCW: Standards of Training, Certification, and Watch Keeping at Sea convention.
- UNCLOS: The United Nations Convention on the Law of the Sea.

Printed in Great Britain
by Amazon.co.uk, Ltd.,
Marston Gate.